Table Talk

Building Democracy
One Meal at a Time

Janet A. Flammang

D1521584

University of Illinois Press
Urbana, Chicago, and Springfield

Library of Congress Control Number: 2016937702
ISBN 978-0-252-04029-0 (hardcover)
ISBN 978-0-252-08174-3 (paperback)
ISBN 978-0-252-09855-0 (e-book)

Joy Harjo Poem (Chapter 1): "Perhaps the World Ends Here," from The
Woman Who Fell from the Sky by Joy Harjo, Copyright © 1994 by Joy
Harjo. Used by permission of W. W. Norton & Company, Inc.

For Alexander Flammang Friedman
and Jacob Flammang Friedman

Contents

Illustrations

Acknowledgments

My thanks to John Finn, Lee Friedman, Wendy Sarvasy, and Jacob Flammang Friedman for reading drafts of this book and providing excellent comments. The following people were very helpful with sources, contacts, and ideas: Shirl Buss, Alexander Flammang Friedman, Karen Gross, Gail Killefer, James Lai, Kira Marchenese, Peter Minowitz, Ann Rankin, Eric Shutt, and Kathleen Wareham. I am grateful for the interviews with Stephanie Bonham, Michael Curtis, Nancy Highiet, Emma Le Duc, Renee O'Harran, Seamus O'Leary, Barbara Scheifler, and Malcolm Sher. Finally, my thanks to family, friends, colleagues at Santa Clara University, and editors at the University of Illinois Press for their support and encouragement.

Table Talk

Introduction

How do we develop a political voice? How do we learn to express our feelings and ideas about authority, a common good, democracy, duty, equality, fairness, freedom, justice, legitimacy, liberty, loyalty, obligation, oppression, order, patriotism, power, repression, respect, responsibilities, and rights? I list these political concepts in alphabetical order in recognition that we all differ in our ranking of their relative importance. Nevertheless, they are bedrock features of politics. I invite you to join me on a political archeological expedition to explore the deep layers of meaning we give to our political understandings. You will notice that my emphasis is not on electoral politics—voting, aligning with a political party, or joining an interest group—about which much has already been written. Instead, my interest is in taking a look at our political worlds from a different angle by investigating the deeper layers of social and cultural relations that undergird electoral politics.

This is the territory of civil society, where we learn that people act, not only selfishly, but also for a common good; where people attend to our basic needs, even though there is not an obvious reason why they should do so; where we are listened to, even when we express thoughts that challenge conventional wisdom; where our experiences are understood, even if they are not approved of; where we learn new concepts that capture what we mean; where we express our feelings and ideas for the first time in our own words. Unless we have these experiences, there is little reason to bother imagining, let alone promoting, any kind of common good.

I propose two helpful guides for our exploration: the art of conversation and table activities. We can develop our civil selves by sharing food and ideas at tables where there are ground rules about listening, sharing, and respect. Of course, not all conversations and table activities have such ground rules. Meals might be marked by tension, rivalries, and tears; conversations might start out well but degenerate into shouting matches and insults. The point

I want to make in this book is probabilistic: that conversations and table activities are *likely* occasions for developing our civil selves, and that not taking advantage of their civilizing potential is a *lost opportunity*. Eating is something we do frequently, and most of us prefer table experiences that are civil. Of course, there are cultural differences in rules about civil tables—who should speak, when and how; what behavior is acceptable; what topics are off limits; and how conflict should be resolved. Indeed, it is our daily exposure to the making, enforcing, and breaking of these rules that constitutes our daily doses of political awareness, growth, and transformation. It is at tables and in conversations that we make sense of the many layers of our experiences with political import.

The best way to excavate these layers of meaning is by telling and listening to people's firsthand accounts of their lives expressed in stories. Stories are rich with emotions and ideas, personal and group history, hopes and dreams. We tell stories in order to make sense of the many facets of our experiences, to put disconnected parts into some kind of whole, and we tell lots of stories in table conversations. When we listen to people's political narratives, we hear contradictions, ambivalences, and nuances, and we want to learn how they make sense of their political world.

The goal here is understanding, not explanation. Understanding gives equal weight to two meanings: that presented by the storyteller and that given by the listener. As the listener, I will present social science studies and concepts that I think help us understand the stories included in this book. But at the same time, I will present people's understandings in their own words in order to honor the variety of human experience in developing a political voice while sharing ideas in conversations and at tables.

In listening to these stories, I am particularly interested in what makes us resilient. In politics many disappointing, even horrific, things happen, and one can reasonably ask why in light of these events people keep imagining and trying to bring about improved political arrangements. My supposition is that there is a cumulative positive effect of being respected, listened to, taken seriously, and trusted, and that these experiences create a reservoir of value and strength for the common good, for a collectivity beyond those in our immediate contact, that can be drawn upon in political setbacks. Stories remind us that others have survived seemingly unbearable forms of being beaten down; that there are novel and creative ways out of apparently hopeless situations; and that humans can relate in ways that generate more light than heat.

This migrant family shares a noonday meal on an Oklahoma roadside in 1939. During the devastating dust bowl, when many people could not afford a table, table rituals helped maintain group cohesion and build resilience.
Credit: Library of Congress, Prints and Photographs Division, FSA/OWI Collection (LC-USF 33-012275-MS).

We become resilient when we feel connected. Stories, conversations, and table activities are important and everyday ways of connecting with others. They might be occasions where we empathize with someone we have not been comfortable with before. A vibrant civil society depends on feelings of respect, trust, and empathy, which in turn make possible the idea of a common good that is worth working toward. It also depends on having people with conversational skills. Conversations take work, and not all people are up to the task or think that it is their responsibility to learn or teach the art of conversation. My hope is that after reading this book, readers will be convinced that mealtime conversations are the building blocks of democracy and that conversational skills can, and should, be learned one meal at a time.

Overview

We begin by setting the table: discussing how to combine academic table studies and people's table stories, followed by an in-depth look at conversations and narratives. We then consider tables at home, tables away from home, and tables and conflict. We conclude with a focus on civic engagement and diplomacy and some important ethical, practical, and theoretical issues raised in our examination of table conversations and democracy.

Chapter 1: Setting the Table

Combining table studies and table stories is a tricky business. As a social scientist, I come to this project with concepts that I think are important to interpreting the stories I hear. These concepts are used by anthropologists, linguists, sociologists, political scientists, psychologists, and nutritionists not only to describe what *does* happen at tables but often to recommend what *should* happen as well. As we shall see, it is hard to get a handle on what really happens at tables. Especially when it comes to family meals, we tend to have idealized notions of what should happen and are tempted to provide researchers with information that makes us look good. Things get even more complicated when studies are used to recommend what should happen at tables. Most table studies are used to weigh in on our *ecological, physical, and social* health, providing recommendations about sustainability, diet, and child development. This book refocuses our attention on our *civic and democratic* health. This chapter begins with a discussion of "table reservations," outlining the difficulties and limitations of table studies, followed by an examination of case studies that have provided many useful concepts. We then consider the social context for this study—what we know about mealtimes for overworked Americans—and take a close look at common tables, stories, and food.

Chapter 2: Conversations and Narratives

Studies of conversations are both empirical and philosophical. Empirical researchers record naturally occurring conversations, look for patterns of speech, and generalize about the meaning of these patterns across ages, genders, cultures, and classes. They ask: Who does the conversation work? Who gets to speak when and how? Who chooses appropriate topics? Political philosophers wonder whether we have a civic imperative to talk to strangers. Everyone agrees that conversations are learned, and here we focus on how they are learned at tables, by children, adolescents, and adults alike. At mealtimes, narratives are a mainstay of table conversations. Telling a story can be an entrée into more complex forms of conversation, providing the building blocks of topic selection, use of hypotheticals and conditionals, turn taking, problem solving, and moral theorizing. Narratives are "on the table" for others to consider and augment.

Chapter 3: Tables at Home

Our discussion of table talk begins at home, where the preponderance of research has been conducted and where most personal food memoirs take place. I am interested in unearthing conversations in the domestic sphere in order to cast light on their significance for civility and democracy. Although the domestic sphere is typically regarded as pre- or nonpolitical, I think that it is foundational to the development of our political selves. We examine the complicated relations of domesticity and family, with domination and control, on the one hand, and care and connection, on the other. We take a close look at kitchen talk, family meals, bridging generations, kids cooking, table manners, talking about one's day, training tables, dinner parties, personal expression, and transition tables.

Chapter 4: Tables Away from Home

Important table conversations also take place outside the home, where things get more complicated as people are exposed to new table rules and customs. We consider in-depth cases of how our civic selves are developed through conversations in settings as diverse as friends' homes, schools, camps, colleges, religious institutions, firehouses, addiction-recovery programs, gang prevention programs, and the military.

Chapter 5: Tables and Conflict

Given my emphasis on civility and democracy, I am particularly interested in difficult conversations, where conflict is profound. In this chapter we examine such conversations not only at the dinner table but also at a school with at-risk youth, among same-sex marriage proponents talking to opponents, at Death Cafes (groups that meet socially to discuss the meaning of death), and at dispute resolution sessions. We examine cultural and ethnic differences and various attempts to use table talk to address stereotypes among Christians, Jews, and Muslims; to educate Americans about Afghanis; and to bridge differences in views about homosexuality. I profile two high-conflict cases: civil right advocates who cooked for racial equality and Pittsburgh's Conflict Kitchen.

Chapter 6: Civic Engagement and Diplomacy

Tables are locations for community building: at swimming clubs, lesbian potlucks, doctor's offices, campgrounds, civic clubs, churches, schools, low-income senior housing developments, and between neighbors and at restaurants in times of need. Studies of civic engagement shed light on how adolescents develop a political voice in families, schools, and communities where their ideas are taken seriously in decision-making processes; how children benefit from political discussions and from speaking up at home and at school; and how political discussion stimulates political action for youth and adults alike. Turning to the issue of civility among public officials, we take a look at gender differences in the conversational dynamics among state legislators, national calls for greater civility and conversations about important topics, civility among U.S. congresswomen, and diplomacy in the State Department's Culinary Diplomacy program and the barbecue diplomacy of Presidents Lyndon Johnson and George W. Bush.

We conclude with a consideration of important ethical, practical, and theoretical issues raised by this study of table talk and democracy. Ethically, whose responsibility is it to learn, teach, and conduct the art of conversation? Practically, how do we learn, teach, and practice this art? And theoretically, how does this book make a contribution to theories about democracy, resilience, and reducing prejudice?

Chapter One

Setting the Table

Table Reservations

We begin with some words of caution about how to interpret what goes on at tables. The first caution is about jumping to conclusions. In recent years, many commentators have waxed effusively about the seemingly miraculous effects of family meals in reducing teens' at-risk behavior, promoting healthy eating, and fostering children's cognitive and emotional development. In interpreting surveys, we must be mindful of potential problems in sampling, question wording, and inferring causation when it is not warranted. People also have a tendency to tell researchers whatever makes them look good, rather than what really is the case, for example, exaggerating how frequently they vote or have family meals. As one anthropologist observes, "In ethnographic interviews in the United States, when I ask people to describe 'real' family meals, most can immediately recite some variation of the normative ideal of family commensality. Only later in the interview, when we are sharing personal family stories, are they willing to talk about the daily reality of their personal experiences, which rarely live up to the ideal."[1] As we shall see, others have found the same discrepancy.

A second caution is about the image that comes to mind when we say "family meal." It can mean anything from sitting together at a table at the same time with no electronic distractions to each family member microwaving his or her own meal and retreating to different rooms to watch TV and read email. It might be shared by extended kin, blended families, and homosexual couples. Anthropologists have a long history of studying "commensality," a term that means the sharing of meals, derived from the Latin *com* "with" + *mensa* "table." Although eating appears to be a universal form of social life, the nuclear family is not the typical unit of commensality. Around the world, most people eat together in age groups, in gender-segregated nonfamily groups, and in family groups both smaller and larger than nuclear families. Married couples frequently live in different households and eat separately. "Even when they live together, men and women may regularly eat with other groups. Children do not always eat with two or even one parent. And in many cultures the numerical majority of meals are eaten in nonfamily groups, causally on the street, in crowds, while working, or in multifamily groups. More people eat on the ground than at a table, and meals are often casual and utilitarian rather than formal, elaborate, or ceremonial."[2] The image of a heterosexual middle-class couple with two children sitting at a dining-room table with pleasant conversation is only one incarnation of a family meal. We will hear stories of many kinds of family meals and focus on those that include tables, mindful that this is not a universal practice.

A third caution is to remember that commensality is an opportunity for, not a guarantee of, conversation, civility, and beneficial effects on children. What matters is not so much the frequency of family meals but rather what happens during them. We want to know the extent to which commensality is a training ground for democracy, an occasion where the voiceless are given a voice. We will give particular attention to children at the table because the process of giving them a voice at the home table is very similar to the processes that give adolescents and adults a political voice as well. Many studies about the frequency and nature of family meals have concluded that family meals have a beneficial effect on children and adolescents. But given hectic schedules and conflicting routines, it is difficult for respondents to recall the exact nature of mealtime experiences. "The categories usually given on surveys about family meals are so broad and ambiguous that they can be interpreted many ways by respondents. On a survey form, a meal where everyone shares jokes and tells stories is the same as one where everyone stares at their plate bolting food silently under the glare of an angry father."[3]

A fourth caution is that even when family meals have a positive effect, it may be short-lived, and, furthermore, family meals may be a proxy for other features of the family environment that might be the real cause. In their summary of academic studies, two sociologists write that adolescents who shared meals with their parents scored better on a range of "well-being indicators" concerning mental health, substance abuse, and delinquency. However, family dinners' associations with these indicators did not persist into adulthood. "Eating together may protect children from depression and risky behaviors by providing a regular and comforting context to check in with parents about their day-to-day activities and to connect with them emotionally. The ability to manage a regular family dinner, however, may also be facilitated by family resources, such as time and money, or it may simply be a proxy for other, more affective, dimensions of the family environment. Indeed, we found more frequent family dinners among families with both biological parents present, a nonemployed mother, and higher income."[4] The positive effects of family meals may change with maturation and have many causes.

Of course, academic researchers are not the only ones to weigh in on the beneficial effects of family meals. Many best-selling works on this topic resonate with the public. One of the most influential is Laurie David's *The Family Dinner: Great Ways to Connect with Your Kids One Meal at a Time*. She is a writer and climate-change activist who produced the Academy Award–winning documentary *An Inconvenient Truth*. She was motivated to write her book because she thinks that family meals are important, even though her childhood experiences of them were disastrous. Her case illustrates that accurately telling a researcher that one sits down for a home-cooked meal five nights a week might conceal an inconvenient truth.

> Honestly, my childhood family dinner experiences didn't serve as very good role models for success. We had a five-night-a-week home-cooked sit-down meal, but I barely remember a family dinner that didn't end with someone crying. Usually it was my older sister or my mother. Occasionally it was me. I dreaded many of those meals. They were something to be gotten through quickly, with the least amount of emotional bruising. As an adolescent, my prevailing thought was always, *Who is going to go down tonight?* followed by, *How fast can I get excused from the table, out the door, and back on my bicycle?* That was not history worth repeating in my own home.[5]

Laurie David was able to put family meals on her table thanks to the assistance of her cook. When we talk about tables and food, a fifth caution is to be aware of the often-hidden labor involved. While the relationship between David and her cook appears to be one of mutual respect and affection, throughout our history, creating civilized meals frequently entailed uncivil treatment of servants and slaves. As one African American cook recounted,

> It was different when company was there. That's when I was really treated as a servant. Mrs. Rawlings wanted everything to be just right and would sometimes bark orders at me throughout such a visit. I remember once I was slow (so she thought) bringing hot biscuits to the table. Mrs. Rawlings yelled for me in front of the guests. Then, as I was coming through the swinging door, she jumped up from her seat and snatched the biscuits out of my hands. "Why the hell didn't you hurry up with the food?" she hollered. She wouldn't have done that if she hadn't had company, I believe.[6]

Caution 6: the kitchen table is not always a rosy place to talk about one's day and expect a respectful response. Many African American cooks survived by "becoming two persons" and not speaking out. "Managing the relationship with her employer was a means by which a domestic worker gained some control over her work. One way that African American women mastered the situation was by cultivating dissemblance, a careful concealment of what she actually thought and felt." One cook put it this way: "They may keep you from speaking out, but they can't keep you from thinking. It's something on the inside. And you learn how to be two persons to live through it all."[7]

For a seventh caution, table conflict results not only from class and race tensions but also from cultural stereotypes and prejudice. At one Christmas dinner, food writer Kim Severson was pleased that her parents had finally come to accept their children's gay and lesbian identities, but cultural and religious differences made for a tense evening. Her mother liked to have a lot of people around the table; she just wanted everyone to be together. Severson brought her Jewish girlfriend, Katia, and her brother brought his Muslim boyfriend. After two martinis, her father turned to his son's boyfriend and asked, "So, why are your people flying planes into buildings?" Severson felt like the snow had suddenly stopped falling, a chill had settled over the table, and the candles had gone out. Her mother asked him not to talk about that because it was Christmas. Her brother's boyfriend said it was fine and launched into "a long, historical lecture that begins with a deconstruction of Christianity and ends, essentially, with an argument that makes it all the Jews' fault." Katia got visibly upset and left the table to wash the dishes. Her mother remarked, "Well, all of that happened a long time ago. Besides, it's Christmas." Severson eventually married Katia and had a daughter, and her brother broke up with his boyfriend and became her daughter's special protector. Her father never did grasp the finer points of Middle East politics, and her mother continued to put out the Spode china every Christmas.[8]

Parents face daily dilemmas not only about who is welcome at family tables and what topics are appropriate for discussion but also about what children should eat. They have an obligation to raise healthy children, and many use some form of forced consumption. This creates a dilemma for advocates of democratic tables. Caution 8: Children are not very likely to value tables as places for civility and democracy if they associate them with nausea and vomiting, which was found to be the case in a study of college students. Two thirds of them reported having had at least one forced consumption episode in their childhood. The most common type involved an authority figure (e.g., parent or teacher) forcing them to consume a novel, disliked, or aversive food, resulting in interpersonal conflict, negative affect, feeling a lack of control and helplessness, and an unwillingness to eat the target food today.

The three most common justifications were healthy food ("it's good for you"), variety in diet ("try something new"), and avoid wastefulness. . . . The most commonly used method [of coercion] was a threat, and most of these involved negative punishment (e.g. "you cannot leave the table until you finish;" "you cannot have desert until you finish your vegetable"). The second coercion technique involved making the target food more appetizing, and was usually accompanied either through the authority figure eating the food and proclaiming its appeal, or adding flavoring to the target (e.g. butter, ketchup). A third technique involved guilt-inducing efforts. . . . Wastefulness guilt involved either *effort* wastefulness (e.g. "Your father worked really hard to cook this meal for you"), *financial* wastefulness (e.g. "I spent good money for this meal"), or *food* wastefulness (e.g. "Think of all the starving children in (name of third-world country) that would love to have this meal"). Emotional guilt was related to the child's health (e.g. "We worry about your health when you do not eat"). Another means of coercing consumption involved the opportunity to earn rewards (e.g. dessert). . . .

[Some] respondents reported that they experienced ridicule because they would not consume the target food, most commonly in the form of being called "childish" or a "baby." Additional forms of ridicule involved questioning one's health, masculinity, or patriotism (one respondent indicated they were called "un-American" because they would not consume a hot dog on the 4th of July.) [Forms of punishment included] staying at the table, going to bed without any dinner, spankings, [and being] deceived into eating the food, either through a lie about the true nature of the food (e.g. telling the child that the liver dinner was really chicken) or preparing the target food in another dish (e.g. cooking pieces of liver in pancakes). . . . Fifty-two individuals reported that they cried, 59 reported that they experienced nausea, and 21 reported vomiting.[9]

Caution 9: assume that there will be sibling rivalry at the table. Parents have adopted various techniques for dealing with it—from minimizing it by meting out equal portions to encouraging it to prepare children for a dog-eat-dog world. George Howe Colt provides some amusing examples from his research about brothers. He grew up with three brothers, and there were nightly battles over who got the largest hamburger, the most cherries in his fruit cocktail, or the biggest slice of pie. His mother's attempts to forestall quarrels by serving identical portions were in vain. On one "pancake night" in James Joyce's household, all four brothers simultaneously dove for the last pancake on the platter, and James got there first. He ran up and down the stairs, claiming to his pursuers that he had already eaten it. Once they were convinced, he removed the pancake from his pocket and ate it up to spite them. The Marx brothers—Chico, Harpo, Groucho, and Gummo—grew up in a crowded apartment in New York City, where they shared a bed more peacefully than their meals. "'There was generally some kind of a brawl at the dinner table over who would get what,' said Groucho, who recalled reaching for the last roll on the plate only to see a cleaver, wielded by the normally equable Harpo, slam down within an inch of his hand." Their father organized competition between his sons to encourage Darwinian resilience. He set out three sweet rolls each morning; "as soon as a brother had wolfed down his breakfast, he was permitted to grab a roll, leaving the slowest eater empty-handed." There were countless fistfights between Joe Kennedy Jr. and his younger brother Jack. At one dinner, Jack grabbed Joe's slice of chocolate pie, gobbled it up, and ran outside and down the beach. Joe chased him, and Jack leapt into the bay. When he was forced to emerge, cold and dripping, the two brothers fought it out on shore. Colt observes that he and his brothers still eat as if they were in a race, but at least they no longer fight over food. "Of course this may be because for some time now, we four brothers are likely to be the ones cooking," he comments. "Not only do we love working in the kitchen together, but this way we can also make sure there will be more than enough food for us all."[10]

The image of four brothers cooking family meals raises eyebrows, hence caution 10: table activities are gendered. As we will see in greater detail later, women typically do most of the food work and the conversation work at tables in the United States. Men are increasingly pitching in, but table work is still "women's work." An anthropological study of the "food rules" of American college students reveals how table activities are gendered. Mothers were associated with cooking, love, and nurturance. As one student said, "Another way I think of food is 'home' and 'love.' When my mom cooks something special, I know it's because she loves us and wants the best for our family."[11] "Bad mothers" could not pull off a peaceful family meal after a hard day at work, and they resented ungrateful children. As one student recounted:

> It started again tonight—I don't know why I expected tonight to be any different. The dinner table becomes a battleground every night around 5 pm. I'm not home very often for dinner, but when I am it's brutal. My mother is the worst. Every night at dinner we hear about how hard she works and how rotten we kids are. . . . Then she starts complaining how tired she is when she comes home from work and how she "puts herself out" to make dinner for us, how ungrateful we

are because we don't eat it. How does she expect us to eat after she's been bitching at us through the whole meal?[12]

Men were often the arbiters of women's diets. Women repeatedly said that eating in the presence of men was intimidating. On dates, they ate sparsely lest they be judged "pigs." Many wrote about how their boyfriends or fathers harassed them about being overweight and eating excessively. One female student reported,

> Ever since 3rd grade my father and I would always argue bitterly about how much I weigh. He would always try to prevent me from eating certain things. It has always upset me that my own father could not accept me the way I was. I know he loves me but I wish he didn't feel like he had to make me change. . . . Even though he made an attempt to make dinner times comfortable, I still remembered how he felt about my weight and I tended to eat less in front of my father, then I would eat more in secrecy, late at night, at stores, at fast-food restaurants, or over at friends' houses. This resulted in me gaining more weight. I resented my father putting restrictions on what I ate. Therefore, I ate more behind his back."[13]

Given the potential for conflict at the table, some families opt out of the fray by turning on the television. Caution 11: While this is an understandable way to keep the peace, especially for exhausted parents working long hours, it means a lost opportunity to deal with conflict. "Many families watch television during meals; according to a Center for Disease Control report, 46% of families interviewed had a television in the area where they commonly ate such as a dining room or kitchen. While some parents considered having television on during mealtimes an educational opportunity (i.e., watching the news or Jeopardy), parents of young children (less than seven years) remarked that having the television on was a way to avoid conflict at the table."[14] Conflict avoidance, however understandable, is an abrogation of adult responsibility to teach children conflict-resolution skills, which are essential for civility and democracy.

Final caution: Gathering to share food can be a civil occasion, but it can also be a place for cruelty, as school children know only too well, when their food differs from the norm, or when there is a stigma attached to "poor people's food." One study found that British children were teased, ridiculed, and bullied when they brought something other than a sandwich, such as cold cooked food, a salad, chicken and rice, or Indian or Chinese food. One Chinese boy who brought chicken legs was called "chicken boy." Children in a school with a high percentage of free meals were embarrassed when they consumed products from a discount supermarket, known to the children for being cheap. One child dreaded trips to this store: "I have to hide if I see anyone from school. I will be screaming because I don't want to go."[15]

In summary, it is important to keep in mind some words of caution about how to interpret what goes on at tables. People tend to idealize and fudge the facts about what goes on at family meals. "Families" are varied in their composition and mealtime practices. "Meals" may or may not involve sitting in the same room eating the same food with people, with diners giving one another their undivided attention. Someone has to work to get meals on the table, and their labor may be appreciated, or it may be hidden, devalued, and unappreciated. Table activities embody race, class, gender, ethnic, religious, and cultural expectations and conflict. Power relations are at play in setting table rules about how to act and who gets to talk. Our purpose is to figure out how to realize the democratic potential of table experiences, given these reservations.

Family Table Talk as Language Socialization

In 1943, James Bossard urged sociologists to study family table talk in order to understand how children became "inducted" into families. He noted both positive and negative features of table talk. On the plus side, people were at ease exchanging family news, diverse interests were expressed during "family council time," individuals revealed and tried out their abilities on each other through conversation, vocabularies were enlarged, children learned how to discuss and to avoid topics of conversation, and positive personality traits were formed by virtue of table talk's intimacy, repetition, and protective nature. On the downside, members were hostile and physically and emotionally upset; habits of family squabbling were learned; people left the table in tears, anger, or disgrace; meals were "family tribunals" where children were reprimanded for misdeeds and nagged about table manners; the stereotype of the strong, silent father was reinforced; and emotions ran high with tension between adults and "duels of silence." Some conversational rules were quite formal, as was the case for a judge who stated a proposition at the beginning of dinner and then asked each of his six children to analyze and debate it. Informal and spontaneous discussions were more often the case. Questions arose in the course of conversation rather than at the prodding of the parent, and children's interests were taken seriously. Children learned their parent's values by listening to how they resolved conflict. And families often had their own words and expressions that had meaning for them but were unintelligible to outsiders.[16]

Today's scholars see many of these patterns of table talk, but they view language socialization less as a way to induct a child into a family unit and more as an interactive process that extends across the life cycle. This understanding is in keeping with my notion of the democratic potential of table talk: as an opportunity for finding one's own voice in a social setting. "Linguistic socialization" is learning to use language "to *maintain* and appropriately and progressively *change* one's position as a member of society" (emphasis mine). Research in sociolinguistics and the ethnography of communication indicates that vocal and verbal activities are socially organized and embedded in cultural systems of meaning, and that higher-order interpersonal interactions are developed through language. Through "guided interaction" (e.g., use of questions, expansions, and attention-getting devices), novices move from collaborative to independent action. There is both continuity and discontinuity of expectations regarding appropriate language behavior across social contexts. For example, white Anglo middle-class children experience more linguistic continuity between home and school than do children from other backgrounds.[17]

Sociolinguist Shoshana Blum-Kulka's *Dinner Talk: Cultural Patterns of Sociability and Socialization in Family Discourse* presents a linguistic analysis of conversations and the "pragmatic socialization" of children. We can extrapolate how these same processes may be used to help all linguistic novices— children, adolescents, and adults alike—to hone their conversational skills to be contributing members of civil society and democracy. Her study of dinner interactions of middle-class professional families found that levels of formality effected conversational behavior. Compared to formal public settings, family dinners were "backstage events"; however, the presence of guests and children at the table often called into play "covert rules for topic selection." Almost no mention was made of three topics: money, sex, and politics.[18]

Blum-Kulka emphasizes cultural differences in views about children as "conversational participants." Many Western, urban, middle-class families treat children as conversational partners at meals, but this is not necessarily the case elsewhere. Views differ about whether infants are worthy of questions and dramatic narratives, at what age children are thought to be capable of conversations, how much to tease, and how much information and structure should be provided in messages to children. All cultures have conversational rules about topic choice, turn taking, modes of storytelling, and rules of politeness. Young children learn turn taking by at least age three. More-complex conversation skills such as entering a conversation, maintaining one's turn, and linking coherently with previous talk take longer to develop. "Once such skills develop, children are recognized by adults as good conversationalists." There are cultural differences in ideas about politeness: how to choose themes, control topics and narratives, respond to requests, and conduct "metapragmatic discourse," which is "comments made to sanction a perceived violation of a conversational norm and, especially in the case of children, to prompt 'proper' conversational behavior."[19]

In Blum-Kulka's study, table conversations were both sociable (enjoyable for their own sake) and socializing (meant to create group members). Even though they were encounters between unequals, egalitarian attitudes prevailed: everyone had the right to talk as well as to listen and was accorded the status of someone whose evaluation of the subject matter was encouraged and respected. She considers dinner conversations as a form of "collective action." "[They] involve a 'we' level of shared intentionality that is not the sum of individual intentions. In ritualized speech events, we-purposes define the desired outcomes. . . . Family dinners have one clear collective we-purpose on the level of action, *having dinner*. This collective purpose is also associated with individual socialization goals (like teaching children table manners) and may be verbalized through instrumental and socializing discourse."[20]

At the table, it was common for adults to ask children questions such as "How was your day?" and "How was school?" These were invitations for children to speak, but they were also impositions on their privacy. When children felt imposed upon, they could exert their power by not responding, thereby challenging the presumption that children were accountable to parents, which parents took for granted. In order to remedy this power imbalance, adults needed to recognize children as an "information givers," people who could be trusted to share with others information known only to them. It was also important to offer "scaffolding strategies": acknowledgments, expansions, clarification questions, and recastings. These strategies gave children practice building coherence through question-answer sequences, adhering to turn-taking rules, constructing autonomous texts, and negotiating moral issues based on personal experience. Children's contributions to family stories helped reduce the power imbalance. "Having your contribution seamlessly woven into the ongoing discourse is a powerful signal of being accepted as an equal, full-fledged conversational partner in the adult discourse world." Narration was a bid for power and participation rights.[21]

Another kind of power imbalance involved gender differences in table conversations about stereotypically male topics, such as politics and science. One study found no difference between husbands and wives when it came to following the news; however, in the presence of their husbands, some women thought that politics was a male domain and displayed a tentative style in talk about it. In Blum-Kulka's study, there was a power differential in the domain of science. When women talked about it, they did not employ a female "powerless style," such as the use of hedges and tag questions. But men demonstrated a "powerful style," presenting themselves as the source of authority and power in family and society and maintaining topic control in spite of several attempts by others to change it.[22]

Preventing others' attempts to change the topic of conversation is typically seen as impolite table behavior. Politeness involves social controls, which impinge on our freedom of action and constitute a threat to face. There is a general consensus among anthropologists and sociologists that "face concerns" are the underlying social motivation for systems of politeness. When people are threatened, they have to make strategic choices in a context of social distance, power, and perceived imposition. There are two basic "face needs"—freedom from imposition (i.e., negative face) and enhancement of a positive self-image (i.e., positive face). Negative politeness celebrates freedom of action, and positive politeness builds group solidarity. Giving children the right to argue their case and showing them respect by providing counterarguments is a form of parental politeness that bolsters the positive face needs of children. Blum-Kulka points out that allowing negotiations over parental compliance teaches children "that the culturally legitimate way to challenge parental authority is through an appeal to reason. Whether successful or not in changing parental attitudes, for children just being listened to seriously while evoking rational arguments is meaningful in this regard. The effort invested in rationally convincing a child why his or her wishes cannot be fulfilled carries the same message." American adults see politeness as speaking properly, taking turns fairly, and censuring untimely interruptions, all of which are consistent with the American ideals of individual rights and equal opportunity. Cross-cultural research has shown that the systematics of turn taking are by no means universal.[23]

For Blum-Kulka, dinner talk is a means of "guided participation," bringing children into the everyday lives of adults. In cultures where children are integrated into the work and social life of adults, guided participation occurs through observation and engagement. However, in the modern middle-class families she studied, adults and children were separated for most of the day, and dinner was one of the few regular times for intergenerational gathering, so guided participation was verbal. She notes, "The family dinner conversations we studied demonstrate how, through guided participation in multiparty, intergenerational talk, adults ease the passage of preschool and school-age children into adult discourse worlds, helping them acquire the pragmatic skills needed to become communicatively fully competent." Parents reported that they were less disciplinarian and more egalitarian than their parents were, as illustrated by their comments: "My parents just laid down the law and 'pulled rank.' No arguing or discussing. We are more attentive and sharing with our children." "We try to be more rational. And I'm much more involved than my parents." "I think [the children] are more coequal members of the family than I certainly was. I listen more. We will tend to explain things longer than my parents would to me as a kid." Developmental psychologists agree that there are beneficial psychological effects on children when parents are attentive, share, reason, and listen.[24]

Children feel they are part of a group when adults pay attention to their needs and preferences. At dinner, when children's food preferences are taken into account, their autonomy is respected. Parental attention to children's food needs often leads to an interest in their conversation needs as well—picking up bids for what linguists call "turn cues" ("Mommy, do you know what?" "Yes, dear.") and engaging in conversational scaffolding strategies. Parents in Blum-Kulka's study granted center stage to children's topics at dinner and helped them gain the skills needed for full and equal participation. However, adults still retained control in subtle ways: the occasional delegitimization of children's topics, the overall prevalence of adult topic control and adult questions to children, and the occasional framing of children as side participants. Parents responded to perceived violations of conversational norms, commenting on the lack of topical relevance, verbosity, nonsatisfactory levels of information, and manner of speech. Children were accountable to parents for their deeds and decisions, and there were high levels of parental conversational involvement with many facets of children's lives, especially schoolwork and attendance and moral issues in peer relations.[25]

Blum-Kulka provides a host of relevant concepts that help us understand civility at the table. Under the broad umbrella of pragmatic socialization are ideas about levels of formality, conversations as both sociable and socializing, conversational partners, conversations as collective action, and guided participation. The area of language socialization encompasses differences in talking to infants, using dramatic narratives, asking questions, teasing, and information giving. Conversation topics are initiated, selected, continued, controlled, shifted, and avoided. There are rules about turn taking, interruptions, coherence, and participation in the creation of narratives. Scaffolding strategies include acknowledgments, expansions, clarification questions, and recastings. Rules of politeness reflect our positive and negative face needs.

Gender differences play out in topic authority, a powerless style of hedges and tag questions, and resistance to topical shifts. Egalitarian conversations foster observation and engagement, welcome arguments and counterarguments based on reason, assume participants have a right to talk and an obligation to listen, encourage and respect various views, and require people to be attentive and sharing. Family dinner-table conversations necessarily entail inequalities based on age, gender, and verbal ability. In the end, adults set most of the rules about topic legitimacy, question control, verbosity, levels of information, manners of speech, and accountability for behavior. But being empowered to change the rules is what civic and democratic growth is all about.

Family Table Talk as Hard Work

Another study that provides valuable insight into table talk is sociologist Marjorie L. DeVault's *Feeding the Family: The Social Organization of Caring as Gendered Work*. Based on interviews in thirty households in the Chicago area in 1981–82, this pathbreaking book emphasizes the work it takes to produce family meals and conversations. Not surprisingly, most people had idealized versions of family meals, often derived from what they had seen on television. Even though actual events fell short of these ideals, they tried to make mealtime calm and social, a finding that bodes well for our purposes. Talk was considered an important part of most families' meals, and people had to work at it. An Asian American woman, married to a white professional man, reported: "At dinner we usually talk about the kind of day that Mark and I had. You know, you try to relate what . . . cute and wonderful thing the child did. . . . We try to talk during dinner. My son will sometimes be very grumpy and grouchy, because 'The whole day went wrong,' and he's told that that's simply not an excuse for not talking."[26] Talking about one's day will be explored in chapter 3.

There were class differences in expectations about whether meals should be times for family interaction. Middle-class and professional women were the most explicit in their efforts to organize family table talk. These class and gender differences will loom large in this book.

> One affluent mother with five children, worried that they might not all have enough of a chance to participate in the dinner talk, had tried to get each child to read a news item each day and report on it at the table. . . . In a few working-class households, talk at the dinner table was an item of contention between taciturn

husbands and their wives, who were striving to construct the meal as a particular kind of social occasion. One of these women argued with her husband over his dinner-table behavior, while another simply gave in on the issue; she explained, "If I sit and start talking, he'll say, 'What the heck, can't you ever shut up?'"[27]

These comments suggest that at least some working-class women, but fewer working-class men, share the more middle-class expectation that meals should be times for family interaction.

Reflecting the unequal power dynamics mentioned earlier, in all households, adults monitored and controlled children's table behavior. Sometimes it was as simple as dealing with children who annoyed each other. Things became more difficult when children were problem eaters and parents had to decide what to do. As one mother put it, "There's a lot of nights when it's, you know, 'Either sit up and eat or leave the table.' And you know, then the whole meal is ruined; it's just an aggravating situation. So the two of us are working on just not letting that happen. We give her real small portions, and just try to encourage her, and praise her when she is cleaning her plate."[28] This is an everyday "democracy dilemma" faced by parents, who have an obligation to raise healthy children and must decide whose food rules govern the table.

Most parents also monitored their own behavior at the table, aware that they were setting an example for their children. One woman said that her young daughter learned to use a cup by imitating others at the table. Another woman began eating more vegetables to set a good example. This kind of interpersonal work was also directed toward the needs of adults. A South American woman whose elderly parents lived with her adjusted the family menu to accommodate her father's dietary restrictions. Social interactions, and even one's own eating, became part of the work that contributed to the production of a family meal.[29] At the table, there is no escaping the fact that food choices have social import: it takes interpersonal skill to be tuned into the needs of others, both younger and older than oneself. Paying attention to these needs creates a climate of trust and goodwill.

In many dual-income households, family dinners were a luxury. The theme of "overworked Americans" will be examined later in this chapter. It is essential to our project of democratic civility that people have the time for shared meals at common tables. There is a tendency to "blame the victims," in this case harried and exhausted parents who cannot pull off family meals on a regular basis. I will discuss possible solutions to this time crunch throughout this book. At this point I want to underscore that it is a mistake to blame working women for the decline in family meals; the blame rests with the economic challenges faced by breadwinners trying to feed their families. One woman, who juggled the demands of full-time work, school, a husband with two jobs, and teenage children, told DeVault that sitting down to dinner every day was a luxury they had to give up. Rick and Robin were a young white couple who both worked full time, he as a delivery truck driver and she as a clerical worker. Their jobs had changed frequently because of layoffs. Robin attended night school in the hope of getting a job that paid enough for Rick to stay home as a househusband. They had two young children. Their dinner routine was a "helter skelter" with no "set patterns." They ate at different times in the living room in front of the TV. Robin regretted that life was not as simple as when she was growing up. Her mother was home and put the meals on the table. Her father got home at a certain time, and they ate together as a family. Then they watched TV. Robin said that her children did not know what it was like to sit down and have a formal family meal.

> "It's such a rare occurrence. The only time we really do that is the holidays. There are a lot of times when I really regret it. I regret not having a family routine. It feels like, you know, your kids are being shuffled around, and you're being shuffled around. And there are times when I get this real craving to stay home, stay home and play housewife. But then you know that there's no way in hell that you could afford it. It's a matter of economics. You have to do it, in order to survive." [Rick added]: "[You're] so damn tired. It's not the time, because you could do it if you wanted to. It just gets to where you're so tired, and fed up with the way the money situation is, and you just say, the hell with it."[30]

DeVault observes that many working parents felt frustrated when they could not arrange the sort of family mealtime conversations they had as children. A married woman who worked as a legal secretary said: "If you have real discussions at the dinner table, like we used to when I was a kid, you can give a person a chance to let you in on their life. What they were doing all day when they weren't with you. You can find out more about that person. That doesn't happen in our house at all. . . . It's time when you can show that you really care about that person in more than just a caretaking role. I mean, I'm their mother, so I attend to certain needs for them. But that doesn't mean I really know them." Workplace flexibility, to be discussed in greater detail later, greatly increased a household's ability to schedule regular family meals. Professional parents were more often able have such meals, even if both were employed. "However, in these households, almost all of the women who worked outside the home worked part-time instead of full-time, and they usually had jobs with flexible schedules, so that they had considerable control over their own activities. They had fewer obstacles to overcome in arranging a regular mealtime routine, and more time to devote to this work."[31]

Some parents were simply too exhausted to do conversation work. Some single mothers reported that they arranged and supervised regular meals for their children, but they themselves ate alone, at another time. One mother with six children who was home all day explained, "I'd rather wait until it's quiet." Another single woman who worked all day as a receptionist said, "We usually sit down and eat. Or I have them in here and I'll—because, you know, I've been working all day, and I might go in and sit in the living room so I'll be by myself for a while." DeVault notes: "In such situations, there is only one person to do all of the family work, and no one to provide any relief, or even help in sustaining conversation. . . . [These] women need some respite. They find that it is simply too much to keep working during their own mealtimes."[32]

Even with limited resources, parents often went to great lengths to produce family meals, table rituals, and conversations. Annie was a white single mom in her late twenties who lived with three of her four children and had worked at a variety of low-wage jobs until she became ill. While recovering from surgery, she began to use drugs. She eventually quit her drug use and reestablished a relatively stable household life. But her health was poor and she had had a couple of nervous breakdowns. Her eldest daughter went to live with a relative, and Annie informally watched over the neighborhood's children as well as her own. By "penny pinching," she managed to purchase supplies and produce family meals. "The meal is on the table, and I tell them if the steam leaves the bowl before they get to the table, the bowl goes right back in the stove and they don't get any supper. So they make sure they get to the table. And then that's our group discussion, this girlfriend played with that boyfriend at school, and—I hear everything."[33]

The living room/kitchen of Annie's apartment contained a couch and television, a refrigerator, stove, and small work counter, a small table for eating, and a table where the children did their homework. Each area in the room had its own purpose and rules. On weekends, she allowed the children to watch cartoons while they ate breakfast. "I don't want them to eat cereal in here [the 'living' rather than the 'kitchen' end of the room]. They could eat here [the table where we are sitting during the interview], but I won't put the TV here because they have to study here. So on Saturdays and Sundays they have to bring a tray [to the couch]. . . . And usually I make a banana shake. . . . They have to bring a tray, they have to have a napkin, their roll's in a bowl. . . . They're real good about it."[34]

American Mealtimes

Taken together, the in-depth studies of DeVault and Blum-Kulka focus on conversation work and dynamics in sixty-four households during the 1980s. In order to make generalizations about tables and conversation, it is important to add to the depth of these studies the breadth of a historical view of American mealtimes. Especially since most studies of table conversations have focused on contemporary middle-class families, we need to keep in mind the historical variety of American mealtimes. In colonial New England, the families of white independent farmers ate a hearty early-morning breakfast, a substantial midday dinner, and a light supper after work was done. Few houses had a designated space for eating meals. A common hall "was used for cooking, eating, spinning, sewing, carpentry, prayer, schooling, entertaining, and even sleeping, occasionally at the same time." Boards were put on trestles for meals and taken down after them. The family usually ate together, but only the men were permitted to be seated. The patriarchal colonial family gradually gave way to the more democratic and affectionate "modern family." Upper- and middle-class business and professional families created the "traditional family meal," a special event that occurred every day and linked good manners and social status. "By the 1850s and 1860s, as standardized schedules of school and work began to impress their rhythms on middle-class family life, there had emerged a carefully ordered progression of breakfast, lunch and dinner, which marked off the middle class from the big lunch eaters down the social scale." Dinner gradually moved from midday to evening in order to accommodate urban work and school schedules. The dining room emerged as a new domestic space and an indicator of a family's status. "Every family member was supposed to be at the table on time, appropriately dressed, and nicely groomed. Conversation, a crucial element of mealtimes, was expected to be conducted in urbane tones and to revolve around instructive topics. . . . Children were usually admitted to the family table at age eight or nine, when they were deemed able to grasp the verbal and unspoken lessons adults would teach them."[35]

After the Civil War, most freed African American women continued to work outside the home for long hours. Sharecropper women served breakfast either in the cabin or in the fields, where they joined the other family members at work. Midmorning they collected firewood to cook the midday meal, which was frequently reheated breakfast leftovers. Supper was often a repeat of previous meals. "Even if freed slaves invested much of their first earnings in kitchen utensils and tableware, the dining equipment that was customary in the middle-class home remained absent from sharecroppers' cabins. Very little formality was attached to meal consumption. The only occasions for elaborate cooking and festive dining were family reunions and certain times of the agricultural cycle." In the early twentieth century, African Americans in northern urban centers ate dinner late in the evening when the family was home. "[They] incorporated the southern breakfast pattern (fried pork, chicken or other meats) with the southern noontime dinner pattern (vegetables) into a single one, coming to resemble the middle-class dinner format. . . . The frequent cohabitation of relatives outside the nuclear family and unrelated boarders was yet another structural factor differentiating poor black households' mealtimes from those of the middle class."[36]

Until the early twentieth century, many white working-class urban workers had no designated space to eat meals. They cooked, ate, worked, entertained guests, and sometimes slept in their kitchens. Sunday dinners were the only highly structured mealtimes. Many of them took in boarders, and family mealtimes had to accommodate these paying guests. Some middle-class observers criticized these households, saying that "proper family meals were unheard of, and food was simply left on a bare table for family members to grab when they could." Social reformers used home economics to "improve" how working-class families had their meals. "This new discipline was originally aimed at middle-class housewives left with no domestic help by the flight of wage-earning white women from domestic service into the expanding manufacturing and clerical sectors. . . . The defense and support of the proper family mealtime in the face of the 'servant shortage' was one of home economics' main concerns." The working class was systematically exposed to lessons in what a middle-class family mealtime looked like. Transformations in food production and distribution enhanced the consuming power of the working class, which adopted the middle-class model of family meals.[37]

By the 1920s, eating out had become a popular middle-class practice. Men had historically eaten meals at saloons and hotel lounges, but Prohibition led to the closure of these venues, which were replaced with restaurants that catered to the growing class of male and female clerical workers and to families with leisure time. In the 1950s, suburban life "separated the male world of work from the female world of the home. The ideology of the separate spheres was never closer to its realization for greater numbers of people than it was in the 1950s. In 1950, 60 percent of American households conformed to the 'male breadwinner/female full-time homemaker' forms the Victorians had set as appropriate a century earlier. . . . [There was] broad observance of the model of a homemade dinner, featuring familial conversation and adherence to standard rules of behavior." Dinner became a "festive reunion meal" in a dining room with very formal procedures, a set time, mandatory attendance, and assigned seating and roles.[38]

Generalizations about table activities must take this historical context into account. Understandably, each of us has a tendency to think that our mealtime experiences are "normal," until we are exposed to practices in other households through historical, anthropological, and sociological accounts of different times and places.

In the contemporary period, research about mealtimes often focuses on questions of time, production, and consumption: For how much time and in what social settings do Americans prepare and consume meals (or, more accurately, food and drink)? People have different reasons for being interested in this question: food and drink marketers want to maximize sales, nutritionists are concerned about public health, government officials monitor public assistance programs, and sociologists want to chart the gender division of labor.

The U.S. Department of Agriculture conducts the annual American Time Use Survey, and here are its mealtime results for 2008.[39] Most of us, male and female, spend about an hour a day on food and drink as a main activity, with those over age sixty-five spending slightly more time. Just over 10 percent of us are "constant grazers," and people who live alone are more likely to eat alone. People in multiperson households eat with household members for just over half of their primary eating time. In half of all households with children, at least one child obtains either breakfast, lunch, or both meals from school, day care, or a summer program. Three quarters of women in male-female households say that they are the ones who are responsible for food shopping and meal preparation. Women who are the usual meal preparers spend twice as much time doing so (about an hour) as male meal-preparers (about half an hour). When meal preparation is shared among household members, things improve for women (down to thirty-eight minutes a day). Wherever and however we eat, time seems to be a huge determinant of what we do at tables.

Overworked Americans

The civilizing potential of table conversations cannot be realized if we don't have time for commensality, which is a real challenge for many households, primarily because of workplace demands. Most Americans feel lucky to land any job, let alone one that pays well, and will work whatever hours are needed for job security and/or satisfaction. By the same token, surveys have shown that many Americans feel overworked. Compared to other advanced industrial countries, Americans work longer hours. The working poor have to hold down "three and four jobs just to make ends meet." Between 1973 and 1998, average annual work hours increased from 1,720 to 1,898. "It is generally more profitable for firms to employ a small work force for long hours. The benefits costs are lower, employers can be more selective about whom they hire, and hours are a simple (if inaccurate) proxy for commitment. Employees who dislike the long hours have typically had to change jobs, or even occupations, to gain free time." In the 1990s, workers made gains in employment and income, but they paid with their time. Overtime hours hit record highs. "By the end of the decade, married couples with children" worked "an additional 151 hours" each year. Prosperity fueled an increased demand for consumer goods, for which many families worked longer hours and went into debt. A 1997 survey found that nearly two-thirds of employees were on the job more than they wanted to be. Compared to Continental Western Europeans, Americans work an additional nine weeks. "For the last half century, America's tendency has been to consume more, rather than work less."[40]

Wall Street and Silicon Valley are notorious for their 24/7 work cultures. In Silicon Valley, tech workers face enormous pressure to produce. Many of them are literally living on the job, where they eat their meals, get their exercise, and return to their cubicles. It is thought to be a badge of honor to work long hours. The "40 is enough" campaign is being waged to put a legal limit on mandatory overtime for all workers, including salaried employees, and to increase the minimum wage so that low-wage earners don't have to work so many hours. Overwork is as much of an issue for low-wage earners as for software engineers. One survey found that the average workweek for janitors was fifty-five hours. Across the country, some workers have expressed a willingness to work for fewer hours with less pay because they value time away from work. "A survey by the Families and Work Institute in New York found that 1 in 3 Americans feels chronically overworked, and a study by the American Sleep Institute found that 50 percent of Americans would be willing to work fewer hours for less pay." Overtime hours average four to five hours a week. And vacations are shrinking due to "all-in-one leave banks that force workers to choose between sick leave and time off." An "AFL-CIO poll found that a quarter of all workers" got "no vacation at all." The Take Back Your Time Movement has a legislative agenda to help overworked Americans: "at least a week of paid sick leave; at least three weeks of paid vacation;

a limit on compulsory overtime, so workers can accept or refuse overtime work; paid childbirth leave for all parents; incentives to make it easier for Americans to work part time if they choose, including hourly wage parity, protection of promotions and prorated benefits for part-timers; and making Election Day a holiday to make it easier for people to vote."[41]

There are some assumptions about the workplace that many Americans do not question: that the forty-hour work week is written in stone, that working longer hours increases productivity, and that vacations are a waste of time. We need to questions all these assumptions. In 1933, in an effort to reduce the nation's 25 percent unemployment rate, the Senate passed a bill to create a standard workweek of thirty hours. Although the bill was supported by "labor and religious leaders who argued that working people needed time for family, education, recreation and spirituality," it failed in the House. In 1938 the Fair Labor Standards Act was passed, creating the statutory forty-hour workweek. Between 1973 and 2000, the number of hours worked by the average American increased 199 hours and "worker productivity per hour nearly doubled." However, worker productivity actually declines at the end of long shifts. America took "its increases in labor productivity in the form of money" and consumer goods instead of time. During this period, the earnings of the very poor declined in real terms, and the largest share of the increase went to the richest Americans. Working longer hours has taken its toll on public health. Stress contributes to heart disease and a weakened immune system. Eating fast foods and having less time for exercise contribute to obesity and diabetes. People complain that they do not have enough time for their families or community involvement. Over the last thirty years, many European countries have decided on a work-life balance that gives workers more time—they work fewer hours for less money and get more paid vacation time. "The average Norwegian, for instance, works 29 percent less than the average American—14 weeks per year—yet his average income is only 16 percent less. Western Europeans average five to six weeks of paid vacation a year; we average two."[42]

Women's groups are active in the Take Back Your Time Movement, in large part because women more than men are responsible for family welfare, as single parents, mothers, and caretakers for elderly parents. Tanya Frazier worked as an office manager at a fifty-employee company. She received a call from her daughter's elementary school "telling her to pick up her flu-stricken 9-year-old." "When she stayed home from work the next day to care for her daughter, she was fired." She said that she had missed only a few days of work that year, but her boss said that "he was tired of her taking so many days off."

Her case is being used by "advocacy groups to argue for more paid time off for American workers," who "feel overstressed by demands on their time" and want "to devote more time to their families, . . . spirituality and . . . communities." Advocates "are seeking legislation in 21 states to give workers paid sick days or paid family leave to take care of infants or seriously ill family members." Almost half of the work force does not have paid sick days. "American workers put in 1,792 hours on average in 2003—three full-time weeks more than British workers and nine weeks more than French and German workers. . . . The average middle-class married woman [worked] 500 hours, or 12.5 weeks, more per year [in 2005] than in 1979." The call for paid leave can unite liberals, who want better working conditions, and conservatives, who promote family values. "Take Back Your Time and the Massachusetts Council of Churches worked closely last fall with the Lord's Day Alliance, an Atlanta-based group, to urge congregants through fliers and sermons to take 'four windows of time' over a month to relax and spend time with their families."[43]

The United States is the only advanced economy in the world that does not guarantee its workers paid vacation. Even when they are entitled to paid vacations, many Americans do not take them. Nor do they always take advantage of maternity/paternity leave and flextime arrangements. Americans have internalized a cultural norm that they are first and foremost workers, and that time away from work shows that they are not serious workers. Given this mind-set, it is hard to convince Americans that having a leisurely meal and relaxing conversation is not a waste of time. We need to challenge this "serious worker" norm. In European countries, workers have the legal right to between twenty and thirty days of paid vacation per year. Workers in Germany, France, and Britain have about six weeks of time off. "In Norway, workers older than 60 get an extra week," and "Austria, Germany, Italy and Switzerland provide extra paid leave for younger workers." In the United States, "vacations and paid holidays are set by companies, union agreements, school systems, states, the federal government and all other manner of employers. In general, our vacations are shorter than those elsewhere. About 90 percent of full-time employees get vacations that average (with paid holidays) about four weeks. . . . For part-time workers, about 35 percent to 40 percent receive paid time off. Not surprisingly, low-wage workers fare the worst. Only about half of the poorest-paid 25 percent receive paid time off." In 2011, Americans worked an average of 1,787 hours a year, longer than workers in other advanced economies—26 percent more than Germans, 21 percent more than the French, and 3 percent more than the Japanese. Americans seem to "draw more of their self-identity from their jobs than do other" people. The "competitive nature of the U.S. economy" might heighten insecurities and make people reluctant to take time off. Many Americans do not take advantage of maternity/paternity leave and flextime arrangements for fear of "being stigmatized as slackers."[44]

In sum, there are many factors that make it difficult for Americans to create common table times. Compared to workers in other advanced economies, we work longer hours and have less vacation time. Overtime hours are at record highs. There is no guaranteed paid sick leave or vacation time, and there are no limits on compulsory overtime. Half of Americans say that they would be willing to work for fewer hours for less pay, but they risk losing important benefits if they do so. One in three Americans feels chronically overworked. We have a low minimum wage, and the working poor need to hold down three or four jobs to make ends meet. We have internalized a cultural norm that we are first and foremost workers. Even when we are eligible for paid vacations, maternity or paternity leave, or flextime, many of us do not take advantage of these benefits lest we be stigmatized as slackers. In some work environments, especially in Silicon Valley and Manhattan, working 24/7 is a badge of honor. Hours are a proxy of commitment. These policies and attitudes have to change to open up time for common tables.

Common Tables

In spite of the host of forces—economic, social, and cultural—conspiring to make it very difficult to find time for table talk, the fact remains that carving out such time is very important. The image of a common table has a powerful attraction as a symbol of the commonplace and the vital, as described by poet Joy Harjo.[45]

> The world begins at a kitchen table. No matter what, we must eat to live.
> The gifts of earth are brought and prepared, set on the table. So it has been since creation, and it will go on.
> We chase chickens or dogs away from it. Babies teethe at the corners. They scrape their knees under it.
> It is here that children are given instructions on what it means to be human. We make men at it, we make women.
> At this table we gossip, recall enemies and the ghosts of lovers.
> Our dreams drink coffee with us as they put their arms around our children. They laugh with us at our poor falling-down selves and as we put ourselves back together once again at the table.

The son of Mark and Jackie Barden (*left*) was killed in the shooting at Sandy Hook Elementary School in Newtown, Connecticut, in 2012. Months later, they and two of their children had dinner at the house of next-door neighbor Karin LaBanca (*third from left*). The ritual of sharing a common table can build community, even when it is painfully difficult to find the right things to say.
Credit: Photo by Linda Davidson / *Washington Post* via Getty Images.

This table has been a house in the rain, an umbrella in the sun.
Wars have begun and ended at this table. It is a place to hide in the shadow of
     terror. A place to celebrate the terrible victory.
We have given birth on this table, and have prepared our parents for burial here.
At this table we sing with joy, with sorrow. We pray of suffering and remorse.
     We give thanks.
Perhaps the world will end at the kitchen table, while we are laughing and crying,
     eating of the last sweet bite.

A table is a place of temporary leveling: social and egalitarian, conducive to chiming in. As one rabbi put it, "Think of homes we had in ancient times. People barely had room to sleep, beds were shared, but there was always one table. And that table was where one studied, that was the table where one argued, where one ate. That was the table where one mended clothes or prepared food. The table was the place where conversation and communication took place. Even today it is the one common space in modern homes and it is still the place where everyone gravitates."[46]

In most Western cultures, a table represents a place to share bread, an activity that gives rise to the word *companion* (Latin: *com* with + *panis* bread). Companions share tables. When National Public Radio's Kitchen Sisters asked listeners to call in with their kitchen stories, they received a call from Larry Lagattuta, who owned Enrico Biscotti Company in Pittsburgh, Pennsylvania, which made biscotti and other Italian pastries. He cooked on wood in a big brick oven and held a bread class once a month. People came from all over the city to get together for breakfast and to make bread, which they took home at the end of the day. Lagattuta thought it was important to teach Americans the history of bread and how it's made, and drinking homemade wine while it was being baked made it even more enjoyable. He praised the companionship of gathering around a communal table: "That's what we provide here, and it's an amazing process. I think if we don't bring it back, we're going to lose this tradition and then lose part of ourselves."[47]

Restaurant tables welcome strangers and encourage conviviality (assuming that they do not discriminate or rush meals to maximize turnover). Of course, restaurants are in business to make money, but many repeat customers frequent establishments where they feel personally welcomed. Writer Adam Gopnik thinks that restaurants teach us that "as important as finding people you have things in common with is learning to live in pleasure alongside people with whom you don't. This may be why, though there's a 'new cooking' every few years, the institution of the restaurant has shown itself so resilient. . . . Home, Robert Frost wrote, is the place where, when you have to go there, they have to take you in. A restaurant is a place where, when you go there, they not only have to take you in but have to act as though they were glad to see you. In cities of strangers, this pretense can be very dear."[48]

Even at restaurants with "power tables" reserved for influential customers, patrons appreciate having a place for conversations. Indeed, according to two Washington insiders, the real business of politics in the nation's capital transpires at restaurant tables. In 2013, the United States learned that the Chinese government had hacked into the computers of some of Washington's most prominent organizations to find out how things got done. According to these insiders, "If the Chinese really want to get a look at where the power decisions get made, send an undercover eater to see who's dining with whom at the Four Seasons for breakfast, Tosca for lunch, and the Palm or Oceanaire for dinner." They maintained that literal transcripts of decision making do not tell the real story. Actual decision makers converse with experts and affected parties to make informed decisions, and "really hearing what was said and accomplishing something afterward requires real work and a lot of relevant, persuasively presented information." Decision makers "take their independence, transparency, and integrity seriously." Washington has increasingly become a "place that rewards *what* you know rather than *whom* you know." In the view of these observers, "it's the nuance and fragments of information that form the mosaic of Washington politics and power. . . . Often it's better to have a short sidebar conversation during a chance encounter at a dinner or cocktails with a 20- or 30-something staffer on a key congressional committee than a courtesy meeting with a member of Congress or a cabinet secretary. . . . You don't need to peep through the keyhole to follow the political maneuvering in Washington; just walk into any good steakhouse and look around."[49]

Common tables bring together people who want an alternative to the anonymity and economic inefficiency of single-family homes. Residents at one cohousing community shared communal meals twice a week with each family cooking once a month. Compared to residents of single-family homes, they had lower utility bills, made fewer car trips, ate out less often, and fulfilled at least some of their social life in the community. One father with three sons remarked that sharing the prep of community meals once a month was more fun than cooking alone, and two nights a week you got to go down to dinner and come home to a clean kitchen. The Common House, which seated thirty people, served as a gathering place for the community and was available for residents' other group activities.[50]

Common tables are valued by young people who want to get off their electronic devices and engage with people face-to-face. For democratic conversations to happen, people need to bring their undivided attention and listening skills to the table. A case in point is Feastly, a San Francisco Bay Area startup connecting chefs, home cooks, and diners to share a meal and conversation. According to its cofounder, "Feastly touches on all of our passions: food, community and technology. It's an online marketplace that allows any passionate cook to offer and serve a meal in their home to any hungry eater." One participant said, "I really liked the idea that it's something to do other than going to a bar. You can sit down, have a meal and spend a lot less money than going out, and you actually get to meet people as well." Another thought that Feastly was "the perfect blend of technology, art and creativity. It is a form of social media, but it gets us off the computer and engaged with people around the table, eating, and in good company."[51]

One group that promotes gathering around tables for the explicit purpose of promoting "conversations that matter" is the World Café, which has a seven-step process for fostering collaborative dialogue. (1) Set the Context:

Clarify the purpose and broad parameters within which the dialogue will unfold. (2) Create Hospitable Space: Assure the welcoming environment and psychological safety that nurtures personal comfort and mutual respect. (3) Explore Questions That Matter: Focus collective attention on powerful questions that attract collaborative engagement. (4) Encourage Everyone's Contribution: Enliven the relationship between the "me" and the "we" by inviting full participation and mutual giving. (5) Cross-Pollinate and Connect Diverse Perspectives: Use the living system dynamics of emergence through intentionally increasing the diversity of perspectives and density of connections while retaining a common focus on core questions. (6) Listen Together for Patterns, Insights, and Deeper Questions: Focus shared attention in ways that nurture coherence of thought without losing individual contribution. (7) Harvest and Share Collective Discoveries: Make collective knowledge and insight visible and actionable.[52]

These principles are consistent with Blum-Kulka's best practices for family dinnertime conversations: establish ground rules, welcome many viewpoints with mutual respect, engage in collective action, and listen carefully. The preconditions for productive "outside the household" conversations mirror those of healthy families: creating a hospitable space and nurturing personal comfort. What is different of course is the expectation for "higher level" conversations, which are essential building blocks of civil society.

Thanks to the internet, today we have global tables. In 2012, the first Feast Worldwide Dinner Party launched over five hundred independently organized dinner parties, where people were invited to discuss a set of important problems and share possible solutions online. The initiative's stated purpose is "connecting with each other over a simple meal and weighing in on a global problem solving session." In 2013, the three discussion questions were: Why is it so hard to turn what you learn at school into real-world skills? Why is it so hard to be healthy every single day? And why is it so hard for vets returning from war to connect with people and services they need? Shared answers created "a global dialogue for good." Feast Worldwide provided an invitation template, meal suggestions, music platforms, and DIY project ideas. It reminded participants: "Be sure to share your answer with others around the world using #feast2013. Keep the conversation going. This isn't the end. Tell us how it went and what you need to move forward!"[53]

Whether it is a kitchen table or a global table, people imagine a place to keep the conversation going. The premise of a common table is the belief that people can connect in a meaningful way and that differences can be dealt with civilly. In cases where it is hard to be civil, we can at least hope that table experiences hold the possibility of preventing uncivil and inhumane behavior in the first place. Adam Gopnik thought about this issue with respect to the French intellectuals who shared tables with their Nazi occupiers.

> How much can the table *truly* reconcile—how sweetly can, or should, the rituals of social life reconcile us to our opposites? It is sentimental, surely, to pretend that the ugliness of life escapes the table; we rightly condemn the French intellectuals and artists who made too easy a social peace with their occupiers. But is it unrealistic to wish that some reconciliation of opposites might yet take place there? It's a hope, at least. Very different people do dine together, or try to. . . . We can't wish away differences, but we can hope for an end to hostilities. Disdain for others is part of life; learning to dissimulate it through manners is as good a cure as we can hope for. While we wait for the reign of Universal Love, we can at least share the premise of the Common Table. . . . Good things do happen when people sit down for dinner. That's itself a faith. Obviously, we don't want to sit down to dinner with Nazis. . . . But we do want to sit down to dinner with people *before* they become Nazis, if it might help them from becoming so. It is not wrong to hope that the revelation of a common human touch, a common taste, shared and relished, can become itself an argument for humanity. . . . We smile, and often, at the countless travelers' tales of violence averted by bread and salt and beer.[54]

Democratic table talk runs counter to authoritarian thinking: listening to opposing views, giving voice to the powerless, encouraging turn taking, and taking responsibility for keeping difficult conversations going. I agree with Gopnik that the diplomatic potential of the common table is based on hope and faith, but I would add that conversational skills play a big role in realizing this potential.

Stories and Food

Tables offer the hope that good things will happen not only because they are common and level but also because they have tasty food and engaging stories. Everyone has table stories and food stories, which seem to sustain us. Writer Toni Cade Bambara thinks stories are lifesavers: "Stories are important. They keep us alive. In the ships, in the camps, in the quarters, field, prisons, on the road, on the run, underground, under siege, in the throes, on the verge—the storyteller snatches us back from the edge to hear the next chapter. In which we are the subjects. We, the hero of the tales. Our lives preserved. How it was, how it be. Passing it along in the relay. That is what I work to do: to produce stories that save our lives."[55]

In conducting their interviews, the Kitchen Sisters asked food questions as icebreakers and found that people's food stories ended up being stories about fellowship, sharing, and community. In their view, the need to be heard and understood is as primal as the need to be fed. We seem, quite literally, to crave connectedness. Food evokes memories and stories; it is our common ground and universal language. They were struck with how there was a "unifying theme to the hours of stories and messages" they gathered—fellowship that came "from tending and feeding each other" and listening. "This need to be heard and understood and recognized seems as powerful as the primal need to feed and be fed. Food and story are a way to kinship with someone whose face you've never seen, whose work you don't know, whose experience is not your own—and a way of discovering perhaps that you share more then you realize."[56]

When we listen to people's food stories, we hear their "food voice," a term coined by dietician and food historian Annie Hauck-Lawson. The idea came to her in the course of her study of the meaning of food in a Polish American family. She explains, "While poring through rich data and reflecting on my observations, I tried to find ways to understand what I saw and heard—people's way with, words about, and meanings towards food. Participants creatively and dynamically engaged with food in different ways to assert aspects of their identities. Food helped them forge cooperative links, extend hospitality and assert power or obligation. Expressing their world views on community, economics, gender, nutrition, ethnic identity, and tradition, their foodways essentially translated into a language."[57]

At a dinner table, what begins as a shared food experience and a personal story might evolve into a life-changing conversation. You never know when that new acquaintance sitting next to you might turn out to be a superb listener like Dr. Martin Luther King Jr., as was the case for art historian William Hood. King asked him why he was studying for a PhD in art history, wondering what he thought art could accomplish, and admitting that he had rarely discussed, or even thought much about, art. Hood recounts, "As I stammered an answer I cannot recall, he listened with the concentration of someone who genuinely wanted to understand. Never before, and rarely since, had I witnessed such authentic humility. It was so simple, so powerful a form of energy that for a few moments it freed me from bondage to myself." This ten-minute conversation changed the way Hood thought about his life: "The determination to use my education to become a famous scholar gradually made room for a half-baked resolution to become a useful art historian. I began to consider the moral or religious content of Renaissance art; and once I got a job teaching art history at an institution whose values encouraged me to develop that ambition, teaching became a means for me to help students identify and examine their own values. That remains my goal. The short conversation I had with Dr. King had a lasting effect."[58]

This is an excellent example of how learning to converse is good for democracy. Who knows when a dinner acquaintance might be someone with whom we want to connect, and it would be a shame (personally) and a lost opportunity (democratically) if we did not have the skills to do so. William Hood was a doctoral student, so presumably he had considerable verbal skills. Still, he was flustered and stammered in the presence of someone he respected. He was so overwhelmed by King's genuine interest in his story that he forgot himself and became part of a collective action called a conversation. This story shows how learning conversational skills is never finished—it is a lifelong project. We are bound to rub shoulders with people who ask probing questions and who tell us interesting stories filled with new experiences and ideas.

A democracy needs to raise children who want to hear other people's stories. Psychologist Anne Fishel is a member of the Family Dinner Project, a group that promotes teaching children the art of conversation. She believes that dinner conversations are the most powerful language experiences of a child's life. Research has found that talking to children during dinner is a more effective way to develop vocabulary than reading to them; that stories told around the table build children's sense of resilience and optimism; that children bring up about six different topics at dinner; and "that families who eat together expect that children will sit and talk for more than a few minutes and each topic usually gets input from several members, so there are multiple viewpoints expressed. This exposure to multiple points of view engages kids in complex thinking and can encourage tolerance for opinions different from one's own."[59] This last point is especially relevant for my argument: hearing multiple points of view and learning tolerance for opposing views are crucial for a vibrant civil society and democracy.

I am particularly interested in difficult conversations. In their groundbreaking book, *Difficult Conversations: How to Discuss What Matters Most*, members of the Harvard Negotiation Project make two important observations.[60] The first is that every difficult conversation is really three conversations: about facts, feelings, and identity. The second is that it is important to reformulate a difficult conversation into a learning conversation, where the goal is understanding and both parties' stories are embraced. "Story" is a central concept here, since it contains the facts, feelings, and identity of difficult conversation work. Fishel joins many other experts in claiming that narrative conversation, or the telling of stories, can be particularly helpful for children. Helping them tell stories that include their thoughts and feelings, rather than just the facts, is associated with their greater well-being.

I am also interested in what makes us resilient in the face of political and social setbacks. Research has shown that children who know a lot about their parents' own childhood and family histories are more resilient in the face of adversity, have higher self-esteem, and see themselves rather than others as responsible for their own behavior. Accordingly, Fishel recommends dinnertime conversations where parents ask their children if they know such specifics as how their parents met, how their names were chosen, what childhood lessons their parents learned, what jobs their parents had when they were young, and what is the earliest story they know about an ancestor. She encourages adults to "piggyback on a story told by a child, in order to tell one with a similar theme. For example, if a teen tells a story about not getting a part in a play, a parent may want to tell a story about a setback he faced and what he learned from it. Stories that start out with something negative but end up positively are associated with greater feelings of life satisfaction." The conversations she promotes in her office as a family therapist are the same kind that can occur at the dinner table. "In therapy and at the table, each family member is encouraged to speak about his or her own experience while being listened to with curiosity and respect. Children and their parents come away from both experiences with the sense that the family is more than the sum of its individual parts: Instead, what is created is something greater—the sense of belonging to a family that has its own set of stories and identities."[61] Telling stories about ourselves that are taken seriously by those we love and respect promotes both psychological and civic health, connecting us to common goods greater than ourselves.

Chapter Two

Conversations and Narratives

Studying Conversations

As we have seen, linguists have developed certain concepts that can help us get a detailed understanding of conversations. To begin with an example with which we are all familiar, they study interruptions, and whether certain groups are more likely to interrupt than others. Linguist Deborah Tannen's analysis of conversations at a Thanksgiving dinner led her to conclude that interruptions were not necessarily displays of dominance. One person at the table had a "high involvement style" with "cooperative overlap." This person talked along with a speaker, not to interrupt, but to show enthusiastic listening and participation. Other speakers used a "high considerateness" style of listening only. This insight made her reluctant to jump on the "men dominate women by interrupting them" bandwagon since cooperative overlap is a form of listening and participation.[1]

In another study, she videotaped males and females at four age levels to look for patterns in body language, topic choice, and topic cohesion. In America, the female pattern of showing conversational engagement was the cultural norm: aligning their bodies, making eye contact, quickly establishing topics, and producing extended talk on a small number of topics. The male pattern was the opposite. Since males and females learned their styles of talking in sex-separate peer groups, they developed different habits for signaling their intentions and understandings. She cautioned that it would be a mistake to characterize the male style as disengagement. In many cultures, respect is shown by casting eyes down and never looking a superior in the face, so avoiding eye contact is the appropriate display of conversational involvement. For men, head-on posture and gaze might connote combativeness, so breaking that alignment might signal friendly engagement. The conversation of tenth-grade boys provided evidence that physical alignment away from rather than toward each other did not mean lack of engagement. "They sit parallel to each other, stretched out in postures that could be interpreted as lackadaisical and careless, in one case occasionally and in the other case almost never glancing at the other. Viewing the videotape with the sound turned off could easily give the impression that these boys are disengaged. But turning the sound up reveals the most 'intimate' talk heard in any of the tapes I observed."[2]

There are gender differences not only in body language, topic choice, and topic cohesion, but also in "conversation work": asking and responding to conversation openers and questions, using "minimal response utterances" to show interest, introducing and elaborating on topics, and filling silences to keep the conversation going. Sociologist Pamela M. Fishman tape-recorded three couples' conversations and found that women did more of every kind of conversation work. They asked three times as many questions, were twice as likely to respond to children's conversational opening "D'ya know what?" question, and were ten times more likely to use the phrase "y'know" to get the other person's attention. Men and women used "the minimal response" (saying "yeah," "umm," "huh," and only that) in different ways: males to convey lack of interest and females to do "support work." "When the men were talking, the women were particularly skilled at inserting 'mm's,' 'yeah's,' 'oh's,' and other such comments throughout streams of talk rather than at the end. These are signs from the inserter that she is constantly attending to what is said, that she is demonstrating her participation, her interest in the interaction and the speaker. How well women do this is also striking—seldom do they mistime their insertions and cause even slight overlap. These minimal responses occur between breaths of a speaker, and there is nothing in tone or structure to suggest they are attempting to take over the talk."[3]

Men produced over twice as many statements, and they almost always got a response, which was not true for women. Many times, a man's comments led to a lengthy exchange, but this was seldom the case for women's remarks. Fishman maintained that men's remarks were not substantively more interesting than women's, but they took on that character by virtue of generating interactions. In one example, a woman made several attempts to start a conversation on a certain topic, and after several minutes, she gave up. Fishman notes, "One might argue that because the man was making a salad he could not pay attention to the conversation. However, while still at work on the salad, the man introduces his own topic for conversation. . . . This topic introduction engenders a conversation when the woman responds to his remark. They go through a series of exchanges which end when he decides not to continue. This conversational exchange demonstrates that the man was willing to engage in discussion, but only on his own terms." For the most part, men defined what appropriate and inappropriate topics of conversation were. Yet women worked the hardest in making interactions go smoothly, whether by being a good listener, filling silences to keep conversation moving, developing others' topics, or presenting and developing topics of their own.[4]

Several of Fishman's insights are relevant to my project. Conversations take work and there are many subtle ways of keeping them going: responding to conversation openers, asking and responding to questions, using minimal responses to show interest, introducing and elaborating on topics, filling silences, and being a good listener. And hers is just one of many studies revealing that women do most of the conversation work.

Researchers have also discovered class differences in parental expectations about conversing with children. Sociologist Annette Lareau attributes these differences to parenting styles: middle-class parents tended to promote organized leisure activities and extensive reasoning, whereas working-class and poor parents tended to organize fewer leisure activities and rely more on directives. The middle-class parents she interviewed, both white and black, engaged in what she calls "concerted cultivation." Their children's age-specific organized activities dominated family life and created time demands, especially for mothers. The parents justified these activities as transmitting important life skills to children. They also stressed language use, the development of reasoning, and talking as their preferred form of discipline. This cultivation approach resulted in a wider range of experiences for children, but it also created a frenetic pace for parents, a cult of individualism within the family, an emphasis on children's performance, and a sense of entitlement in children. By contrast, the child-rearing strategies of white and black working-class and poor parents emphasized the "accomplishment of natural growth." These parents believed that as long as they provided the basics—love, food, and safety—their children would grow and thrive. They did not focus on developing their children's special talents. Their children participated in fewer organized activities and had more free time and deeper, richer ties within their extended families. Parents issued many more directives to their children and, in some households, placed more emphasis on physical discipline. This child-rearing approach encouraged a sense of constraint in children.[5]

Lareau provided examples of household conversational dynamics. In middle-class families, parents elicited information and promoted reasoning and negotiation. They gave children opportunities to develop and practice verbal skills, including how to summarize, clarify, and amplify information. They expressed interest in children's activities, which often led to negotiations over small, home-based matters. There was a general pattern of reasoning and accommodating. Life in the working-class and poor families flowed smoothly without extended verbal discussions. The amount of talk varied, but overall, it was considerably less than in the middle-class homes. Parents joked with children and discussed what was on television. But they did not appear to cultivate conversation by asking the children questions or by drawing them out. Often their remarks were brief and direct. One mother listened to her children's complaints about school, but she did not draw them out on these issues or ask for details. When her son said that his teacher was mean and had lied, the mother listened, but she did not encourage him to support his opinion with more examples, nor did she mention any concerns of her own.[6]

In terms of understanding the development of a political voice, it is interesting to see how these conversational dynamics played themselves out when families interacted with groups outside the home: teachers and school officials, health-care professionals, and government officials. Although families addressed similar problems (e.g., learning disabilities, asthma, traffic violations), they did not achieve similar resolutions. Middle-class children's sense of entitlement worked to their advantage, and a sense of constraint disadvantaged working-class and poor children.

> Both parents and children drew on the resources associated with these two child-drearing approaches during their interactions with officials. Middle-class parents and children often customized their interactions; working-class and poor parents were more likely to have a "generic" relationship. When faced with problems, middle-class parents also appeared better equipped to exert influence over other adults compared with working-class and poor families. Nor did middle-class parents or children display the intimidation or confusion we witnessed among many working-class and poor families when they faced a problem in their children's school experience. . . .
>
> Working-class and poor children seemed aware of their parents' frustration and witnessed their powerlessness. At times, these parents encouraged their children to resist school officials' authority [and use physical force against classmates]. . . . Middle-class parents' superior levels of education gave them larger vocabularies that facilitated concerted cultivation, particularly in institutional interventions. Poor and working-class parents were not familiar with key terms professionals used, such as "tetanus shot." Furthermore, middle-class parents' educational background gave them confidence when criticizing educational professionals and

intervening in school matters. Working-class and poor parents viewed educators as their social superiors.[7]

Class differences in everyday conversations raise important questions about finding a democratic and political voice. On the one hand, as Lareau correctly points out, it is a mistake to see either child-rearing approach as intrinsically desirable. Drawbacks to middle-class child-rearing are often overlooked: exhaustion from intensive mothering, frenetic family schedules, a sapping of children's naïveté that leaves them feeling too sophisticated for simple games and toys, an inability to fill "empty time" with creative play, and dependence on parents to solve boredom. There is an important distinction between standards that are intrinsically desirable and those that facilitate success in dominant institutions.[8] On the other hand, in order to cultivate a political voice, one needs to learn the conversational skills used in dominant institutions. In my view, such skills should not remain horded among the middle and upper classes. Democracy is best served when all people are able to join a conversation, and democratic conversations need to begin at home. But care has to be taken when well-meaning government programs attempt to define and address "problems" of class differences in everyday conversation. A case in point is the "word gap."

The discovery of "the 30 million word gap" between poor and rich children set off a lively debate about what, if anything, government should do about it. A study of forty-two families found that in four years, an average child in a professional family was exposed to 45 million words, as compared to 26 million in a working-class family and 13 million in a welfare family. Differences in exposure to words among three-year-olds predicted language skills at age nine to ten. The authors were concerned that poor children would be disadvantaged in their cognitive development. They also noticed that average children in professional homes had a much higher ratio of affirmative/encouraging words to prohibition/ discouraging words than did working-class and poor children.[9]

In 2014 President Obama convened a White House conference to "bridge the word gap," and cities initiated programs to encourage low-income parents to talk more frequently with their children. In a program in Providence, Rhode Island, children wore devices that recorded adult words, child vocalizations, and conversational turns. Caseworkers provided parents with graphs to see how well they were doing. Providence's mayor was a self-described "Head Start to Harvard" son of immigrants who wanted to provide opportunities to low-income residents. Critics raised a host of concerns about governmental responses to the word gap: emphasizing quantity of words rather quality of conversation; adopting an overly rigid developmental framework; using an intrusive technology; imposing middle-class values on poor people; and perpetuating a blame-the-victim approach to language and poverty. Poverty can be stressful and dispiriting, making it "difficult to summon up the patience and playfulness for an open-ended conversation with a small, persistent, possibly whiny child." A Boston researcher who had helped establish a program to encourage parents to talk to their children convened focus groups with low-income parents. Some were overwhelmed and exhausted working three jobs, and when they got home, they had to cook, clean, and do the laundry. So they put the kids in front of the TV. He said of word gap interventions: "Maybe we have the model wrong. Maybe what we need to do is come in and bring dinner and help with the laundry and free up a parent to engage in more play with their child."[10]

The "word gap" controversy underscores several themes of this project: that conversations are hard work, that table talk is a luxury for exhausted parents, that cultures have different expectations about which types of verbal interaction are appropriate for infants and children, and that Americans tend to look for silver-bullet solutions to complex problems. More talk does build vocabulary, and a large vocabulary helps in school and at work. However, the quality of talk also matters. For our purposes, civil conversation requires the skills of listening, turn taking, respecting the views of others, and providing evidence. All kinds of families can help children develop the social and emotional intelligence needed for conversations, even if not all of them build their children's vocabularies at the same rate. Language socialization is a lifelong personal and civic project.

In households that encourage civil conversation, people gain a sense of comfort in a group setting where their experiences and thoughts are taken seriously. This makes them more likely to seek out similar group settings. Indeed, it may be in familiar settings that the most public-spirited and open-minded conversations take place. This was what a sociologist found in her research about citizens' everyday political conversations. She participated in three types of groups: volunteer, recreational, and activist. The nature of people's conversations differed depending on whether they took place in private or public settings. People had curious and open-minded private conversations and avoided political talk in wider circles. A cycle of "political evaporation" set in when people assumed that talking politics in a publicly minded way was out of place. The further "backstage" the context, the more public-spirited conversation was possible. People thought that in public they had to couch their motivations in a politics of self-interest, even though this was not true, as in the case of volunteers. Or they had to speak "for the children," engaging in mandatory "public Momism," and wax nostalgic about community. The silencing of public-spirited conversations was the volunteers' way of looking out for the public good: they did not want to ruin positive feelings or alienate anyone. Each group created and enforced manners for political conversations. "Cultures of talk" told them when they needed to hide their fears and when talking helped work through fears. The democratic norms that really mattered were unspoken rules about conversation, manners, civility, and tact that made them comfortable engaging in freewheeling political conversation: "companionable ways of creating and maintaining a comfortable context for talk in the public sphere."[11]

This study raises some interesting dilemmas about the relationship between backstage settings and public arenas. People felt freer to speak their minds in smaller, more comfortable settings, and in wider circles they censored what they said according to their understandings of what "public speech" meant: self-interested, "for the children," "public Momism," or "nostalgic community." If their true feelings did not fit into any of these preordained frames of reference, they silenced themselves in public. They also refrained from speaking if they thought their views would damage group harmony by hurting people's feelings or alienating them. On the other hand, groups developed norms to help people talk through their fears and engage in freewheeling conversation, and these norms created a companionable context for public talk.

Norms regarding political conversations and the common good have social origins—varying by age, gender, education, race, and class. These differences played out in a study by a political scientist who observed elderly, middle-class white men at a corner store and women at a church craft guild. Women evaded political topics for fear of disrupting the air of politeness, and men were much more likely to talk politics for several reasons: they had more shared experiences and acquaintances, interacted daily as opposed to weekly, met for social rather than instrumental purposes, and convened in the same room as "others" (blacks, women, and youth), enforcing a group solidarity of "us" versus "them." Both groups developed a collective perspective based on their group identification, and they made sense of politics using that shared view. The "elite frames" of experts and pundits mattered, but through conversations people transformed and circumvented these frames by applying their identity-based perspectives to supplement news stories. These socially rooted perspectives were often more important than partisanship. People did not act on behalf of a predetermined public good; rather, ideas about a common good were worked out in group interaction. Although such interaction fostered trust and clarified social identities, it also reinforced the exclusion of nonmembers. I agree with the author that given this trade-off between community and exclusion, more social interaction by itself does not necessarily bolster civil society. Community-wide intergroup dialogue is essential.[12]

It is interesting to see how group solidarity affects conversations through self-censorship, excluding others, and modifying elite frames of reference. Churchwomen did not want to disrupt group harmony by talking politics. Group solidarity, when it is not based on exclusion, is good for civil society because it fosters bonds of trust. It is possible that their group bonds would have been ruptured with divisive political discussions. On the other hand, one has to wonder if members had the right kind of conversational skills, would they have been able to broach political topics with more ease. Men felt freer to discuss politics, but their group identity was formed in part by distinguishing themselves from "others." Civil society is better served by groups that do not define themselves in this way. As for the power of elite frames, they seem to be subject to modification by groups with strong social bonds. Civil society benefits when groups empower themselves to question dominant ideas and institutions—that is what a strong democracy needs.

It is not only social scientists who have thought about various forms of conversation in a democracy. Some political philosophers maintain that citizens have a moral obligation not only to engage in conversations but also to exercise conversational restraint. We are never going to see eye to eye on many important issues, but, pragmatically speaking, we have to keep talking about them since it is part of the human condition to "all be in this together," to be stewards of our common planet. I agree with legal philosopher Bruce Ackerman that dialogue is the first obligation of citizenship. He argues that when two people have reached different conclusions about an important question, the only way "to find out how matters stand" is for them to talk to each other

> to consider the way they might live together despite this ongoing disagreement. . . . Somehow or other, citizens of a liberal state must learn to talk to one another in a way that enables each of them to avoid condemning their own personal morality as evil or false. Otherwise, the conversation's pragmatic point becomes pointless. . . . The history of liberal thought can be read as a series of efforts to provide conversational models that would enable political participants to talk to one another in an appropriately neutral way.[13]

When people have profound moral disagreements, sometimes conversational restraint is called for. Rather than searching for "some common value that will trump" the disagreement, or translating it into some "neutral framework," or calling upon an "unearthly creature [to] resolve it . . . we should simply say *nothing at all* about this disagreement and put the moral ideals that divide us off the conversational agenda of the liberal state. . . . We need not lose the chance to talk to one another about our deepest moral disagreements in countless other, more private, contexts."[14] Such restraint means that no one is obliged to say something false.

> Having constrained the conversation in this way, we may instead use dialogue for pragmatically productive purposes: to identify normative premises all political participants find reasonable (or, at least, not unreasonable). . . . Rather than require people to say things they believe are false, I am asking them to make a special kind of emotional sacrifice . . . Each must try to repress their desire to say many things which they believe are true, but which will divert the group's energy away from the elaboration of the pragmatic implications of the [propositions that could be used for conflict resolution].
>
> This kind of selective repression is, I think, a familiar feature of social life. It is continually required by the ongoing exercise that sociologists call role playing. Each social role can be understood as a set of conventional constraints upon acceptable symbolic behavior. . . . All roles are constraining, placing vast domains of conversation off the agenda so long as the participants are acting within a particular role framework. . . . [Liberalism] calls upon us to reflect upon the pragmatic imperative to talk to strangers as well as soul-mates; and to consider whether, despite the strangers' strangeness, we might still have something reasonable to say to one another about our efforts to coexist on this puzzling planet.[15]

As we will see later, because female senators from both parties have adopted Ackerman's pragmatic approach, they have been able to accomplish things in a highly partisan, dysfunctional Congress. He helps us think about the conversational dilemmas we have raised. In a democracy, who has a moral imperative to talk to others and under what conditions? When is topic avoidance a good idea? Is it more important to maintain group harmony or to speak the truth? I agree that in order for a democracy to work, citizens cannot cut themselves off from dialogue with others. As a pragmatic matter, we know that for the most difficult issues, things will rarely be resolved to everyone's satisfaction, but we must find a way to live together despite this ongoing disagreement. Citizens must learn to talk to one another in a way that avoids condemnation. If we have a fundamental moral disagreement with another citizen, it is fine to say nothing at all about this disagreement and put the moral ideals that divide us off the conversational agenda. In restraining ourselves in this way, we can still talk about our deepest moral disagreements in other, more private, contexts. We should use public dialogue for pragmatically productive purposes: to identify normative premises all political participants find reasonable and can live with. He echoes sociologists' ideas about "backstage" roles and conversations as being more forthcoming and about public roles requiring more restraint. We have a pragmatic imperative to talk to strangers as well to as intimates, and despite strangers' strangeness, with a little curiosity and imagination, we might have something reasonable to say to one another about our efforts to coexist.

Learning the Art of Conversation

To some extent, learning to converse is a science. There are building blocks of alphabet, vocabulary, and grammar, and basic rules about turn taking, interrupting, topic coherence, and narrative flow. But for the most part, learning how to converse is an art: an interaction that requires active listening with an open mind, a willingness to alter one's thinking, and curiosity about new imaginary roads—depending on what the other person says. Interaction raises social, creative, and moral questions: How should I respond, if at all? Whose language should I use, my vocabulary or theirs? How much do I censor my thoughts or formulate them in a polite way to keep the conversation going? Elementary school teachers are charged with teaching both the science and the art of conversation. One of them, Susan Engel, thinks that engaging in extended and complex conversations is key to children's intellectual development and literacy. She argues that our current, test-driven educational approach is at odds with scientific findings about child development and has created a curriculum that stifles both children and teachers. Developmental precursors, such as saying the alphabet, "don't always resemble the skill to which they are leading," such as reading. "But having extended and complex conversations during toddlerhood" does help children learn to read. Children in elementary school should not "cram for high school or college" but rather "develop ways of thinking and behaving that will lead to valuable knowledge and skills later on." She imagines a third-grade classroom where "children would spend two hours each day hearing stories read aloud, reading aloud themselves, telling stories to one another and reading on their own." They would also spend an hour a day writing things that had actual meaning to

It is difficult to practice and teach the art of conversation when people are on their cell phones. Women do most of the "conversation work" at tables and many people are trying to figure out new rules about cell phone table manners. Credit: Frank Van Delft.

them. And "teachers should spend time each day having sustained conversations with small groups of children. Such conversations give children a chance to support their views with evidence, change their minds and use questions as a way to learn more."[16]

In confirmation of Engel's views, child development researchers have found a correlation between kindergartners' expressive vocabulary and their reading comprehension as adolescents. An effort is under way to have children begin kindergarten with an expressive vocabulary of around 2,200 words, and many experts think that dinnertime conversations build such vocabularies. Dinner is the time when parents sit down with their kids for about twenty minutes and everyone is together. If they're not watching TV, it is a good time to have extended conversations, since people are not preoccupied with other chores and the opportunity for concentration and connection is there.[17]

Without good role models growing up, it is very difficult, but not impossible, to practice and teach the art of conversation. When Laurie David interviewed people about their childhood dinners, many of them said: "No one spoke; we just ate." Her ex-husband, a professional comedian, was not skilled at table talk: "His own childhood family dinners were about yelling, *not* talking, and meals were about refueling, not socializing." Her family had a hard time talking as well: "It was more like tiptoeing around sensitive subjects, accidentally wading into the wrong territory, lots of arguing, and then tears. There were also those miserable awkward years from eleven to thirteen when all we talked about at dinner was how accident-prone I was." In spite of these experiences, David thought that one of the greatest benefits of family dinners was the opportunity to teach children how to carry on a conversation. "Basic skills like listening, waiting your turn to speak, and not interrupting others are all modeled and learned at the table. A friend reminiscing about her family dinners wistfully said to me, 'I loved our dinners because I really felt listened to.' A common thread of family dinners among previous generations was the expectation that everyone came to the table ready to talk and share. I heard this repeatedly from people I interviewed for this book. Being a good conversationalist is a skill that will serve your kids well their entire lives, but it requires practice."[18]

For many children, being asked to join adult conversations, at dinner tables and social gatherings, sends a message that their thoughts matter, that adults are genuinely interested in what they have to say. This is an important building block of their civic selves. Here is how one student I interviewed described the importance of being taken seriously as a participant in adult discussions.

> I am an only child. My parents have always felt that I have been mature enough to go to some of their friends' dinner parties. They include me because they feel like it is important to my development as a person to understand what people talk about and to know the issues of the time. At family meals, we talk about elections, but we don't necessarily spend too much time focusing on them because there are often negative connotations for both sides of whatever the argument is. We like to crack jokes because it makes it easier to enjoy the experience. They feel it is important for me to be part of the discussions because I am a third of the family. They include me in important decisions, like where I go to school or what I do for extracurricular activities. They have never really forced me to do anything, which I think is nice. I enjoy the independence that they have given me to make responsible decisions, and I think I have shown that to them. So it's really proven to them that these family meals are important.[19]

Of course, not all adolescents are eager to join in adult table conversation. When teens become surly and keep to themselves, many parents give up and retreat from the battlefield of uncomfortable meals. I believe that such a retreat is an abrogation of parental responsibility. When in doubt, one can always tell a story, or even play a game, to replace a third-degree atmosphere with one of diversion and fun. On those occasions when no one has the energy or skill to do the conversation work, it is still a good idea to maintain group cohesion by trying something, however light-hearted. As one woman put it, "We kind of blew it when our daughter hit adolescence. She got so surly and uncommunicative that in an act of self-preservation, we stopped sitting at the table and started eating in front of the TV. If I had thought to play games at the table, I think we could have gotten through that stage better." Here are some table games that caregivers have found useful.

> Getting-to-know-you games: pet peeves and idiosyncrasies; limitations and virtues; my special talent is; something I like about myself; what I know about you

or what I like about you; I remember when; would you rather; and name change. Conversation starter questions: your highs and lows today; something you are afraid of; three places you would never go; three things you would want on a desert island; perfect birthday dinner/day; all pets you have had; something that makes you nervous; your dream vacation; two things you do to relax; grossest thing you have ever eaten; how middle school differs from elementary school; remember lines from a school play; who is nicer in high school, boys or girls; ever been a victim of peer pressure; your best feature; what you are more courageous about today than you were two years ago; why parents were grounded; parents tell kids about places they have traveled; and describe a recurring dream. Word games: spell it, define it, use it; SAT words; list things in a category; ten questions; my favorite; what am I; what I want to be when I grow up; alphabet game of picking words beginning with that letter; once upon a time telling story going around the table adding to it; and telephone.[20]

Another table tactic is checking the newspaper for current events. David was struck with how many of the prominent public figures she interviewed told her that their political views and social advocacy interests were formed during nightly discussion of current events at the family dinner table. She recommended these ground rules: "1) Everyone has to listen to others' opinions or views without interruption (at least try). 2) No one can allow the conversation to devolve by hurling insults or making fun of another person's position. 3) Understand that the 'right answer' might not exist or a conclusion may not materialize by the end of the meal—it's great when the discussion can be ongoing. 4) It's your choice whether you want to wade into controversial topics. My view is, if not now, then when? Any opportunity to spread a little life wisdom is an opportunity we should grab."[21]

In addition to discussing current events, another crucial aspect of civic development is engaging in conversations about moral dilemmas. When adults model a respectful consideration of such dilemmas, it helps domestic table democracy translate into public table democracy. David agrees that this is a good use of dinner table conversations and that religion and politics should be on the table.

> Discussing and debating moral dilemmas is a good way to teach your kids deductive thinking and to get a read on where they stand on issues. Of course, it's also a perfect opportunity to insert some parental guidance on how to deal with tough decisions. They will be faced with many of their own dilemmas in life—they probably are already grappling with some—so we want to prepare them to think critically and find their own voice. I think the old adage of never discussing politics or religion at dinner should be retired along with "children should be seen

and not heard." Debate is healthy, disagreements a part of life, and we want our kids to hear opposing viewpoints and practice responding in a mature manner. Someday I want to hear my kids say, "I respectfully disagree." When they do, that will be my parenting high for the week . . . Discuss people's motivations for what they say or do, including your own . . . Understanding others' perspectives helps kids develop empathy and avoid conflicts. Talk up to kids.[22]

Travel often exposes people to new models of table conversation that are worth emulating. When journalist Miriam Weinstein lived in Paris, she was impressed by how children were included at tables, with delicious food and civil conversation to keep them there. All the women among her acquaintances had jobs, but everyone got off work at five o'clock, and evenings were spent with family and friends. Children came home from school and started their homework. On their way home from work, mothers shopped for meat, vegetables, and freshly baked bread. Dinner began at seven and was leisurely, with lively conversation and "the pleasure of being together." The food was fresh and delicious, with "many separate courses" that were small by American standards. Weinstein remembered "a wholeness, a balance; everyone sitting around the table talking or laughing or arguing or just listening, feeling comfy with the good food and the wine." Children drank diluted wine, "cut their fruit into neat squares," and ate "whatever was on their plates." The parents "didn't worry about" whether they liked their food or were "behind in their schoolwork or out of touch with their friends." The children were not "subjected to [an endless] round of lessons, practices, . . . and games; their parents and siblings weren't" condemned to hours of "chauffeuring, waiting, and cheering. It was assumed that the kids would learn something from meeting a variety of informed, chatty people in a relaxed setting; that in time they would grow up to become friendly and civil and balanced and well informed themselves, able to take part in the give-and-take of cultured people, capable of discriminating between a pear, or an argument, that was ripe and one that was still green."[23]

It is a good idea for parents to include their children's friends in table talk. Some children may learn more conversational skills away from home than they do within it. One student I interviewed noticed how many of his friends enjoyed coming to his house for dinner, not only to eat good food, but also to be included in the conversation.

All my friends really like my mom's cooking and think that my parents are pretty nice. I have had a number of friends whose parents are divorced and not gotten back together, or they haven't found a new partner, so oftentimes they are in a house where they are not necessarily eating dinner as a whole family. I think they often enjoy that my parents make a point of including them in the conversation. My dad likes to crack jokes for other people, so he tends to be pretty funny. He knows my friends and makes the conversations relevant for them. And so does my mom. I have a lot of friends who are interested in my mom's work. I think it is really cool for my friends, and for me, when she talks about her work because it is information that we don't really get at school, and I think that's another reason they tend to enjoy coming to my house.[24]

I interviewed another student who had a friend whose family never ate dinner together. Surveys have revealed that this is increasingly the case for many children. What I found fascinating about this student's account was the extent to which his friend seemed to crave conversations; he could not believe that such an activity was possible, let alone so enjoyable.

I had a friend whose family never sat down for dinner. I would sometimes be over there and his family would argue and it made me sad because they didn't look very together as a family. I was curious how much that related to the fact that they didn't sit down at dinner, and I realize now it possibly was a large factor. I don't think he and his mom talked all that much. When he came over to our house and he talked, it seemed like this was something he wasn't used to and he seemed almost weirded out by the idea but he enjoyed it. I feel he wanted that for his family, and I hope that they got that experience at some point because it is something I think everyone needs and should have in their lives.

At first he was kind of shocked that we all sat down and ate together. He said, "Is this unusual?" and I said, "No, we do this every night." And afterwards he came up to me, and he said, "Your family is really awesome and fun and funny." He was smiling and said, "I wish I could do this at my house." That made me smile because it showed me that, even though he couldn't do that, I could tell that he wanted to. I think that if he has kids some day, he will probably go by that. He was part of the conversations we had, and he smiled while he was eating. Not because he got his problem on his math homework done, but because he was hearing stuff, he was listening, he got to tell stories about his day, and that's something that you can't do on a regular basis if there's no place to meet and talk. And that place is dinner for my family and I hope for others as well.[25]

There is something about a table that makes it a great place for learning the art of conversation. Kim Severson asked food writer Marion Cunningham whether she thought that the dinner table was the modern-day tribal fire, the place where everyone gathered to share news of the day and build a culture. Cunningham responded, "I have always believed that the catalyst for social interaction is cooking and eating together." She lamented the fact that strangers cook most of our food and that we live "like [we] are in motels," grabbing fast food and watching TV. They talked about the "lessons of the table, about how serving food family-style teaches [children] to share," and about how "sitting next to someone and eating creates a kind of intimacy and gently teaches the art of conversation and the importance of community."[26]

Table Narratives

There is a particular kind of table talk that is especially crucial to developing our civic selves: narratives. When we tell first-person stories, we exercise agency. When we add to others' narratives, we are co-builders of a shared story. Even when we simply repeat an existing narrative, such as family folklore, we are imagining ourselves as part of something larger than ourselves that extends backward and goes forward in time. In short, narratives connect us to people beyond ourselves.

The Emory Center for Myth and Ritual in American Life has analyzed many hours of family dinnertime narratives. They have found that families do not talk about any one thing for very long, with parent-initiated topics shifting from food to school to family issues to problem solving. Interlaced with food content are the emotional and psychological "meat and potatoes" of family narratives—passing on stories, understanding experiences, teaching, learning, defining identities, and establishing a secure home base. Here are three examples that illustrate these various functions of family dinnertime narratives.[27]

In the first example, a child discusses "a current school science project." Both parents are "immediately interested in hearing about" it. The father wants to make sure that "the child knows the material at a [certain] level," so the "what happened at school today" conversation "turns into a science quiz, . . . done with good humor and lots of laughter. The child is learning that his schoolwork is important [and that] his parents value what he is learning, but very much in a secure and affectionate context." The discussion then turns to the Mexican Revolution, which "the younger brother is studying in school." The family is of Mexican descent, so "the conversation about what happened that day at school becomes an important lesson in family and individual identity."[28]

In another case, the family is preparing dinner, and the mother is "trying to get the father to converse." Then the child asks them "about the beginning of their relationship, 'Love at first sight, huh?' Although the story of how the parents met never gets fully explicated, . . . when the mother asks, 'You think it's gonna be love at first sight for you?'" she is "making an explicit link between the parents' history and the child's future. While this is going on in the background, the process of learning about food preparation is in the foreground. So we see the interweaving of the formation of family and food as a deeply interconnected relation."[29]

In the third example, a family identity is "formed in contrast to other families" and different places of origin. The parents tell a story about "a dinner out with another family" and discuss "the individual characteristics of one of these family members." They also tell "how this is the same and different from yet another family (and implicitly from [their own] family . . .). All of this focuses on where these individuals came from (England) as an important part of their identity and how it is expressed."[30]

The Emory Center has also found a connection between children's participation in family narratives and their development of a sense of agency and resilience. In addition to taping family narratives and dinnertime conversations, the researchers used seven measures of family functioning that were completed independently by the mother, the father, and the child. The "do you know?" measure is "a 20-item yes/no questionnaire that assesses an individual's knowledge concerning his/her parents and family." The "locus of control" measure is the perception of "connection between one's action and its consequences," whether people "believe that what happens to them" is due to "forces beyond their control (external control)" or "that they in some way affect what happens to them" (internal control). Locus of control is "a master variable in psychology . . . a factor that has been shown to be related to so many other behavioral, emotional, and psychological variables that it may be considered a unifying, central concept." Another important measure is self-esteem, which "seems to buffer children against the negative impact of external stressors." The Emory Center has found that there are "significant correlations between the amount of family history known by a child . . . and that child's locus of control, level of self-esteem and perception of family functioning."[31]

As I mentioned earlier, I am particularly interested in what makes citizens resilient. What enables us to be hopeful that we can recover from setbacks such as war, social injustice, or partisan defeat? One key is psychologists' concept of locus of control. To the extent that we believe that what happens to us is the result of forces beyond our control, we will be less motivated to take action than if we believe that we can somehow affect what happens to us. A second key is high self-esteem, which acts as a buffer against the stress of life's challenges. Since participation in family narratives appears to bolster internal locus of control and high self-esteem, it should be encouraged to strengthen civil society and democracy.

Family narrations have the same social dynamics as conversations: norms about participation and assistance, relations of hierarchy, creation of and challenges to social identity, and maintenance of face. One study of family dinner-table narration focused on accidents and near misses riding bikes. The stories, told mostly by males, portrayed a world in which danger was confronted by bravery and skill. Females were an attentive audience. Patterns of family hierarchy appeared in the arrangements for conversations, seating, and food transfer. "[Discourse] coherence in the conversation was not simply a matter of topic but involved as well the social identities and modes of social participation of the interlocutors. . . . There were issues of personal and collective display; performing for and playing to diverse audiences within the family, maintaining face, showing attention and interest, alternating between the keys of irony, humor, and seriousness. . . . Thus, topic, social participation structure, and family structure were somehow related in the family's conversation at the dinner table."[32]

Psychologists link children's well-being to narrative rituals, insofar as they provide occasions for belonging, trust, and expressing emotions. However, if family rituals are exclusionary and mistrustful, there are negative consequences. When researchers asked parents to tell their child a story about their own childhood dinners, there was generational continuity in story themes and parent-child interactions. "Parents who recounted their family-of-origin mealtimes as warm, supportive, and opportunities to gather together as a group were more likely to express positive affect at the dinner table with their own children. Their children were also less likely to evidence problematic behaviors." By contrast, creating a group identity through exclusion and lack of trust in others created unhealthy social dynamics. "Relationships are seen as a bother rather than a source of reward, and planning revolves around how to avoid others rather than relying on others as sources of support. . . . When rituals are marked by patterns of exclusion and used for opportunities to degrade rather than support, group membership is compromised, and family identity is characterized by alienation. Indeed, one would question why anyone would want to belong to such a group."[33] Positive narrative rituals bolster civil society, and negative ones erode it.

Another lesson from this research is that clear and direct communication is essential for problem solving, negotiating difficult conversations, and hearing everyone's voices. The free exchange of information makes it easier to get mealtime tasks done, reducing the stress associated with trying to feed a hungry group. Forthright communication supports positive emotional exchanges, contributing to the well-being of all family members. "Validating feelings and knowing that the family provides a safe place to express troubling thoughts can most optimally occur when these thoughts are relayed in a clear manner. . . . When emotions can be expressed in a safe place, there are added opportunities for problem solving. Whether it is being rejected by peers in kindergarten or a difficult conversation with a coworker, being able to problem-solve with other family members may provide multiple solutions to a difficult situation and also send the implicit message that your voice will be heard."[34]

As we have seen, there are cultural differences in how parents elicit narratives from their children. Hawaiian children's "talk stories" are "rambling narratives about their personal experiences, usually enhanced with humour, jokes, and teasing . . . [and a] joint performance, or cooperative production of responses by two or more speakers." African American children describe past events in their narratives in an oral-strategy (or poetic) narrative, and European American children produce a literate-strategy (or prosaic) narrative. A study of Japanese, Japanese American, and Canadian mothers and children found differences in evaluation, verbal acknowledgment, description requests, turn taking, question asking, humor, jokes, teasing, joint performance, and expression of choice. Compared to English-speaking mothers, mothers of both Japanese groups gave less evaluation and more verbal acknowledgment. Japanese mothers in the United States requested more description from their children than did those in Japan. English-speaking mothers encouraged their children to take long monologic turns by asking descriptive questions. Japanese mothers facilitated frequent turn exchanges.[35]

One useful way to look at a family narrative is as a kind of political activity. Linguists Elinor Ochs and Carolyn Taylor describe the family as a political institution constituted through conversational interaction: "Families are political bodies in that certain members review, judge, formulate codes of conduct, make decisions and impose sanctions that evaluate and impact the actions, conditions, thoughts and feelings of other members. Such administration of power is characteristic of families everywhere and may occur whenever family members interact."[36] Ochs and Taylor studied power dynamics in narrative activity at family dinners, often the first time in the day when family members interacted as a whole for a sustained period of time and when reports about that day's activities and experiences were aired in front of the group. Stories of personal experience drew in the participation of the entire family as "co-narrators," who often made significant contributions to the narrative's settings, actions, consequences, and psychological responses.

Stories and reports at dinner tended to focus on children as protagonists, yet children exerted little control in some critical aspects of the telling of these narratives: they tended not to introduce (either elicit or initiate) narratives, even when about themselves; they were rarely primary recipients of others' narratives; and they rarely problematized the actions, thoughts, etc., of other family members as protagonists and narrators. . . . Parents, especially mothers, tended to assume the role of report/story introducer, thus administering power by deciding whose actions are to be verbally revealed to the family and when; parents, especially fathers were, overwhelmingly, the chief narrative problematizers, exercising power principally by evaluating others' actions, conditions, thoughts and feelings—as either praiseworthy or problematic. [There is] an underlying pattern of narrative role preferences that is not reciprocal but largely hierarchical and which impacts *who* contributes *what* to family dinnertime narrative activity.[37]

All family members above the age of three participated in narratives: asking questions and supplying information critical to understanding and interpreting the significance of the narrated events. Children were socialized into "joint construction of narratives and collective problem-solving in which alternative perspectives on events [were] weighed and family members rework[ed] several oral drafts of a narrative, sometimes laying out first what did happen then what should or could have happened if the protagonist(s) had shared the world-view of the co-present family." When dinner narratives centered on a complaint against a nonpresent nonfamily member, the family's redraftings of events often supported the family member who initiated the story. There was also a divisive side to family dinner co-narration: judgmental reckonings of a family member's actions and stances. Narratives were initiated with the understanding that they were "on the table" for others to consider, so in this sense they were fair game for critical commentary. Family membership entitled those present to narrative privileges.[38]

Parents were often tempted to turn the dinner hour into a nightly inquisition. They understandably wanted to hear about their children's day and became frustrated at their children's reticence. The challenge was to find a way to obtain information and show interest without being overbearing or interrogating. In some families, parents had to "pull" narratives out of their children. When children became upset with the power imbalance of having to reveal more about themselves than their parents did, they engaged in resistance through "*reluctances to comply* with parental elicitations of their narrative accounts and in their sometimes *ironic stances* vis-à-vis parents' narrative expectations. . . . Children's flights (or attempted flights) from the dinner table may in part manifest sensitivity to—and desire to escape from—certain injustices and disempowerments in family co-narration. While the restlessness of many children to leave the dinner table might be readily written off by some as reflecting simply children's drive to play, to be more active, etc., it can also represent a political counter-offensive—a resistance to a discursively manifest hierarchy that manipulates children."[39]

It is not surprising to find that caregivers, even those who want to minimize power imbalances, are often at a loss to know how to engage children in conversation at the dinner table. Anthropologist Amy Paugh provides this daunting summary of conversation work.

> Linguistic devices like conversational turn-taking procedures, interactional sequencing, and the management of miscommunication exhibited in everyday interactions with caregivers or others in their verbal environments socialize children to understand social relationships and activities, to acquire problem-solving strategies, and to learn to express and interpret expressions of affect. Furthermore, as children acquire language, they also acquire cultural and social practices, values, and ideologies, such as those concerning class, ethnicity, gender, morality, knowledge, and language itself. Caregivers often make explicit for children's benefit cultural rules and knowledge that are usually tacit. They call attention to children's breaches of etiquette, correct or expand children's utterances to be socially appropriate and grammatical, repeat and paraphrase their own speech and the speech of others, and may model linguistic behavior for children through explicitly prompting them to "say" or respond to interlocutors in particular ways.[40]

In Paugh's study of family dinnertime conversations, children acquired narrative and analytical skills through taking part in and overhearing their parents' conversations about work. They were exposed to moral theorizing about events at work through intonation, grammatical marking, and nonverbal behavior, as well as explicit appraisals of work-related experiences. Narrating parents portrayed themselves as competent and morally just at their workplace. When a co-narrating parent called into question a teller's workplace competence, it led to additional discussion about moral standards for acceptable behavior. Children participated as co-narrators, posing questions in nearly half the narratives. They requested information about the workplace and occasionally contributed to the problem solving provoked by their parents. Children's questions always received a response from one or both parents. Children evaluated workers' competence and the morality of their actions. In one example, after a three-minute narrative initiated by the father and co-narrated by the mother, their two daughters joined in when his competence and training as a lawyer were called into question by an opposing attorney. The family jointly collaborated in making sense of this event and in casting the father in a more positive light: praising his competence and offering an alternative scenario where he could have challenged the lawyer about his training in return. The children were supported in their contributions to the problem solving and moral casting of the narrative.[41]

As daunting as mealtime co-narration might be, it is an essential building block of finding a political voice: learning about expected behavior, grappling with moral dilemmas, and being taken seriously as an active participant with something important to say. Psychologists Catherine E. Snow and Diane E. Beals have studied how mealtime narratives and explanatory talk contribute to children's linguistic and cognitive development. Family mealtimes vary widely across social class and race in the amount and style of talk and in discussions and explanations of current events, world knowledge, and abstract general principles. Mealtime talk provides an opportunity for everyday problems and proposed solutions to be discussed at the table, often in the context of stories. For many immigrant families, mealtime narratives provide an opportunity not only to reinforce the home language but also for bilingual children to negotiate control over familial language use. "Even in cultures in which a high level of formal politeness is the rule, family talk at mealtimes tends to be fairly direct and hardly every characterized by extremely polite indirectness. Nonetheless, dinner table conversations constitute an opportunity for explicitly teaching aspects of politeness ranging from not talking with one's mouth full to not interrupting to using *please* and *thank you*. . . . Children learn what appropriate topics are, how to stay on topic, how to give enough information to the listener, and what the socially acceptable means of communication are."[42]

Mealtimes offer a distinctive opportunity to learn because of the availability of "extended discourse," which is talk centered on a particular topic that extends over several "utterances" or "conversational turns." There are two kinds of extended discourse: explanatory talk and narrative talk, both of which help create a political voice insofar as they involve questions and answers, understanding, nonpresent topics, complex language structure, hypotheticals and conditionals, and sophisticated vocabulary.

> Explanations can be initiated by genuine child questions (for example, "Mommy, what does 'budget' mean?") or by parents trying to ensure their children understand something (for example, "So why do you think the firemen carry oxygen tanks with them?"). Explanatory talk brings with it the introduction of sophisticated, nonpresent topics and the opportunity to learn about the world. Mealtime narratives, in contrast, often emerge as part of catching-up talk—in response, for example, to questions like, "What happened at preschool today?" Narratives are often about relatively familiar topics but may require the use of complex language structures, for

example, to keep track of who is who and what happened when in the stories being told. And they can be opportunities for considering hypotheticals or conditionals (for example, "Let's consider why that made your sister mad at you"), which introduce complex language forms. In addition to offering opportunities for extended discourse, mealtime talk often introduces relatively sophisticated vocabulary, typically in the middle of narrative or explanatory discourse. Knowing sophisticated words like *budget, oxygen*, and *consider* become important to children's success in participating in classroom talk and reading after grade 3.[43]

The families they studied shared certain cultural norms: that mealtimes were family time, that they should last more than a few minutes, that pleasant conversation involving all family members was appropriate, and that all family members should be present and contribute to the conversation. "These norms were embraced by low income families with low parental education . . . as well as by middle-class families. . . . Dinner table conversations are used . . . as opportunities to catch up on the day's events, plan the next day's activities, reminisce about shared experiences, answer puzzling questions, seek explanations for strange happenings, and solve problems." Not surprisingly, there were gender differences: "Mothers and children together accounted for approximately three-quarters of the talk. Fathers, even when present, contributed relatively little to the conversations." And as for duration, "mealtime conversations varied enormously in character across the families. They ranged in length from two to forty-seven minutes, averaging about twenty minutes."[44]

In summary, narratives are a foundational component of democratic conversations. Difficult conversations operate at three simultaneous levels—facts, emotions, and identity—and constructing narratives involves all three. They are a safe way for us to begin to add our two cents to a collective conversation. We all have personal stories, and we feel connected to others when we are encouraged to tell them. Listening to others co-narrate, we see ourselves as part of a larger story: of a family, a neighborhood, a culture, an ethnic group, a religion, a country, a planet. Explanatory talk is also foundational to civil and democratic discourse because citizens need to expand their vocabulary, use reason and evidence, develop hypotheticals and conditionals, and hone argumentation skills. At domestic tables, we have everyday opportunities for extended discourse—both narrative and explanatory—that will serve us well when we venture out of our households into more challenging political environments.

Chapter Three

Tables at Home

Domesticity

For most Americans, table talk is learned at home. The table is a powerful symbol because, given its domestic associations, it simultaneously represents inegalitarianism and egalitarianism, parents and children, hierarchy and democracy, domination and care. As bell hooks describes the contradictions of the family table, "Usually, it is within the family that we witness coercive domination and learn to accept it, whether it be domination of parent over child, or male over female. Even though family relations may be, and most often are, informed by acceptance of a politic of domination, they are simultaneously relations of care and connection. It is this convergence of two contradictory impulses—the urge to promote growth and the urge to inhibit growth—that provides a practical setting for feminist critique, resistance, and transformation."[1] Especially for groups subject to social hostility, the home-place is political. She recalls traveling across town to visit her grandmother's house when she was a child, a journey from her segregated black community into a poor white neighborhood.

> I remember the fear . . . those white faces on the porches staring us down with hate. . . . Oh! that feeling of safety, or arrival, of homecoming when we finally reached the edges of her yard. . . . In our young minds houses belonged to women, were their special domain, not as property, but as places where all that truly mattered in life took place—the warmth and comfort of shelter, the feeding of our bodies, the nurturing of our souls. . . . [Black women] for the most part worked outside the home serving white folks, cleaning their houses, washing their clothes, tending their children. . . . Then they returned to their homes to make life happen there. . . .
>
> Historically, African American people believed that the construction of a home-place, however fragile and tenuous (the slave hut, the wooden shack), had a radical

political dimension. . . . One's homeplace was the one site where one could freely confront the issue of humanization, where one could resist. . . . It was about the construction of a safe place where black people could affirm one another and by so doing heal the wounds inflicted by racist domination. . . . Whatever the shape and direction of black liberation struggle (civil rights reform or black power movement), domestic space has been a crucial site for organizing, for forming political solidarity.[2]

Feminists criticize domesticity as a site of gender inequality and praise it as a location of resistance, inclusion, and transformation. Although the domestic has frequently been associated with the nuclear family and hostility to people who live outside its norms, domestic cultures are not inherently heterosexual. Nor have public and domestic life ever been truly separate. The home has historically been a place where women's unpaid labor has kept them dependent on men, but some of this labor has been inherently rewarding. For example, cooking is "a key home-*making* practice which not only physically sustains household members but is also a form of emotional labour that helps to create the meaning of a home. . . . Cooking can be thought of as both leisure and labour." We need to appreciate the dual nature of domesticity—as an imposed ideology and as a location of transformation.[3]

Many gay and lesbian couples value the domestic sphere as a place where they can express themselves and take refuge from hostile social norms. In one study of how couples forged their identities and resisted heteronormativity in domestic spaces, many respondents described their homes as places where they could "be themselves" and as "sanctuaries from wider social sanctions against same-sex relationships." Pressured to refrain from same-sex-intimacy in public spaces, homes were primary sites for affection. Shared spaces in their homes were important for relationship building. Two women "spent a lot of time together in the family room and kitchen, cooking, conversing, and relaxing." For another couple, the kitchen, dining room, and living room were particularly important for consolidating their relationship. "That's a really big part of our lives now—we cook, sit down, and we actually eat our meals together. And we're talking to each other about what we did during the day and what happened at work." One man reported: "I think that a lot of the things that we bought were domestic items, things for the kitchen and things that maybe if I wasn't in a partnership I wouldn't have purchased. . . . So I think the fact that you're buying kitchenware and things like that is really a sign that you have a home together and a partnership."[4]

Gay and lesbian couples who want to create a family identity face many of the same gender, ethnic, and class role expectations that straight families do.

Sociologist Christopher Carrington analyzed these dynamics in his study of lesbigay (lesbian, bisexual, and gay men) families in the San Francisco Bay area. Many of them pointed to "the continuous preparation of daily meals and/or the occasional preparation of elaborate meals as evidence of their status as families. . . . Families with strong ethnic identifications reported more shared meals," with class differences.[5]

> When comparing the appeal of ethnically identified foods to the upper strata of the lesbigay community (mostly Euro-Americans) with the appeal of such foods to the Asian and Latino participants it becomes clear that the food symbolizes very different things for each group. For the affluent lesbigay families the food represents creativity and contributes to the entertaining atmosphere of the dinner party. It carries status due to its exoticness and the difficulty of its preparation. In contrast, among Asian and Latino lesbigay participants, food expresses ethnic heritage and symbolizes ethnic solidarity, and sometimes resistance to cultural assimilation. Many Asian and Latino participants pride themselves not on the variety of cuisine but on the consistent replication of the same cuisine and even the same meals."[6]

Food work was considered to be women's work, even when men engaged in it. Many participants downplayed its complexity and significance. Even those who actually did the feeding work said that they did not do much of it.

> Those who feed often lack the vocabulary to articulate their effort to others. . . . [Many] participants diminish feeding because they don't want to face the conflict that a thorough accounting . . . might produce in their relationship. Moreover, given the potential for stigma that exists for the men who feed, and the women who don't, it becomes even clearer why the work of feeding remains particularly hidden in lesbigay households. . . . Concealing foodwork reflects the cultural tendency to romanticize domestic activities. Recognizing feeding as work raises the impertinent question of why the effort often goes uncompensated, a question that leads directly to issues of exploitation and inequality, issues ripe with the potential for social and family conflict. Given the social precariousness of lesbian and gay relationships, mostly due to the lack of social, political, and economic resources, the tendency of the participants to avoid such conflicts is probably essential to their long-term survival. Those with economic resources have an easier time avoiding this conflict since they can purchase meals. For those with less means, feeding looks different: routine, fatiguing, nutritionally compromised, and symbolically arid (in the sense that the capacity of feeding to produce a sense of family is compromised). Participants rarely conceive of eating ramen noodle soup on the couch as constitutive of their claim to family status, but they frequently conceive of eating a nutritionally complete meal at a dining-room table as constitutive of such a claim.[7]

For these households, creating families was an ongoing process of inclusion and exclusion based on partnerships, friendships, and extended kinships. The gender, ethnic, and class dynamics of their domestic spaces were many. Feeding work was seen as women's work, even when men engaged in it. Non-Latinos seemed to be envious of the frequency and extended-family nature of Latino meals. For affluent families, food represented creativity and entertainment, and status was derived from its exoticness and difficulty of preparation. In Asian and Latino households, food symbolized ethnic solidarity and resistance to cultural assimilation, and more value was placed on replication of the same cuisine than on variety. For many, sharing meals and conversation was constitutive of family. Consistent with other studies of family meals, people had a hard time talking about the labor involved. There was a tendency to reduce its complexity and minimize its significance. Many of those who did the food work not only lacked the vocabulary to articulate their efforts, but also downplayed such efforts to avoid conflict in the relationship—making others feel guilty or obligated. Food work was also hidden because of the stigma applied to men who fed others and women who did not.

Domestic relations become complicated when couples decide to have children: whose food and table traditions should be perpetuated and how? One lesbian couple had experimented with different Jewish observances until children changed their attitudes and limited their flexibility. "I want Jordan and Zach to see candles lit, to taste wine and challah every Shabbat. I want them to know how to observe holidays, how to sing Hebrew songs and to know Jewish stories, to incorporate Jewish values into their lives. Betsy knows how important this is to me and has been willing to compromise in many ways. . . . Our sons will live Jewish lives. But I also compromise. Our home is only a modified form of kosher; our Shabbat observance is limited; our conversation rarely revolves around Judaism. We have both become more adept at compromise."[8] Such household compromises about food and table practices are beneficial for creating and maintaining civil society.

Households have to decide whether watching television should figure into mealtime practices. An anthropologist who conducted fieldwork among families with and without televisions from three different U.S. ethnic groups—Navajos, Spanish-Americans, and Euro-Americans—found that in describing family mealtimes, there is often a disconnect between what people report and what they actually do. Every family with a television spent a lot of time watching it, especially in the evenings, and it reduced the diversity of family activities. "Navajo families of varying degrees of traditionality who had no television, for example, performed a large array of activities—family discussions, butchering, weaving baskets, making quirts and inexpensive necklaces, playing with young children, talking, grooming horses, and so on." Television viewing also reduced the number of places where activities occurred, "since the set was usually located in the living room and most activities revolved around it."⁹

> In [one] urban Euro-American family . . . television viewing was the dominant evening activity even when friends visited, in which case conversation usually alternated with television. Although the television was watched sporadically by the female head of this household and her children throughout the day, it was watched continuously by the entire family on weekends (especially during the football season). Snacks and occasionally dinner were eaten in the living room so that the family could watch television while eating. The children rarely played outside, even though the weather was sunny, albeit a little cool. In another Euro-American home, family members ate, folded clothes, did homework, read magazines, and so on in the living room in order to watch television at the same time. Breakfast was usually eaten at the kitchen table, since there was little that interested them on television at that hour. Lunch and dinner, however, were eaten in front of the television. The male and female heads of the household usually ate at the kitchen table before joining the children in the living room to watch television.
>
> One of the most interesting households from this point of view was a rural Spanish-American one in which the television set was broken when I first arrived but later provisionally repaired. Once the set was functional, television viewing became the dominant evening activity, and the types of activities and the locations in which they were performed became noticeably less varied. . . .
>
> When the female head of [a Euro-American family] was asked where meals were eaten, she mentioned the dinette table and the table in the formal dining room, the latter of which was actually only rarely used. She did not mention that about two dinners a week were consumed in the living room while watching television (which was the pattern I observed). The ideal behavior according to many middle-class Euro-Americans is to eat meals at a table in a formal and routine food-consumption locus, and this was the response elicited by my questions at the end of my stay with this family. The real behavior was quite different.¹⁰

This study suggests that television is a distraction from the kinds of mealtimes that are optimal for civil society, where people can give each other their undivided attention and engage in extended discourse without the lure of entertainment designed to grab our attention and to be more engaging (or glamorous or shocking) than the people sitting next to us.

Domesticity blends nicely into civil society when household dynamics operate simultaneously in the community, as is frequently the case for newly arrived immigrants. For example, research on the adaptive strategies of a community of Vietnamese refugees revealed that women's domestic social networks were central to the organization and survival of the community. Sociologist Nazli Kibria reports, "While 'hanging out' at informal social gatherings, I observed women exchanging information, money, goods, food, and tasks such as child care and cooking. Given the precarious economic situation of the group, these exchanges played an important role in ensuring the economic survival and stability of the households."[11]

At the turn of the twenty-first century, the idea of domesticity got a fresh appraisal from second-wave feminists' daughters and granddaughters, who wanted to reclaim a "do-it yourself" (DIY) domesticity to challenge industrial food and wasteful consumerism. But they also worried that it might be a step back for women. "Our tech-saturated generation craves creative hands-on activities, and nostalgic hobbies such as canning, knitting and baking fit the bill. We've realized that just because something was historically devalued as 'women's work,' that doesn't mean we have to shun it to be taken seriously in the world. . . . Suddenly, learning the old-fashioned skills of our great-grandmothers seems not just fun, but necessary and even virtuous." However, as Emily Matchar observes, this new domesticity "can be seen as an effort to repair on an individual level what isn't being fixed at a governmental or societal one. Pro bono. Because, as important and fulfilling as housework may be, it's unpaid. And in a world where college-educated women still earn, over the course of their careers, about $713,000 less than college-educated men, that's no small thing. Women like me are enjoying domestic projects again in large part because they're no longer a duty but a choice. But how many moral and environmental claims can we assign to domestic work before it starts to feel, once more, like an obligation?"[12]

Domesticity is being redefined not only by do-it yourself-ers, but also by "boomerang kids." Throughout the twentieth century, most young adults left their parents' home for good once they found jobs, went off to college, or joined the military. But the twenty-first century saw a sharp increase in the number of young adults who never left, or who moved in and out of, their parents' home. These "accordion families" pay the private toll of global competition and need to renegotiate domestic table rules and practices. Here are three illustrative examples.

Accustomed to preparing meals for four or five, empty-nest parents may stop cooking in favor of expedient take-out meals. They put a lot of thought into nutrition when they were raising growing children, but why bother for just one or two? Lucy Tang, a Newton resident who hails from Taiwan, works for a health-care company as a nutritionist. Even though her business is healthy food, in the absence of her kids, she stopped thinking about what she was putting on the table. But when they returned home, there was a reason to be interested again, and the kitchen turned out to be the place where Lucy bonds with her kids. "We sit in the kitchen," she explains, "We have a nice meal, we have nice conversation, enjoy the laughs." . . .

Dan Morton tried to contribute to the household. Almost every workday, he called his parents from work to see if they needed anything from the store. He was usually home for dinner three or four days a week. "They seem to have adjusted their dinner to when I get home, around 7:15 p.m. . . . They wait for me to cook. . . . I was a chef for two and a half years. I know a lot of tricks; I teach [my mother] how to do certain things that she never knew how to do. I inspired her to grow an herb garden in the backyard." . . .

Teddy Yoo and his parents were conflicted about how autonomous he should be. He resented his parents' surveillance. . . . "I really don't like being asked all the time. Because I feel it's not that I am doing bad things, [and] I never even have had a girlfriend, it's just that they say, 'We want you home for dinner, so you should tell us where you are going and if you will be home for dinner.' When you have a bad relationship with your parents, even them asking you where you are going is bad. Because you relay it to them badly. Even the littlest thing brings up the bad relation, so you can't cope. So I tell them, but sometimes I don't tell them. I say I'm going here, but I go somewhere else because I think they don't understand. They say, 'Oh, you just want to spend money again.'"[13]

Domestic spaces are increasingly inhabited by "blended families," consisting of some combination of custodial parents, noncustodial parents, and stepparents, along with their biological children and stepchildren. Child-development specialists emphasize that blended families are cohesive social units where table traditions are negotiated just as they are in other families. As a rule, younger children have an easier time adjusting to blended families, and adolescents, particularly those of the same sex as the stepparent, are more likely to resent the stepparent. Children generally adjust better to a stepparent after the death of a natural parent than after a divorce. Following divorce, adults' attitudes contribute significantly to a child's adjustment, with positive attitudes more beneficial than negative ones. Family traditions provide opportunities for enjoyable new experiences, but they also cause conflict. Children in blended families often bring to the table resilience, flexibility, and experience with conflict resolution. "Stepchildren often learn to adjust to different value systems. Thus they may adapt more easily and flexibly to

new traditions and situations. These children generally know how to negotiate new situations and compromise when necessary. Consequently, when
situations require new behaviors (new schools, teachers, etc.), the child from
a blended family may have already developed some important coping skills
that can be generalized to these other situations."[14]

To summarize our discussion of domesticity, it is a domain of contradictions: inegalitarianism and egalitarianism, hierarchy and democracy, domination and care, gender inequality and gender transformation. For many
groups, it is a safe refuge and homeplace. Meals are provided, but food work
is often hidden or devalued. Meals represent creativity, entertainment, status,
and ethnic and religious solidarity. Households differ in the amount and
nature of connections within them (e.g., how frequently the TV is on during
mealtimes) and outside them (e.g., sharing community resources). Domestic
spaces are populated with a wide variety of people: do-it-yourselfers, gays
and lesbians, custodial parents, stepparents, stepchildren, and grown children
moving in and out of the parental home. Given our interest in resiliency and
conflict-resolution skills, it is noteworthy that children in blended families
have had to learn to adjust to different value systems, negotiate new situations,
compromise in order to make a new domestic situation work, and resolve
conflict between hostile parties, namely, their divorced parents.

Kitchen Talk

Domestic table talk often occurs in the kitchen, a place where women have
historically spent a lot of time. Writer Paule Marshall values "women's kitchen
talk" as "highly functional." She remembers kitchen gatherings serving "as
therapy, the cheapest kind available to [her] mother and her friends. . . .
It restored them to a sense of themselves and reaffirmed their self-worth.
. . . But more than therapy, the freewheeling, wide-ranging, exuberant talk
functioned as an outlet for the tremendous creative energy they possessed."[15]

Political scientist John E. Finn analyzes how women's "kitchen voice" is
expressed in "kitchen confessionals," an important literary genre that captures
the ambiguity of kitchens at the boundaries of private and public, comfort
and conflict, and spiritual and physical.

> Unlike other varieties of confessional literature, the kitchen confessional recalls
> and underscores the importance, the sanctity, and the ambiguity of the kitchen as
> place, as the intersection of both the spiritual and physical appetites. An apprecia-
> tion of the significance of the kitchenplace is critical if we are to understand the

intersection and continual renegotiation of gender, politics, and domesticity. In kitchen confessionals, the kitchen as place is polysemous—a source of comfort and conflict, personal and social. Moreover, the kitchen exists at the boundary of private and public. The household kitchen is a private place, distinct from the professionalized restaurant kitchen, for example. But in many homes, and especially in certain cultures, the kitchen may be the most public of spaces, the kind of space where friends are welcomed and guests entertained. This balance between the public and private dimensions of the kitchenspace mimics the confessional voice more generally, where the act of confessing makes public the most intimate and private details of our lives. . . . Kitchen confessionals contribute to our understanding of gender politics by showing how the kitchenplace is a site not simply of oppression, not simply victimization, but rather a site subject to continual renegotiation and kitchenwork.[16]

African Americans have subjected the kitchen to this sort of continual renegotiation. As slaves and servants, even though they produced and served the meals, when company came, they were confined to eating in the kitchen and denied a seat at the table. The kitchen voice of African American cooks spoke of being relegated to the kitchen, unable to taste the very food they had prepared, and humiliated by a social caste system. Idella Parker recalled her elaborate preparation of a ham: "It was a lovely sight to see, and *without even tasting it* I know it was good."[17] When a cook was allowed to dine in the house, she could eat the food that she prepared only in the kitchen, and only after everyone else had eaten.

Idella Parker remembered the distance that existed between her and her employer. "She usually took her dinner in the dining room, and I would serve her each course just as I did when guests were there. Then I would go in the kitchen to eat my dinner. Even though it was only the two of us, I still had my place as a servant; she never once invited me to sit down at the table with her to eat." Employers reinforced such discrimination with their children. A young white woman from near the Mississippi River observed in 1954: "I came in late to lunch one day. Everyone had eaten except the cook, and I started to sit at the table with her and eat. My mother asked her to move. I didn't understand it." In the employer's mind, the cook's lunch took third place—after the family's main meal and after the tardy teenager.[18]

In response to these conditions, African American domestics created survival networks. "In their own homes, cooks overcame the daily isolation of their jobs through a 'work culture' among female relatives and neighbors that allowed them to share secrets about how to perform certain tasks, to exchange recipes, and to pass on survival strategies for handling demanding mistresses, long hours, menial work conditions and lack of respect or autonomy."[19] Many children of African American cooks first realized the racial differences in kitchens when their mother brought food home from work. Anne Moody recalls, "Sometimes Mama would bring us the white family's leftovers. It was the best food I had ever eaten. That was when I discovered that white folks ate different from us. They had all kinds of different food with meat and all. We always had just beans and bread."[20]

As a general rule, domestic kitchens are very different from commercial ones. However, chef Gillian Clark sees parallels in the family dynamics of both settings. She raised two daughters and for years ran the popular Washington, D.C., restaurant Colorado Kitchen. She thinks that being a chef and being a mother helped her become better at both. At staff meetings, she had to deal with language barriers, learning disabilities, alcoholism, and educational differences. She wanted to create a set of "family values" by cooking together. She watched staff in action to get to know "what made them tick." After her divorce, she created a new set of family values for her daughters by cooking together and "taking into account what they had to say."[21]

In setting up her restaurant, Clark wanted to replicate meals at her grandmother's house. In a bid for historical accuracy, she included certain features, such as commercial icons and Aunt Jemima's red bandana napkins, which offended some customers. Kitchen memories run deep, and it is often difficult to juggle personal and political meanings. She chose the name Colorado Kitchen "to provide a dining experience that resembled a relaxed meal of comfort food taken at the kitchen table." She explains, "My goal was to re-create the kitchen table meals at my grandmother's house. We never ate around the table in her formal dining room. The stemware and candelabra were in that other room. That didn't matter. Nana's soup was best served at her chrome-banded kitchen table with the yellow vinyl chairs." She also wanted to connect to the community: "There were plenty of places to get a sub or a single beer passed to you through a bulletproof glass. There was no place like Colorado Kitchen. Our focus was access and openness. The first thing we did when we took possession of the building was to remove the security bars from the windows and door. A restaurant can't have security excess and atmosphere at the same time."[22]

Another story about restaurant kitchens is provided by English professor Meredith E. Abarca, who was raised in restaurants owned by her mother and grandmother along the Texas border. Like Gillian Clark, she thinks that kitchens embody family values and are connected to the community. She says that the categories of academic feminism, which relegated the kitchen to the suspect domestic sphere, did not make sense to her while she was conducting her research with family and friends. She interviewed these women in their kitchens with *charlas culinarias* (culinary chats) over a shared meal, where she heard about the kitchen as women's space, as opposed to women's place; about *sazón* (the sensory logic of cooking); and about recipe stories. Using the metaphor of a "borderless boundary zone" to capture the array of different social spaces women created in their kitchens, she argues that for working-class women, the appropriation of their kitchen space was crucial since they usually could not afford to leave their kitchen work to someone else.

> For Liduvina Vélez, neighborly sharing was part of a daily exchange of food with *la güera*, her neighbor: "I remember that *la güera* and I would share each other's food. . . . Yes, whatever she would make, she would send me, and I would send her some of what I made. I think we did this every day, depending on what we had cooked for dinner." . . . Carving out a public *space* from within her private *place* represents the first stage of Vélez's survival politics and her first negotiations in maneuvering inside her *borderless boundary zone*. The rage she felt seeing her children's hunger and shabby clothing led her to transport the kitchen to the front door of her house. . . . "Every afternoon, I would put my little table there in the street, at the door of the house, without chairs or anything. People would eat standing up there or would take the food to their houses." Her *puestecito*, the table she located outside her door, does not constitute a conventional "political institution," and the struggle within this site represents an economic one. . . .
>
> The informal economic practice helped increase Vélez's assertiveness in stating her opinions . . . [and] helped her gain a confidence and self-esteem that helped her change her *destino* (destiny) as well as her children's. [She and her children escaped from the man she called "the" husband, a drunkard, abusive womanizer, and she went to work in a restaurant owned by her mother.] There, she had a public kitchen that her children took as their private kitchen and ate to their heart's content.[23]

Using a kitchen to carve out a public space from a private place illustrates the fluidity of what are often thought to be rigid boundaries: between private and public, personal and political. It allowed women to gain self-esteem, speak their minds, and escape from abusive relationships. And it strengthened civil society. Abarca saw her informants as speaking from public kitchens, which created not just family wealth but also vital community resources. She was raised in public kitchens—the restaurants of her mother and grandmother. Her mother "raised seven children by selling food" after leaving an alcoholic husband. "After three years of gathering and sharing *charlas culinarias* (culinary conversations) with women who own[ed] *puestecitos* [food stands] in Cd. Juárez, Chihuahua, and El Paso, Texas, [she] coined the term 'familial wealth' to capture the meanings and values women [gave] to their own work." Owning a business brought more than financial gain; it benefited family and community by promoting collaboration, reciprocity, and citizenship. "For many customers public kitchens replace their home's breakfast, lunch and dinner tables," she explains. "I am aware of at least one regular *homeless* customer, often described as "*casi de la familia*" (almost like family), who always receives his daily meal at no cost. Furthermore, many patrons convert the public kitchen into a meeting hall where the current local politics are discussed or romances unfold." Maria Luisa Gonzales and her daughter Cecy ran a twenty-two-stall market that functioned as a day-care center for children and grandchildren. Marketers kept an eye on one another's children, protecting them from strangers. Many customers were regulars. Once a customer asked Cecy for a bowl of *caldo* [clear beef broth] "for her mother who had just returned home from the hospital. Cecy got the biggest container she could find and filled it to the top. When she gave it to the lady who had asked for it, Cecy refused to accept any money saying, 'No, no forget it; just take it to your mom. Hopefully she will get better soon.'" One day, Gonzales's nephew, a high school student, took more than twenty of his classmates to have lunch at her stall. She "refused to take money from them"—her nephew's happiness and recognition of her culinary talent was enough. "They left very happy," she remarked. "Those are beautiful details in life that you do not forget. You remember them always." Gonzales was proud that she provided people with a place of employment, a chance to learn about reciprocity, a space for social services, lessons about entrepreneurship, and exposure to local politics.[24]

As was the case for Abarca's family, the kitchen talk of urban immigrants is often crucial for their economic and cultural survival in a new land. Home kitchens were the center of immigrant life in late nineteenth- and early twentieth-century America.

> Where urban immigrants ate was almost as important as what they ate in the preservation of group life. In the tiny apartments that the newcomers found affordable, the kitchen was not only a place to cook and to eat, but it was the place to talk and work. It was the social nexus of the immigrant family. At the wooden kitchen table, the man of the family read newspapers, the women prepared the food and the school-age children did homework. Southern and eastern European

families often took piecework from garment manufacturers, and that work was frequently done in the kitchen. In the wintertime, the presence of the oven made this room the coziest in the apartment, and children or boarders slept on cots near the stove. Kitchens provided an opportunity for sociability, a place to maintain identity in the face of many pressures to abandon it. . . .

The state-supported hot lunch programs, designed to help the new arrivals, violated Italian tradition by keeping the children away from home at lunch time. Often, Italian parents insisted that their children come home at noon. Historian Richard Gambino fondly remembers coming home to a "good home-cooked lunch of the *paese*, for example, fried eggs and potatoes on Italian bread." To Gambino, and to many other youngsters, this fare was "indescribably delicious" and much preferred to the school's institutional "balanced meals." Eating with relatives or close friends rather than *stranieri* (strangers), as a child's schoolmates would be, was a deeply-rooted aspect of southern Italian tradition. Ironically, one could only ascend from the status of stranger to that of intimate friend through the rite of sharing a meal, or any food or drink, "a symbolic entering into the ceremony of family communion."[25]

Kitchens were crucial for identity formation in other ways as well. Food writer Kim Severson sees them as places where cooks exercised power and taught life lessons about community and resilience. She notes that the art of cookie baking had, on several occasions, made her "the most popular person in the room." Food was power. Her heroes were "women who never abandoned the kitchen" and "use[d] cooking as a source of strength," keeping families together and saving communities. "They have made political change through their love of food." In times of crisis, they fed people "something soothing." They taught that "food is the best antidote for anything life throws at you." Cooks helped her "figure out what [she] really believed in, how to remake [her] life and re-create a family, and finally, how to face death." Acknowledging that not everyone's life paths and lessons were the same as hers, she ventures, "We could sit down at a kitchen table and find that parts of our paths look just the same. Like me, you learned from people who navigated life before you and then took the time to tell you how they did it. For me, those guides were these women. And their kitchens were my classrooms."[26]

Family Meals

Table talk takes place in kitchens and at family meals. There are many types of family dynamics, and meals lose their civil potential when power is wielded arbitrarily and rituals are stifling. Miriam Weinstein reports a story about a father who set a timer to thirty minutes, after which time the food would be taken away. In another case, a mother set her timer to ten minutes, and if you didn't finish your food in time, you got another helping and had to start eating all over again. Family meals and rituals can also be pleasurable, setting the stage for enjoyable conversation—socially and physiologically. "Rituals have great power for smoothing over the rough spots, helping us to regroup and heal. Because we are sharing a pleasurable sensuous experience (the only one that's public, it's been said), we reinforce pleasurable associations with family members. The rise of the hormone oxytocin after a meal is linked to feelings of calm and connection."[27]

When they asked people across the country about sharing tables, the Kitchen Sisters were struck with the variety of families they encountered, ranging in size from two people to scores of people. Whatever the group's size, it was the ritual connection that mattered, the civic glue. A woman who was raised in a traveling circus described how when the cookhouse flag went up on the big tent three times a day, everyone gathered for a communal meal. Even when "a tornado took the circus tent, [or] an animal got loose, [or they] were up all night in the mud tearing down the tent," they gathered on big picnic benches to eat. Another woman told about her job as a cook for an eighty-three-year old, classic WASP Boston man. He would pick her up at college, and they shopped for dinner ingredients in small neighborhood grocers on the cobblestone streets. They shared stories over dinner. She told him about her college life, and he read her poetry and played her records by composers he wanted her to know about, both classical and modern. She reflected, "It was a remarkable way of connecting across generations. I think young people seem to be increasingly isolated from anyone over the age of sixty in any real way. It seems to me that this is being lost."[28]

As we have seen, many health-care professionals recommend frequent family meals to prepare children for adulthood and citizenship, as described here by a pediatrician.

> I encourage you to think of family dinner as your child's nightly dress rehearsal for adulthood, a protected space for him or her to master patience, conversation, and cooperation . . . *one meal at a time*. . . . My parents cooked almost every night, and my sisters and I set the table and handled the cleanup. Even today, a warm little grin fills my heart when I remember the scent of chocolate pudding bubbling on the stove or the savory perfume of my dad's garlic-roasted chicken. I remember getting into fights with my sisters over who would get the only two wings. As you might imagine, with three kids and only two wings, these fights always ended with one of us getting a refresher in the art of *taking turns*. . . .

When my wife and I raised our family, dinners together gave our daughter a chance to share her daily ups and downs . . . to feel heard and respected. We tried to encourage her confidence in her own ability to problem-solve by not rushing in to rescue her with our opinions and ideas. These meals gave us an opportunity to see the world from her point of view; for us to learn about iPods and Facebook. Family dinners gave us a chance to recount our experiences growing up to give her insight into why we hold the beliefs that we do. Having a regular dinner routine also helps build family unity. Joint meals won't end all domestic squabbles, but sitting together—even the night after a fight—gives kids practice talking through disagreements, forgiving and forgetting, and seeing the world as a bit more complex than right and wrong.[29]

Teachers have also weighed in on the importance of conversation at family dinners, calling parents to task for overscheduling their children and policing proper eating instead of listening and learning.

Family dinner isn't considered important. Too often it's just squeezed in and rushed through. There isn't much joy, conversation, or bonding in rushing through meals. Dinnertime is an opportunity to build and deepen relationships. The foundation of our family is loving, respectful relationships. All of us, adults and children, learn through our relationships, not only about others but about ourselves, too. At dinner, when parents sit down at the table, they are generally focusing on the wrong things. They focus on how much food the child is putting into their mouth. They miss the opportunity to have a connecting, joyful experience, to listen to their children and engage in a shared dialogue. For the most part, we don't know how to listen well. The ways our culture is eating today—fast food, solitary eating, eating on the run—don't support relationships. Parents are not slowing down, and this can mean a missed opportunity every day to build our sense of belonging through shared mealtimes.[30]

It takes a concerted effort to routinize family dinners. Of course, this is easier to do when you can afford to hire a cook, as was the case for writer Nora Ephron. But even without such help, parents can try to make dinner the central event of an evening. Ephron goes so far as to define a family as a group of people who eat the same thing for dinner.

I would have to say that if we had a religion at all in our house, it was the family dinner. We all ate together—my parents and my three sisters—at least five nights a week, in the dining room. There was a sideboard, and my father carved the meat, and one of us helped with the vegetables and potatoes. The food was absolutely fantastic—over the years we had two great Southern cooks, and they could make ethereal yeast rolls and the flakiest piecrust you've ever had. The food was traditional American—pot roast, stews, roast beef, fried chicken, and always fish on Friday nights because (as my mother said) Friday was the day when the fish was freshest because of the Catholics. Before dinner (which was at six thirty), we all met in the den, where my parents had a couple of drinks and there was a cut-glass dish filled with what are now known as crudités but were then known as celery sticks and carrots and black olives.

Dinner was truly our time to be a family, and everyone (including the four of us) told stories about our day. I really do think that sharing food at the table is the way to friendship and family. A family is a group of people who eat the same thing for dinner. You don't have to serve "great" meals. You can serve the simplest meals. The point is that it should be the event of the night. My dinners as a parent were much more informal that the ones I grew up with, but I did have the same rule my mother had—you don't have to finish it if you don't like it, but at least you have to taste it. The best thing I did with my kids was to sit down for dinner with them.[31]

The civic and democratic potential of a family dinner cannot be realized if everyone consumes it in a different room. A student I interviewed had a friend who did not have family dinners. Everyone ate a different meal. "I don't like it when families do that. I think children become picky eaters and they don't try new things and there is no bond over food—it's fuel instead of food. It was hard going over there. We would make mac and cheese out of the box and go to the TV or her room. There would not be any socializing. I don't think they are really close as a family. The dad stays in his room a lot of the time, and they are just not as open with each other as they could be if they were meeting for a meal every night. She probably thinks we are strange too. She definitely was not used to just sitting down and having a meal together and talking."[32]

Elementary school teachers frequently hear from their students that family meals are microwaved and eaten in separate rooms while watching TV, conditions that are hardly conducive to conversation. I interviewed Barbara Scheifler, who taught fifth grade for ten years. An assignment in her nutrition unit asked students to keep track of their meals for one week.

Dinner would be cereal or mac and cheese or ramen noodles. They ate by themselves in front of the TV or in their bedroom. If there were other people in the house, they were doing something else. They got out of school at 2:05, so even if the parents lived there, the kids were home four hours before their parents came home. In middle school, most kids went straight home; they didn't go to day care after school. They had eaten breakfast at 7:00, had lunch at 11:00, and by 4:00 they were hungry. So they would eat some snacky something, pick up something on the way home, make cereal or a sandwich, so they weren't necessarily hungry for dinner at 6:00 or 7:00 when Mom or Dad came home, tired from their days. I think it was just the economic strain of both parents working different shifts. Often they wouldn't see each other. When I asked students to have their parents sign a form, oftentimes they would have to put it on the pillow of Mom and Dad's bed because by the time the parents came home, the kid was asleep, and the parents were still in bed when the kid got up.

Even if they had a community area, they would eat their cereal or grilled cheese sandwich in front of the TV, and there wasn't a lot of mixing. Certainly not for breakfast, and for lunch everybody was out. But for dinner, even on the weekends, when I think they weren't necessarily working, it wasn't big family time. A lot of the families did not live near their relatives, so they weren't going over to relatives' houses for dinner. Friends came over for parties, but they were almost too big to share. There wasn't much shared daily time. About 75 percent of them had no concept of what a pleasant dinner conversation was.[33]

Scheifler's story illustrates many obstacles blocking the civic potential of family meals: harried working parents whose schedules do not allow them to be in the same room at the same time to share a family meal, children whose hunger cycles do not make it easy for everyone to be hungry at the same time, dinners consisting of everyone eating something different in separate rooms, no rituals of common meals, even on weekends, and, not surprisingly, unfamiliarity with the notion of a pleasant dinner conversation.

The opportunity for meaningful family meals can present itself in many settings, so long as there is face-to-face communication and a willingness to listen. One student I interviewed described memorable meals at diners on road trips with his father. He voiced a theme echoed by many of the young people I interviewed: it is important to laugh and have fun at meals. He also reminded me that, for all the attention to family dinners, sometimes there can be more-meaningful connections at breakfast, especially if one is a morning person. "I very much enjoy family breakfasts because you are a whole different person in the morning than you are at night. Sometimes at night you are really stressed out, or maybe you haven't had that good of a day. But in the morning you're such a fresh mind that you don't have any real reason to be very upset. You're calm and collected, and you are just there being yourself instead of being someone who's been manipulated by a day that maybe wasn't up to par."[34]

Many teenagers associate family meals with being mortified by the stupid things their parents say. Sometimes, they come to appreciate those things or at least the rituals that accompanied them. For Molly Wizenberg, it started when she was a freshman in high school. Sitting at the kitchen table eating dinner, whenever her father remarked, "You know, we eat better at home than most people do in restaurants," she would blush hotly and shrink into her chair, "mortified by the weird pleasure he took in [their] family meal." But she came to realize that he was right. It was not that the food was particularly good: "It was the steady rhythm of meeting in the kitchen every night, sitting down at the table, and sharing a meal. Dinner didn't come through a swinging door, balanced on the arm of an anonymous waiter: it was something that we made together. We built our family that way—in the kitchen, seven nights a week. We built a life for ourselves, together around that table. And although I couldn't admit it then, my father was showing me, in his pleasure and pride, how to live it: wholly, hungrily, loudly." As an adult, she felt the presence of her parents at her kitchen table and at all the meals she ate. She remarks, "Food is never just food. It's also a way of getting at something else: who we are, who we have been, and who we want to be." She loved "the familiar voices that fall out of the folds of an old cookbook, or the scenes that replay like a film reel across [her] kitchen wall. . . . Everything interesting, everything good, seemed to happen when food was around."[35]

Teenagers know when they are being respected and when they are being dissed. The more they feel valued at family meals, the more they will want to spend time at the table. They also notice whether their parents respect their friends. Miriam Weinstein interviewed a high school senior who split his week between the houses of his divorced parents. He enjoyed having dinner with his parents because of the love they'd shown him. He appreciated all the time his mother spent with him. It made him feel good, and he liked sitting down to talk with her. "I think the more respect a parent shows to their child, the more apt they are to sit down and talk and have dinner with them," he observed. "I know if my dad or mom's not treating me right, I'm not gonna want to sit down with them." When his friends came over for dinner, the conversation changed because his mother would ask how they were doing. When it was just the family, they would talk about what they did that day. "There's a little time in your day, in your lives, your whole family's together and doing one thing," the young man reflected. "It's a time to like share with everyone. I can talk with my brothers all at once and hear all their input."[36]

Family meals can build self-reliance. Among the Gullah, descendants of slaves who live in the coastal South, motherhood is not limited to a biological relationship; it can also include "othermothers," women who share household responsibilities with blood mothers. Neighbors jointly prepare and share meals, and parental permission is not required for children to eat at a neighbor's house.

Women of all generations, as mothers and as extended-family members, play a critical role in fostering self-reliance and a sense of collective memory in their children of both genders. They do so through the daily preparation and eating of traditional foods and by using informal conversation to teach family history and cultural traditions. I learned about the use of informal conversation when I attended a funeral at the home of a Gullah family. In the evening, after the funeral ceremonies were finished and most people had left, all the women of the family sat together in the living room with their children at their feet, eating and telling each other family stories. Someone asked about the people in a family photograph. My hostess described the context in which the photo was taken (which happened to be a family meal) and recalled each family member present, including the wife and mother, who was in the kitchen cooking when the photo was taken. Because children are expected to eventually manage their own lives, both sons and daughters are taught the skills of self-reliance through cooking. Parents believe that their children must know these things to survive in the wider culture.[37]

The beneficial effects of family dinners have received a lot of media attention. As we have seen, social scientists caution against overclaiming, noting that their purported positive benefits may be due more to other factors, such as having the resources and ability to organize common mealtimes, than to the meal itself. And of course, other family rituals may be just as conducive for conversations. There is no point in guilt-tripping parents who are not able to organize frequent and successful family meals. To shed light on these issues, journalist Jan Hoffman interviewed both experts and harried parents. Psychologist Philip A. Cowan cautioned that "there is not a proven cause and effect" relationship between more family dinners and fewer behavioral problems. "To say that family dinners are associated with good outcomes is not the same as saying that family dinners cause good outcomes," he said, adding that "the most likely explanation for the Center on Addiction and Substance Abuse (CASA) results . . . is that families who place importance on eating together . . . are those who are more likely to produce good outcomes for their children" for other reasons. Dr. Amy Middleman noted that "the dinner table may be the last place a teenager chooses" to be forthcoming. "There's too much time to see your parents' reaction and their over-reaction," she said, adding that teens "prefer to drop [bombshells] just as they're getting out of the car." Even though she believes in the importance of family dinners, especially for patients with eating disorders, "she is not certain that the fundamental element" of a family dinner is actually the food. "The family dinner research may be telling us that some of the more important elements may be about slowing down, organizing our lives with a little bit less harried time," she said. "There just needs to be some element of structure and reconnection during the day. And I don't know that it has to be 'meaningful.' It could be a drive, a walk, a regular conversation." Teenagers need to separate from their families in a healthy way and to be reassured that "when they come back, what they left will still be there. And so whatever it takes to make that clear is probably what we're getting with 'family dinners.'"[38]

As for harried parents, Hoffman interviewed a divorced mother of four with an hour-long commute from home to work. The woman said she typically got home around 7:00 p.m. and described "the exhaustion, laundry, silliness and homework that converge when she walks through the door." She managed family dinners three times a week and the rest of the time it was "Do it yourself. Leftovers. Cereal and bananas," explaining, "By the time I'm home, they've already eaten and I can grab a kid, make a run to Target. Then you get the one-on-one time. I think there are different ways to get to the same place." A frenzied Manhattan lawyer with two young children declined to give her name, fearing social embarrassment. "I don't know why dinner has to the meaningful thing," she said. "Having my kid eat four snacks so she can wait for a 15-minute dinner with us and go to bed right away doesn't work. What's important to me is creating time with my kids that clients don't infringe on." For her, that time was during breakfast and walking to school. An accountant who got up at 5:30 a.m. and got home at 8:00 p.m. said that she and her husband rarely had dinner with their children, but there was a lot of talking in their house. She went to sleep at 10:00 p.m. "My son comes in every night, sits on the bed, talks about his day, kisses me good night and tucks me in." A county Web support worker with two teenaged daughters was usually home by 6:00 p.m. They never dined together; everyone ate in a different room. "Dinner is refueling," she said. "It's another chore." But when the three of them watched television, they paused shows and talked a lot, and on weekends they often rented movies. She usually drove her daughters to school, and her office was close enough for them to visit. "At lunchtime, the girls call[ed] to chat." When they asked her about her day, they did not accept a one-word answer, "Fine." They wanted to hear about her projects. She laughed at the fact that her daughters wanted her "to spill it," admitting, "So I do." Joseph A. Califano Jr., the founder and chairman of CASA, admitted that he was rarely home for family dinners: "I spent four years working for Lyndon Johnson as chief domestic aide, . . . and I wasn't home for dinner much. My wife had dinner with the kids. But I spent every moment with them on Saturdays and Sundays. You have to try." He agreed with the experts that "family dinner" could be read as a surrogate for parental engagement.[39]

Generations at the Table

At the family table, children hear stories from older generations, both relatives and nonrelatives. They learn about family, cultural identity, and how loved ones have met life's challenges. Teenagers sometimes think they are the only ones who have experienced injustice, been disrespected, or had their hearts broken. They can learn about resilience from older generations who have been down similar roads. The vice president of Ancestry.com, the largest family history website, said that many Americans lack basic information about their personal histories. "A lot of kids don't connect to their history because they are not sitting down together at the table. The family dinner is the number one place where most of this information usually gets passed on."[40]

Mealtimes at the Japanese American war relocation center at Manzanar in 1942 brought generations together. Table rituals helped them remain resilient in the face of the political adversities of being unjustly relocated and deprived of their property without due process.
Credit: Library of Congress, Prints and Photographs Division, FSA/OWI Collection (LC-USZ62-128823).

As we have seen, researchers at Emory University's Center for Myth and Ritual in American Life have found that sharing personal histories builds children's self-esteem and resilience, in part because it provides a larger context for their immediate lives. "It teaches them that there is more than just their few years. There are people who came before them; there are people who are connected to them, experiences that belong to them because they belong to their family's story. These narratives give us a sense of consistency and continuity, and even when things are bad, Grandpa will tell you 'it was bad before and we got through it.'" Their "Do You Know" game asks children questions about how their parents and grandparents met and where they grew up; what was going on in the world when they were born; the source of their name; the person in their family they look and act most like; their family's national background; when and how their family emigrated to this country; the jobs their parents had when they were young; and things that happened to their parents when they were in school. When relatives and old family friends are invited to dinner, kids can hear embarrassing stories, laugh, and make family history.[41]

Cookbook author Bryant Terry describes the context provided by the stories of his grandparents, who hailed from rural Mississippi and grew their own food.

> Both sets of my grandparents grew tons of food in their backyard, and tended fruit trees in the front yard. . . . They grew so much that my grandfather would give it away to neighbors and church members. . . . [My maternal grandmother] had a seemingly never-ending pot of greens cooking on the stove. . . . We often ate them with her homemade chow-chow. She had this huge pantry where she kept all of her preserves and pickles and chutneys because that's what they would eat for the leaner months. We would spoon that over the greens and sop the juices up with corn bread. . . . I use the terms *African-American cuisine* and *soul food* interchangeably. The cuisine has constantly evolved and changed throughout history. It's not just the obvious comfort foods like deep-fried fatty meats, sugary desserts. That's certainly part of it, but people need to widen their notion of what soul food is. . . . Just two generations ago, my grandparents were growing their own food and cooking everything fresh and in season. Who's to say what they were cooking and eating wasn't authentically African-American cuisine? Ironically, what they were cooking is the same type of food that many of my haute cuisine chef friends are cooking: farm to table food, fresh, local, seasonal, sustainable food. . . .
>
> I worry that we risk losing so much knowledge and connection to our ethnic backgrounds. When I think about family and food, I think about my grandpar-

ents' connection to the land and how important it is to pass down these recipes, traditions, and stories. Without that, our generation will lose a big part of what it means to be a family living in America. We have to hold on dearly to those memories and honor the knowledge that came before us. . . . My grandmother always said, you cannot know where you are going if you don't know where you came from. Boy was she right.[42]

Stories about grandmothers' cooking are so commonplace that people often tire of hearing them. Indeed, when the Kitchen Sisters began their journey in search of cooking traditions across America, they told listeners not to clog their hotline with such stories. In hindsight, they were glad that almost everyone ignored their plea. One woman told the story of her grandmother, who made pies for families of people who had died. On the day of her death, the woman received fifty empty pie plates, all with her grandmother's name on the back, from pies she had made for the community.[43]

Many immigrant grandmothers brought with them the food and the culture of their homeland, and the kitchen was their domain. Nikki Silva's grandmother emigrated from Portugal when she was twelve, married at thirteen, and had five children by the time she was twenty. "Narcissus was the matriarch of our family, holding everyone hostage with her *soupage* and *carne vino d'alhos*, her legendary Portuguese soup and meat. She canned, preserved, and tended a little kitchen garden. She held court at the stove—bestowing and withholding approval and love to her sons, daughters, and grandchildren who arrived unannounced throughout the day for coffee, cookies, and to make sure their position as 'her favorite' was secure."[44]

The Kitchen Sisters thought that it was often up to grandparents to preserve traditions of the table through recipes and stories. A case in point was a woman who taught high school nutrition classes for thirty-five years. She required her students to cook something at home, which she found was becoming increasingly difficult. Many students did not have any kitchen utensils at home, so she bought some for them. One girl said that she had never eaten a home-cooked meal, just take-out deli food. The teacher lamented that the childhood food memories of her current generation of students will be of frozen pizzas and microwave burritos, instead of a pork roast cooking. "We are losing a generation of food memories—of what Grandma cooked, childhood memories of the house smelling good." The Kitchen Sisters were surprised in their "search for vanishing kitchen traditions" that the family dinner table was among them. Grandparents' recipes and traditions "held part of the key to gathering the tribe around the table. The kitchen, it conjures up conversation, comfort. It's the room in the house that counts the most, and that smells the best, where families gather, where all good parties begin and end. The room where the best stories are told."[45] Notice the civil significance they attribute to kitchen tables: gathering, conversation, comfort, aromas, parties, and stories.

When cookbook writers want to transmit their ancestral history to future generations, they often pass along the wisdom of their grandparents. Jessica B. Harris wanted to "fix the taste of cornbread, beans, collard greens, okra, chilies, molasses, and rum on our tongues for generations to come."

> Traditional foods trace a gossamer thin line as far back as I can remember or discover in my family. It is a tradition that I maintain and will pass on. Grandma Jones's banana fritters—born of the necessity of feeding a family of twelve during the Depression—cut the bad spots off the overripe bananas that no one wants and make fritters—have become a food that I now crave. . . . Grandma Harris insisted on fresh produce and some of my earliest memories are of her gardening in a small plot where she lived, tending foods that I would later come to know as African: okra, collard greens, black-eyed peas, and peanuts. . . . The heavy black cast-iron pots, caldrons, and skillets are a leitmotif of Black cooking in Brazil, Nigeria, Barbados, and the United States. . . . Grandma Harris presented my mother with a caldron and skillet when she got married. These utensils, though at first disdained, have done over half a century's yeoman's duty in our kitchen. One day they will be mine. . . . My mother, who trained as a dietician but was discouraged from work in the food presentation field in which she excelled because of her race, took her talents home. Each night was a feast. No frozen dinners or cake mixes ever crossed our threshold. Made-from-scratch cakes, flaky pie crusts, and intricate finger sandwiches went along with the traditional African-inspired foods that my father loved.[46]

For some grandmothers, meals and cookbooks are a repository of family stories, and they are eager to share them with their grandchildren. A student I interviewed spoke of how her immigrant grandmother had a story for each one of the recipes in her family cookbook.

> I really enjoy having dinner at my grandmother's house. I know it is important to her. A lot of times the stories that she tells are based on meals she has had with friends and relatives. We talk a lot about food and how she learned to cook in America. She can go through each cookbook and tell you where she got a recipe and what it means. One of the cookbooks is from Austria right after World War I. It has recipes that they used on the front line, like goulash. That cookbook inspires stories about her dad, who was in World War I. They had goose and it

would be a weeklong thing and they would use every part of the bird. She would talk about her mother cooking and the help they had in the house cooking. She cooked Yugoslavian dishes to re-create what my grandfather knew growing up.[47]

On the other hand, some children have no contact with, or knowledge about, their grandparents. They are not able to construct a family tree and have never asked their parents to do so. Teacher Barbara Scheifler thought that this may be due in part to the fact that they were not spending time at family tables where they might hear stories about their ancestors.

At my family meals growing up, we heard about family history, where our relatives emigrated from. When I was teaching and asked the kids to go home and fill out their family trees, they asked who could be on the tree, and I said, "You can put your stepparents, step kids, foster kids, and anybody you want. You can have as many branches as you want. I don't care; it's for you." They said that they did not know anything about their families. "Don't you talk about this at the dinner table?" "No, we don't talk at the table. We don't eat together." When I was the librarian, I was curious about the names of some of the kids who checked out books. When I asked them, about 25 percent of the kids had no idea where their names came from. Or they said it was an American name. Well, we all are but we came from different places, and they didn't seem to be curious. So many of the kids are from split families and aren't living with their biological mom and dad. They might live with one parent and occasionally see the other parent. Or they live with stepparents, boyfriends and girlfriends of the parents; their siblings are halves and steps. In terms of family history, that muddies the waters. One time I had a parent say, "It is none of your business who is in our family tree," and I said, "You are absolutely right, and how would I know? You could say anything. And why would I care? All I care is that the tree is filled in and that Marco has some concept of who is on his tree."[48]

When curious children notice that their friends do not share family meals, they reflect about whether it is a tradition worth saving. One student I interviewed was aware that his parents were raised with family meals, and because they valued conversations, stories, and fun, they continued the practice with him.

When I was younger I had a friend, and his family ate in different rooms. He and I went into his living room to watch television while eating pizza, his mom was up in her office working, his dad was up in the bedroom watching TV, and his sister did homework in her room. It's like they almost didn't seem to get along as well as my family. They didn't have this point of getting together. I talked to my parents about it and asked them why we all sat down to dinner together. They told me it's because they want to talk to us and they feel like dinner is something that can bring us together as a family and they don't want us to grow apart. They enjoy dinner; it's how they were raised. They ate dinner as a family together; they talked and had good conversations. They both had a bunch of siblings, so they had lots of stories to tell. I guess they want us to have the same fun experience they had. I want to have children, and I want them to have the experience that has really kept me close to my parents and my sister at dinner time and having fun. I want to hear what my kids have to say later in life, and maybe they want to hear what I have to say. Maybe they don't. I don't know.[49]

Curious children also notice when their relatives are silent about their past, causing them to speculate about the reasons. For example, domestic workers in the South often had painful table memories that were difficult to share. "Annette Coleman recalled that her employer in Georgia in the 1920s expected her to eat table scraps, which had to be shared with the employer's dog. . . . Richard Wright remembered waiting for his mother's employers to finish their meals so that he could learn what his own dinner would be." Florence Ladd wondered whether the hard work of housekeeping and cooking for priests had taken its toll on her "often silent" grandmother: "Had years of domestic chores, in the service of others and in her own domain, rendered her quiet (as well as visibly weary)? Had she been silenced, over the years, by the labor required to purchase the land and building materials for a house, acquire furniture, buy a piano, provide piano and organ lessons for my mother, then send her to Winston-Salem Teachers College? After years of rearing her own children, Mama Willis had three grandchildren thrust upon her. Had her voice been stilled by duty and responsibility?"[50] Sometimes *not* talking at a table speaks volumes about how we might learn to empathize with others.

Ritual family meals can be an occasion for adult children to pay their parents a visit, sometimes with friends in tow. A librarian I interviewed told me how her children, a thirty-year-old daughter who lived locally and a nineteen-year-old son away at college, would occasionally show up for Friday-night Shabbat dinner. Growing up, her daughter had always been around for family meals. But her son was more athletic, and it was challenging to arrange common meals, depending on the time of year. "But we're Jewish, so we always have Shabbat dinner," she noted. "And obviously food is huge in Jewish culture. Our daughter is living with someone now who is not Jewish, and last Friday night she brought him and her friend from high school over for dinner on Friday night because they requested it. Neither one of them is Jewish. The high school friend lives elsewhere and came back to town and asked to come. She wanted to see us and asked, 'Can we do Shabbat dinner with your parents?' We have always included our kids' friends in Shabbat and Passover seders."[51]

For many immigrants, family dinners are both a link to a homeland and an adaptation to conditions in the United States. Children pressure adults to "eat American," and labor-intensive food items disappear from household menus, as seen in the case of Bengali-Americans.

> Eighty five percent of Bengali-American respondents claimed that dinner is the most important meal of the day, mostly because it is the only meal that all members of the household eat together. Many claimed that dinner is important because it is the only *Bengali* meal of rice and fish, and some underlined its importance as the most "relaxed meal." This is the other side of the decay of breakfast and lunch as commensal meals. As modern work schedules have made breakfast and lunch less important, dinner has moved to the center of the re-enactment of ethnicity and "culture." Thus, it is not surprising that two out of three respondents claimed that dinner has not changed since migration. . . .
>
> Children often prefer pasta and hamburger sandwiches to rice and fish. Adult second-generation members are typically equivocal about their choices among rice, pasta, and bread, but for *first*-generation Bengali-Americans, pasta and bread are not considered filling staples. . . . *Rooti* [wheat flatbread] has been replaced by rice as the carbohydrate anchor of dinner in the United States. Clearly, the reason is convenience. *Rooti* is probably the most labor-intensive ingredient of a meal, and its preparation is typically assigned to servants among middle-class Calcuttans. In the absence of servants, *rooti* has effectively vanished from Bengali-American meals.[52]

Preparing meals is an act of generosity, which some children take pleasure in reciprocating for their parents. In a study of mother-daughter visits, one older mother said of her daughter, "She fixed me lunch. It was a really wonderful soup. She'd gone to a lot of trouble to think of what I might like." One daughter explained, "Most of the times when I see her, she comes to visit at my house and we feed her and she loves my husband's cooking. And it's nice to see her get fed. She's fed everybody so much. She really appreciates how much we put in. She's very appreciative."[53] Such norms of reciprocity bolster civil relations.

Some women say that they learned to be black and female in their mothers' and grandmothers' kitchens. Here are three stories.

> A thirty-two-year old mother of two said: "Grandmama is a very good cook, and I watched her. Mama is a good cook and I watched her. I'd pick up on things.

Gradually, they'd let me do little things here and there. If I cooked something, I don't care what it was, they would eat it. I made some dumplings one day that were just like rubber balls! They ate them. They never complained about them. I enjoyed cooking. You know when people act like they enjoy your cooking, even when you know it's bad, you do it, and the more you do, you get better at it. I enjoyed cooking so much that I took over a lot of the cooking from Mama, especially during the week."

As explained by one woman, [household] activities started early in childhood: "We bought food, clothes, or whatever we needed. We took great joy in doing it but Mama didn't tax that on us. She just raised us to be thoughtful about the household. If I was working and came home and we were out of bread, I went and bought some. My nine-year-old brother would do the same thing. He'd come home from that coal house and if we didn't have any bread, he'd turn right around and go back to get some."

A forty-seven-year-old woman said: "Any one of my children could have paid my bills, could have told you how much money I made, how much I was going to pay in church, how much grocery I was going to buy and what week I was supposed to buy what grocery when they were twelve years old. You see, what I did was let them in on the real facts of how we were doing it. I didn't play no games with them. We didn't pretend we had what we did not have. They knew exactly what we had."[54]

When restaurateur and author Maricel Presilla was growing up, generational learning occurred at the main midday meal, when the whole family ate together. She observed, "Once you share a meal something changes. It brings a level of wonderful intimacy and it relaxes everyone." Her four aunts were fantastic cooks who prepared an extended family meal at her grandfather's house every Sunday. "The preparation of that lunch was a ritual," she recalled. "I saw so many wonderful traditional foods prepared in my grandfather's kitchen, seasonal foods like tamales. I come from eastern Cuba and corn season coincided with carnival time. The making of the tamales was a big family affair. You need a lot of people to help, and I remember my aunts each doing a chore and then the kids husking the corn or helping to grate it. The smell of damp earth that corn has when you're boiling the tamales is something that I will never forget."[55]

Kids Cooking

Adults have to decide how much to involve children in getting meals on the table. There are many benefits of including children, even if all they do is set the table. As a student I interviewed put it, "One thing that might lead to sitting down to dinner at least from my experience is that we're all part of the preparation for dinner. My parents cook a lot of the meals. I or my sister usually set the table, so we're all part of the preparation for dinner. We're not all in separate rooms; we're all contributing toward the meal itself."[56]

As a child, chef Gillian Clark was a shy bookworm whose voice was rarely heard, until she put dinner on the family table. When her father cooked dinner for five hungry teenagers, she thought that he was the most important person on earth, and she was determined to enjoy that kind of power and attention. At school and at home, her voice was rarely heard. As the youngest child, she found it difficult to get attention. She often spent entire evenings with her nose in a book without saying anything. But once she put dinner on the table, she got everyone's attention.[57]

Learning to cook as a child gave food writer Kim Severson a sense of security. The kitchen table was her refuge from the storms of trying to fit in. She was desperate to stand out, yet more sensitive than she let on. When she arrived home at the end of the day, the kitchen "brought instant relief." Getting to the dinner table on time was the one rule she wanted to obey, even when she enjoyed breaking rules as a teenager. She felt safe at the table; it was home. While she was in elementary school, her mother taught her how to put dinner on the table, giving her "everything [she] needed to know to make a safe home when [she] grew up."[58]

For some parents, asking children to pitch in preparing meals is pragmatic—they are harried and need help. Lynn Fredericks was the mother of two sons. At dinnertime, she dragged them from the living room TV to the kitchen TV. While they ate, she picked at her own dinner, walked around, or talked on the phone. One night she handed her one-year-old a bunch of basil and told him to rip off the leaves to help her cook. She shifted her focus from how quickly she could get a meal onto the table to how she could include her children in the process. She gave them age-appropriate tasks and praised their efforts. "Once their egos and skills were involved, they stopped rejecting foods out of hand." She got used to a messy kitchen. "When she let them choose menus and ingredients, she was surprised at their adventurousness and creativity. She began taking them to the supermarket, and to farmer's markets—real eye openers for city kids." She eventually shut off the TV and moved dinner into the dining room. "When she introduced table linens and cloth napkins, . . . conversation improved." Before dinner, they said a short blessing in which they enumerated what they were grateful for that day. The blessing "was the last bit of glue that mended [their] broken family." The children took the blessing very seriously, and Fredericks learned a lot about their values from what they said was important to them on a daily basis. Her older son, who was seven when the project started, began to link cooking to foreign countries, asking, "What culture are we cooking tonight?" The confidence he learned through cooking helped him through some difficult times at school. Fredericks noted that many children find it easier to talk when they are doing something. One night when making dinner, she could not persuade her son Stephan to sing a song he had learned at school until she praised his cooking skills, whereupon he jumped off the stool and sang it.[59]

This story is chock full of lessons for civility and democracy: asking a one-year-old to participate in a common good; turning off the TV and the phone to give others your undivided attention; being mindful in the moment of the process of feeding and connecting to others; relaxing standards of neatness to promote creativity and self-esteem; counteracting the invisibility of food preparation by including children in trips to markets; eating at a common table with rituals to promote conversation; expressing gratitude; listening to what children value; encouraging cultural exploration through food; and appreciating that for some people, conversing might be easier when they are doing something.

A child can feel empowered by cooking for adults, even when she or he is an only child in a household with one parent. Chef Anna Kovel recalled "the time when she was twelve or thirteen and living with her father. When he insisted on eating 'family dinners,' she objected that it was just the two of them, and that she'd rather be out playing with her friends. But when he would call her up from work and tell her how to put the chicken in the oven, she remembers feeling empowered by her chicken-cooking skills."[60]

When children are asked to play a special role in producing a collective good such as a family meal, they are likely to be in a position to articulate its value, not only to themselves but also to outsiders, as Shavreen Pooni did when she shared delicacies with her friends and teachers. When her grandparents emigrated from India and moved to her parents' grape farm, it enabled her family to continue many traditions and rituals, such as making *saag*, a green spinach dish typically served with a yellow corn tortilla, *makhi de roti*. Eating *saag* during winter became a family ritual because of her grandmother's dedication and skillful cooking.

> My favorite part of creating *saag* comes after the spinach has been planted and picked. Preparing the *saag* is my favorite part because it's a family affair. Everyone

plays a special role and makes the process more unique. This is different from the traditional way of cooking in India where only the women would handle the food and no one else was allowed in the kitchen. Similar to the way *saag* was created in India, we also made it on an open fire pit in my American house. . . .

My grandma always prefers to grow her own vegetables and make her own spices and *achars* [ginger and chili peppers] from fresh ingredients. We usually buy our corn flour and wheat flour from the Indian stores because it tends to be of better quality for our *rotis* than the flour sold at grocery stores such as Vons. Every year during fall quarter I come home with hopes that my grandma has made some fresh *saag*. Even some of my teachers from elementary school and extended family members will call the house to see if there is any fresh *saag*. This extended love for my grandma's *saag* has allowed me to appreciate and accept my culture's cuisine. Before I would be scared to talk about it and share it with my friends, but I now boast about my easy access to home made Indian food. Moreover, seeing the time and effort my grandma puts into the process of *saag* shows me how food plays an important role in our culture and family. Instead of making it on the stove and buying all the ingredients from the store, my grandma always wants to make it in the traditional way because it brings the family together. As a result, making *saag* and *makhi de roti* is a regular family ritual that involves some traditions brought over from India and some new ones created in America.[61]

Many adults assume there is no point in asking teenagers to help prepare meals. But as Pooni's story indicates, this is a mistaken notion if we care about promoting an appreciation of different cultures, an awareness of gender roles in mealtime production, and the self-confidence and resiliency that result from sharing important parts of who we are with others. A surprising number of young people think it is unfortunate when adults do all the cooking and exclude them. A student I interviewed was active in her high school's Slow Food Club, whose members enjoyed preparing and sharing meals.

Every year we went to the farmers' market. Everybody pitched in three dollars, and we bought food and brought it back to my house to make a big lunch. I know my friends really enjoyed that, and I did too. It was good because there was a lot of stuff to do, and everyone felt involved and needed in the process of making a meal. Things are different at their homes. One of my friend's mom does all the cooking; for other friends, the dad does all the cooking. When there are specific adults who do most of the cooking, children are not as involved in it, so I think it was pretty meaningful to get together as friends and peers and all make the lunch together. They definitely liked bringing their own recipes to the lunch, sharing their own cultures and rituals. Parents should have their kids be more involved in the kitchen. Too many times, they will take care of everything even when the child wants to help out. It is what the parents are used to. My peers are generally open to new foods, and they do not see cooking as women's work; they are not into stereotypes.[62]

Group participation means less stress on any one individual and more opportunity for relaxation, enjoyment, and conversation. Here is how a student I interviewed put it.

> Our meals have become more organized so that we can all sit down and enjoy the meal. We've been efficient about the preparation of the meal to the point where when everyone's home we've got maybe an hour before dinner when the food's cooking and the aroma is going through the house. I can do homework, or maybe watch TV or do whatever, and then once we're ready for dinner, I usually set the table. We split up the cooking a lot too, so there are a lot of opportunities for everyone to share the process of making the food. Once the food's ready, we get to just enjoy it instead of worrying about other things that may be stressing us out. It's also a good opportunity to talk about what is stressing us out and what we're worried about, which usually does not end up being that much. It's been nice to have those family dinners because we all love to cook and love food. It's a very central part of our lives I think in the sense that we enjoy it so much.[63]

When sociologist Elaine Bell Kaplan interviewed middle school children, she discovered a wide range of involvement in making meals. Their stories portray the complex ways in which food is a metaphor for care and a signifier of gender, culture, and class. A fourteen-year-old girl "recalled seeing the movie *Soul Food*, [which was] about a Black family reunion." She got "excited about its focus on family togetherness" and convinced her mother to make such a dinner once a month. She enjoyed seeing all her relatives, and because her mother did not always feel like cooking, she learned how to cook collard greens, macaroni and cheese, deviled eggs, and potato salad. Some children "saw cooking . . . as a way to assert their competency and creativity to themselves and their working parents." A twelve-year-old boy said that he had been cooking since first grade. He got inspired watching his mom and asked if she could help him make the juice, crack the eggs, and cook the grits. Like most of the children Kaplan interviewed, his first cooking experience was making eggs. And sometimes he made steak. A thirteen-year-old girl wanted to learn about ingredients, especially what her mom put in her peach pie.[64]

Kaplan was struck with how many children "saw cooking for their families as a way to repay them for their care." Twelve-year-old David told her that the night before he was hungry, and his sister "kept on bugging [him] to cook some chicken or something like that." He explained, "I did that for her, cause sometimes she does it for me. And if it's Mother's Day and I don't have any money, I might make my mother breakfast in bed or something like that." An eleven-year-old girl cooked a dinner of soup or eggs for herself and her four-year-old brother because her mother "left home every morning at dawn" and came home tired from her hour-long commute and stressful job. Josie was the daughter of a single mother who "had managed to get her family off welfare by working at various part-time jobs. On Tuesdays and Wednesdays her mother left home at 6:00 a.m. for a six-hour job as a clerk at a local cleaner. In the afternoon, she left again for another six hours of work as a janitor at a hotel, and for four hours every Friday she sold Avon products door-to-door. Although she was always home when Josie arrived home from school, most often she was 'asleep or tired,' Josie said." She appreciated that her mom tried to find the time to talk to her and her brothers. "I know that she'll find space in between sometime. Like when she's off from working, she [will] come and sit down, kinda talk to [my brothers and me] for five minutes. When she has a budget, she sometimes has to break it to provide for us. Like yesterday, we asked her if we could go to the store, and it was off her budget, but she let us anyway. [Me and my younger brother] got her a king-size Hershey [candy bar] because we feel that she deserves it." A twelve-year-old girl said that she often cooked because her mother was "so stressed out" that she wanted to help. "Whenever my mom is like down or something, I make her this nice little meal, she gets all happy." Although she wished that her mother would cook something other than microwave food and she "felt burdened by her cooking chores," she wanted "to be emotionally supportive of her mother." And a fourteen-year-old girl wanted to give back to her family: "My mom does a lot for everybody. My family, they're really nice. So I make things that are simple, that I know they'll like. Like tuna."[65]

Not all children looked so kindly on the fact that their mothers did not cook "real food" for them, and they resented having to pick up the slack. A fourteen-year-old girl "thought that dinnertime should be central to her . . . mother's identity as a good mother." She realized that her mother worked but thought that she should be home in time to fix something other than frozen food. A thirteen-year-old boy compared his stepmother's frozen-food dinners with those of "his 'real' mother, who cooked 'real' food." During most of the dinners with his father and stepmother, there was little conversation, bad food, and arguments about something he did. He preferred to eat alone. But he enjoyed dinners at his biological mother's house, and sometimes he made her dinner because he liked to cook. A thirteen-year-old girl "complained that she had to do all the cooking for her mother. . . . 'My mom leaves before I do [in the morning]. And I don't eat breakfast. My mom, she can't cook. Like for Thanksgiving, I cooked the whole dinner.'"[66]

Nick was a twelve-year-old whose parents had demanding professional jobs and "left for work an hour earlier than he did for school: [He complained,] 'Nobody fixes my breakfast. Well, I'll either not eat breakfast or maybe go out or I'll just get it myself. . . . I always tell them to make breakfast every morning before I go to school so I can wake up.'" His parents' community involvement and work demands affected dinnertime. His mother was active in the PTA, and she was "often on the phone discussing school issues or work problems," and his father was frequently in his office or on a business trip. "I ask them a lot, 'Why don't we do things [on the holidays]?' I'll like ask them all the time, but they just don't have any answers and they don't tell me why." His fourteen-year-old sister said that she did not do anything to care for her family because they always yelled at her. She was angry that her parents served microwave food. Kaplan observed that many children had a food hierarchy: at the top was "'real' food cooked from scratch (by mom most likely)," and at the bottom was microwave food. Many children "equated . . . parents' ability to cook 'real' food with their ability to care for [them]."[67]

At school, food was a signifier of class. For example, when Kaplan asked Stacey, Amanda, and Letia who fixed lunch for them, Amanda replied, "Sometimes, when I don't have time, when I go to school, I just grab a cup of noodles, warm it up there. The teachers are nice; they let me." These girls helped out at home and did not expect their working parents to make them lunch. Amanda said that she could get a free lunch at school but chose not to. Stacey said there was a stigma on free lunches. "You're supposed to be poor." All three girls chimed in: "[You're] on welfare!" "Amanda's and Letia's families were part of the growing black middle class," and the girls tried to shape their new class identity in three ways: "Avoid being seen receiving food at the free lunch counter, being seen bringing lunch from home, or (and the best rule of all, the kids seem to be saying) being seen paying for food at the snack bar. From their point of view, free food would cost them a sense of self." Stacey, who could not afford to buy lunch every day, "covered" her lower-class status "by accepting free food from Amanda and Letia, but not from the school where she could be seen receiving it. According to the girls, receiving food from a friend carries with it a different connotation than the one associated with accepting free institutional food."[68]

Pediatricians think that there are many benefits—social as well as nutritional—to be derived from parents and grandparents cooking with children and sharing family recipes. I would add that some of these benefits are civil and democratic as well: participating in an everyday common good and building self-esteem and communication skills. Here is some of the advice posted on the WebMD site. The author admits that including children in cooking requires time, patience, and extra cleanup, but she says it is well worth the effort.

Some of the short-term benefits: it encourages kids to try healthy foods; kids feel like they are accomplishing something and contributing to the family; kids are more likely to sit down to a family meal when they helped prepare it; parents get to spend quality time with their kids; kids aren't spending time in front of the TV or computer while they're cooking; and kids generally aren't eating junk food when they're cooking a meal at home. Some long-term benefits: learning to cook is a skill your children can use for the rest of their lives; kids who learn to eat well may be more likely to eat healthfully as adults; positive cooking experiences can help build self-confidence; and kids who cook with their parents may even be less likely to abuse drugs.

Be caring and supportive of your child. Parents get many opportunities to compliment and support their children while they're in the kitchen together. Open the lines of communication. Kids having fun in the kitchen, elbow to elbow, are likely to interact with each other and with their parents. Cooking together gives parents and children time together to talk and share thoughts and stories. "Communication doesn't start when your child is 17," says [a doctor]. "It should start when your child is 3." Eat dinner together regularly. Involving your kids in the kitchen is a big stepping-stone to getting them to appreciate family meals. Because of challenging work, school, and sports schedules, many families struggle to sit down to even one daily meal together. But you can start by maximizing weekend opportunities to eat together. . . .

For many of us, dinner offers the best opportunity for cooking with our children day in and day out. One tip: Set out some washed and sliced fruits and vegetables to munch on, and nutritious or zero-calorie beverages to sip while you're cooking. This means the children (and you!) will be less likely to nibble on the dinner ingredients while you work. . . .

Set your kids up for success. Structure the work area so they are less likely to spill. You can also have them do their measuring with a jellyroll pan underneath to catch any spills. Remember that the easier dishes are to prepare, the more likely the kids will try making them again. Start with things like breads, muffins, pasta, smoothies, and fun sandwiches. Slowly work your way up to the fancier stuff.[69]

Table Manners

Cooking together provides an opportunity for parents and children to talk and share thoughts and stories. It also increases the likelihood that children will want to sit at a table to savor and discuss the fruits of their labor. In order to facilitate conversation, tables need rules about polite behavior. Needless to say, these rules are subject to considerable debate, and Americans frequently turn to adjudicators such as Miss Manners to get help. Our concern here is not about deciding which fork to use but about creating democratic tables that facilitate conversation. As Miss Manners reminds us, "The dinner table is the center for the teaching and practicing not just of table manners but of conversation, consideration, tolerance, family feeling, and just about all the other accomplishments of polite society except the minuet."[70]

Democratic tables need some level of formality. In one study of family dinners, formality increased children's verbal interactions with both parents and siblings. Measures of formality included waiting to begin eating together, getting parental permission to leave the table, staying seated during the meal, and waiting for everyone to finish his or her meal. Mothers tended to be in charge of meals: preparing and serving the food and directing verbal interaction. Large families were more child focused, less orderly, and noisier than small families. The more formal the meal, the more likely were young children to interact verbally with older siblings, and older siblings to talk to younger siblings and mothers. During mealtime conversations, there was a tendency, regardless of family size, for mothers to direct talk to be more formal.[71] There is civic virtue in having table rules that promote conversations among people of all ages with different skill levels.

Learning how to behave at a table for a common purpose is a primordial form of citizenship training, according to Kim Severson. As a youth, she ate most meals at a big table in the kitchen. The fancy table in the dining room was used only for "Christmas dinners and birthday parties and visits from relatives." But the "real action" was at the kitchen table. The five children were instructed on "how to become good citizens and helpful guests. We learned to be part of a tribe. And we figured out how to behave. Making my sister, Keely, laugh so hard that milk poured from her nose wasn't cool. Bringing home a good report card was. Depending on the day, I arrived at the dinner table happy, sad, angry or bored. As a teenager, I sometimes showed up stoned. I once sat at that table for hours, refusing to eat green beans despite my father's declaration that my freedom could be earned with just three bites."[72]

A basic table rule concerns where and for how long one is supposed to sit. Teacher Barbara Scheifler explained rules she used at a residential camp for sixth graders, most of whom had little experience sitting at a table for a meal.

For ten years (1985–95) we took forty sixth graders a year to a Point Reyes residential camp for a week of environmental education. The students were ethnically across the board: Filipinos, whites, African Americans, Hispanics, and Indian Americans, and roughly half girls and half boys. Lunch was potluck outside, but for both breakfast and dinner, the kids lined up outside in different ways—by shoe size, height, month they were born, dates they were born—so that they would end up sitting with different kids in the dining room. When we were lining up outside, we sang a welcoming song to calm them down.

At each table there were six sixth graders, one or two tenth-grade high school counselors who had been on the program when they were younger, and one adult. The adult and the counselor sat at the foot and the head of the table, and the kids sat facing each other. They went through the tray line, sat down, and couldn't eat until everyone had sat down. "Why can't we eat yet?" "Because everyone hasn't sat down yet." "But my food is here." "I know, but we will wait for everybody to sit down." They gobbled their food really quickly. When they were finished, they were ready to take up their tray and head back to the kitchen to put it down. "Oh no, we can't leave until everybody's finished." "Well, I'm done." "I know but everybody isn't done." "Well, what do I do?" "We make pleasant dinner conversation." "What's that?" "Well, watch. Maria, how was your day? What did you like about today?" And Maria would answer back, and then I would say, "Mariano, what did you learn today? What special thing did you do today?" And then he would answer back.

Each meal was a different conglomeration of kids because of the way we lined them up outside. They did not always sit with their buddies or partners or tent mates. Each conversation involved a different grouping of six or seven kids and a different counselor and adult. We wanted the table conversations to vary from meal to meal. Sometimes it was predominately boys, sometimes girls, but most of the tables were fairly mixed. The meals were pretty simple. It wasn't really about the food; it was more about the conversation at the table. At the beginning of the week, it was really awkward; they wouldn't have anything to say, and I felt like I was conducting an interview at the meal table. Because we sat at different tables, we didn't know what the kids had said the day before. During the early part of the week, the conversation was really stilted, and it was like pulling teeth to get them to say anything.

By midweek, they all understood that they were going to line up, and they asked, "How are we lining up today?" They started asking each other, "Oh yeah, did you see that? I saw such and such at the beach today." Of course, by this time they had more common experiences to share as well. Throughout the day, we put the kids into four groups so that they would go to the stream, the art center, the hill, and the pond. So by Thursday, the kids would have gone to each of these four areas, but not necessarily with the other kids at the table. "Oh, when I went to the pond, I found a this and a that." "Oh, I didn't see one of those, but I saw in my little insect box a such-and-so." "And I found some three-colored leaves."

They had some shared experiences to a point, but each one experienced it slightly differently, so then they could start sharing that. By the end of the week, you could see that they didn't have the need to rush off. They didn't say, "When can we go?" They actually could pause and share things.

We called it our Point Reyes family. You felt like a family by the end of the week because you were the only ones there and only you had that shared experience. When you went back to school, you'd remember who was there, so there was a sense of bonding. Everyone was on the same footing. They were the same age, so there wasn't any pecking order—oldest to youngest or smartest to dumbest— nobody had been there before. They all came equally ignorant, as opposed to the family where there is a built-in pecking order. It was a safe place.[73]

This account highlights the importance of insisting on table rules that facilitate learning conversational skills. The camp made a concerted effort to mix conversants at each common meal. This environment was conducive to learning given the children's age equality, their common adventures giving them something to talk about, and the clear goal of "a pleasant dinner conversation." Notice her inclusion of the work "pleasant." Pleasant things are easier to learn than dreary ones. Scheifler had learned the art of conversation at the dinner table as a child. Her large family had rules about seating and participating. "The little ones waited their turn or raised their hands. 'I colored a pig today.' 'Great, Anita.' They saw that the way you participated was by sharing something. Mom was aware that it was important for the little ones to get a word in. For the rest of us, it was the survival of the fittest. We had assigned seats at the table. My parents tried to make sure the kids wouldn't bug each other and kick and poke and stuff. The youngest one was furthest away from the other three siblings, so she had to communicate through Mom in order to participate."[74]

Another common table rule is to avoid fighting words. Modeling civil discourse is good not only for democracy but also for personal safety. When Gillian Clark opened her restaurant, she applied rules she had learned at her parents' table growing up, in part to avoid the fights she had heard about at other restaurants.

Growing up, we were never to use the words "shut up" or to call a sibling "stupid." My mother found these words inflammatory and provocative. With five kids in the house—all pretty close in age—a parent had to be creative to keep fights from breaking out. I didn't let my two little ones use those words either. It also became a rule in my [restaurant] kitchen. And surprisingly, it was adhered to with more discipline than simply coming to work on time. No cook, dishwasher, or busboy ever insisted someone "shut up" or declared that a coworker was "stupid." There were disagreements in the small, hot space, but nothing escalated to the knife-jabbing brawls I'd heard about.[75]

Cultures have different table rules when it comes to the timing of eating and talking, and acceptable types of noise. For example, cookbook author Buwei Yang Chao compared Chinese and American table manners.

> The typical [Chinese] family meal has several dishes all served at the same time. In families, in shops, and on the farm, people eat together, and share a little of several different dishes, and never have one dish belonging to one person. . . . The result is you feel you are all the time carrying on a friendly conversation with each other, even though nobody says anything. I wonder if it is because the American way of eating his own meal is so unsociable that you have to keep on talking to make it more like good manners. . . . Certain hot foods are best when eaten very hot. The technique for eating them is to draw in air over a narrow opening so as to hasten evaporation and diffuse the flavor. This is most effective when the air roughens the surface of the liquid. That is why hot soup, hot soup-noodles, hot congee, etc. are best when sucked in with as loud a noise as possible. . . . I feel an inner conflict when I remember how I was taught that in foreign countries one must drink soup as quietly as possible. On the other hand, I can never bring myself to blow my nose in public, as people do in America, since this operation tends to be much louder than eating noodles and sounds much less inviting.[76]

At democratic tables, it is inevitable that children will contest adult-generated table rules. How this conflict plays out sends an important message to children about their rule-making power. In a study of Australian families, parents promulgated these table rules, which children obeyed, questioned, and resisted.

> Speak with an empty mouth; close mouth when eating; keep hands and feet away from others; make as little mess as possible; behave at the table (no acting "silly"); no use of salt; eat with cutlery (no fingers, drinking from cereal bowl, or licking plate); ask to be excused from the table; no snacks close to the next meal; ask for required food and drinks; eat an appropriate amount in one mouthful; eat all food; sit at the table to eat; keep hands off food not about to be consumed; once a meal is finished there is nothing else to eat; some fruit is to be consumed each day; some vegetables are to be eaten for the evening meal; utensils to be used to serve food; eat nicely, no playing with food; elbows off the table; children can get their own drinks; parents put salt on food; no toys at the table; food dropped on the floor is to be picked up; parents decide how much chocolate, ice cream, etc., children can have; youngest child fed by mother if an inappropriate amount of vegetables

eaten; physical punishment (smacking) used during the meal if the youngest child not eating properly; if child chooses not to eat, still required to sit at the table; if child is not eating the meal, no chips, milk or soft drinks allowed; knives stay out of mouths; child's food preferences have some influence over what is eaten; speak nicely at the table; sit appropriately at the table, with feet on the floor.[77]

When mothers gave their children choices about what they wanted to eat, girls tended to make decisions quickly and without much fuss; boys were more likely to use these opportunities to challenge their mother's authority. Girls were expected to help their mothers prepare, serve, and clean up after meals; boys were called to the table just before the food was served, and then they were required to sit down and eat.[78]

Linguists use four approaches to study polite table behavior. The *social norm* view says that each society has a set of explicit rules about polite table behavior. The *conversational-maxim* approach assumes that conversationalists are rational individuals interested in efficiently conveying a message. The *face-saving* view says that polite speech maintains "face," that is, self-esteem or public image. And the *conversational-contract* approach assumes that each party brings an understanding of rights and obligations that will determine what participants can expect from one another, for example, take turns, use a mutually intelligible language, speak sufficiently loudly, and speak seriously.[79] For our purposes, each perspective focuses on different, and equally important, aspects of table conversations: explicit rules, rationality in conveying messages, saving face, and rights and obligations.

Developmental psychologists elaborate on the parent-child power imbalance when politeness is taught and learned at the table. Those who participate in a conversation are polite insofar as they address others' face needs, both positive (to be respected and held in high esteem) and negative (to avoid being disrespected or imposed upon). Parental teaching can take the form of direct explication of the rules or indirect manipulation of the situation. Parents can mitigate (make less hostile) their requests of children, or they can use unmitigated imperatives (demands). They can ask simple yes-or-no questions or more complex "wh-questions," which are formed with an interrogative word (what, who, whom, whose, which, when, where, why, or how) that expects an answer that is more elaborate than a simple yes or no. With each of these interactional choices, parents decide the extent to which conversations with children are democratic—explicating rules, mitigating requests, asking "wh-questions," and addressing face needs. Reducing a face-threatening act depends on the social distance and power differential between people. "Thus, a relatively slight request between two social equals who know one another well might require only the minimal concession to face needs represented by conventional politeness (*Pass the salt, please* or *Could you lend me a quarter?*). Similar requests of relative strangers or of persons in positions of power might involve strategizing so as to address either the positive face needs of the interlocutor (*Would you be so kind as to pass the salt?*) or his/her negative face needs (*Do you think you could lend me a quarter for my meter, just until I get upstairs and get some change?*)."[80]

In one study of politeness, parents rarely taught the rules directly; they were more likely to manipulate situations so that children could observe how rules of politeness related to language forms and to teach children which forms to use in various situations. During family meals, parents' social interactions empowered their children and respected their positive and negative face needs. When they asked children to perform acts that went beyond their minimal obligations as members of the family, they mitigated their requests as they would for adults. When they wanted to express disapproval of children's actions, American mothers used unmitigated imperatives, as compared to Japanese and Korean mothers, who used extremely indirect speech forms such as wh-questions.[81]

Some families have "insider" norms to guide polite table behavior when guests are present. Civil conversations need people's good manners not only among family members but also with guests and strangers. When it comes to saving face, some families have devised codes to communicate when awkward situations arise: "F. H. B." means "Family Hold Back," so the guests will have more to eat; "L. K. F." indicates "Lick and Keep Forks," so that there will be enough flatware for everyone; "M. I. K." designates "More in Kitchen," and "stretching it" means adding a couple of extra potatoes and slicing the roast thinner. Other awkward moments result when a host or hostess monitors a guest's plate too closely, when a guest attends only to the food and not to the conversation, and when the last piece of food calls into question the abundance of the food available, the modesty of the guests, and the equality of the portions.[82]

Talking about Your Day

A good way to maximize a table's democratic and conversational potential is for adults to ask children about their day because this sends a message that both the *events* of their lives and their *interpretations* of those events matter to adults. A crucial practice in developing a political voice is defining what is important in life and why—what gives it meaning. Children, along with all conversants, need to be welcomed to contribute to the table's discourse. A child's narrative might be added to family folklore and serve as a springboard for other topics of conversation. Being asked to talk about one's day is usually a sign of respect, but as we have seen, it can also be interpreted as an unwanted inquisition.

One student I interviewed recounted how she was more willing than her brother to discuss her day. He was not interested in talking about himself but joined the conversation when it became more general. The topic comfort level of children, like that of all conversants, varies over time and by social context, and skilled conversants are sensitive to such nuances.

> Family dinners are something that I have come to expect. I am used to sitting down with my family every night for dinner. We all sit together until we are all finished, and we have discussions about different things. They helped foster my interest in political science because that is when we have the time to sit down and talk about what is going on in the news. If I have any problems in school, it also helps. Frankly, when I am invited out by friends to eat out or something, I usually decline, saying I have to be home for dinner. The food at home is usually better than what I would eat out. I would feel bad if I did not come home for a family dinner, not like it is some obligation that I don't want to do; it is something I want to do, something I enjoy and am used to. When I was young, we talked about things from our school day. I was pretty open, so I talked about what I want to talk about; but my brother was not a very open person, so he did not talk much about his day, but he joined in the conversation. So we still had a conversation going even if it was not too personal.[83]

Even though not all children are eager to talk about their days at dinner, if the event is enjoyable, they will be more likely to want to do so. The goodwill created during happy times can be drawn on to alleviate the stress of demanding days. The themes of table fun and creating reservoirs of goodwill and resilience were striking in another student's interview.

> It's really rare that we don't sit down together as a family for dinner, and it's so much fun. We have conversations that I don't think I would have anywhere else. We usually talk about our day; we talk about the fun things that happened. We often tell stories like, "Oh this happened today," or "This happened last week." We laugh a lot at dinner. Sometimes if we're bored and don't have much to talk about, we come up with a little game, like go through the entire alphabet and name a food, or an animal, or name five things you think of when I say this word. Even if it doesn't provide laughing and conversation, it often leads to conversation.

We have interesting and often long, really enjoyable conversations at dinner. My sister is thirteen, and I am fifteen. I like hearing what other people have to say. If I've had a bad day, I might hear about something my sister did that day that was really wonderful and that makes me happy and it's one of the reasons if I've had a bad day I look forward to dinner because I know either my parents or my sister will have a story to tell that will cheer me up and make me happier. I laugh and I smile at dinner every night. It's something that really sort of helps me if I'm feeling down that day. I know that sometimes it will be the reverse, like I might have a great story to tell and my sister might not have had a good day and I feel almost obliged to tell that story to help cheer her up because I know I am in that situation too sometimes.

I don't want to sit alone in my room eating dinner by myself where I don't get that cheering up and I don't share my stories. I feel like engaging with my family over a meal makes it much easier to just be with them because oftentimes we're not together; we are busy doing homework, and they're working. Dinner, at least for my family, is that meeting place where we can all just sit down and talk about our day with people we love and enjoy spending time with. We may not get to spend that much time with them. I feel that is what dinner is.

My parents talk about their days a lot too. One of my parents is a stay-at-home, and the other works. My mom at work will mention a funny story. We have two dogs, and my mom at home will sometimes mention a funny story about the dogs. We all have equal things to share. My sister always talks about her friends at dinner. She always has a story to tell. I feel like she often feels she doesn't talk enough at dinner. We want to hear her because at other times we can't hear her and she won't be able to tell those stories. I feel that dinner in our family is that place where we tell stories and engage in good conversation.[84]

Gillian Clark thought that her restaurant's staff needed to let off steam and talk about their days, just as her family did at home. It was good for morale. The "family table" at her restaurant was a safe place "to let it out and be yourself." The staff got to know one another at a common meal that broke the stress of the day. Before the crowds arrived, the staff "[searched] the walk-in refrigerator for something to throw together to 'feed the family.'" These shared meals allowed waitstaff and kitchen staff to bond. "There are tense moments on busy nights and mistakes are made on both sides of the line. The staff needs to be able to move on and let go in order to recover and work together the following night no matter how much shouting and name-calling went on the previous night."[85]

Sometimes, talking about one's day works better at the kitchen table instead of the dinner table. Table opportunities should be taken advantage of whenever and wherever they might arise, as Clark realized with her daughter Magalee, who stopped paying attention in class after her parents' divorce. Homework assignments were met with headaches, tears, and tantrums. Clark helped Magalee get through this "bump in the road" with an "after-school bowl of stew" and going over what she had missed in class. The stew settled her down and was grounding. "It showed her it was safe to eat for no other reason than she wanted to, that she was hungry or unsatisfied—it wasn't to please a parent but for her own personal health and satisfaction. Maybe I could beat back the headache of her missing father and help her think of herself and of school. . . . If it made her eat less at dinnertime, that was fine, too."[86]

Clark thought that talking about one's day at the table was an occasion to get reenergized and build resilience for the next day.

> Having dinner was and always will be an opportunity for my family to let the air out. We could defuse the tension of a day at school or a day in the kitchen by sitting down together. It could be delivery pizza, a roasted chicken, or the teriyaki pork chops my mother taught me how to make. What mattered was that it was like time in the locker room with our own team. Whether we were celebrating a win or rubbing away the sore of a loss, dinnertime was not only a half hour of enjoying the company of those who knew us best, but also a time to plan a strategy or a new angle of attack. The next day we could go back to school or work stronger.[87]

For writer Arianna Huffington, talking about her day was an important bonding ritual with her mother and sister. "The three of us would talk about what happened at school, about our teachers, schoolmates, challenges, aspirations, and our dreams. We would talk about boys, girlfriends, family, books—anything and everything that was on our minds. It was our ritual—one filled with love and life lessons. It would leave us deeply satisfied, or as my mother used to put it, 'with body and soul fed.'"[88]

The ritual of talking about one's day occurred in a middle school kitchen where children prepared meals using produce from the school garden. The chef-teacher hoped that students' "kitchen confidence" would enhance their self-esteem and carry over to other domains at school. "We want to slow them down, to bust a hole in their day," she said. Students often came back to the school kitchen to reminisce about mundane tasks. "It's the simple things they remember and talk about, like helping me with the kitchen laundry or sitting at a table and folding napkins and talking about their day. Our students are so stimulated with 'stuff' all day long that they don't always stop and get the feeling of doing ordinary things for pleasure. . . . I want to bolster their self-esteem and hope that it radiates out into other situations—in the hallways, on the playground, in the classroom. I want them to leave this program with enough confidence that they can improvise in the kitchen."[89]

Training Tables

The ability to talk about your day, use good manners, and engage in conversation might come in handy one day, even at a job interview. A magazine publishing director said that when she was serious about hiring someone, she took that person out for a meal. "You learn so much in a meal. It's like a microcosm of life. How they order, what they order, how they give instructions to a waiter, can they keep a conversation going . . . these are all the things I look at."[90]

Parents who want to prepare their children for high-level professions and public service often see the dinner table, quite literally, as a training table, where children can practice discussing a wide range of topics. Such was the case for Robert F. Kennedy Jr., son of Robert Kennedy Sr. and Ethel Kennedy, and his siblings. Dinner was served at 6:00, and everyone had to be on time with hair combed and nails cleaned. Children under the age of seven sat at a small table and were not expected to participate in adult conversations. The parents sat at each end of the big table. His father "came home for dinner whenever he could." He would talk about his civil rights cases at the Justice Department and ask the children about their views on the issues of the day, such as the Vietnam War and drugs. His mother insisted on a single conversation. At Sunday dinners, they discussed current events and recited poems from memory. On Saturdays, they wrote down in notebooks three newspaper stories or recited biographies of prominent figures. They also played games at the table. Kennedy marveled at how his mother had the discipline to orchestrate family dinners night after night. "It was such an important part of our family life. We were all expected at the dinner table, we were all expected to participate, and we were all expected to perform." Even when famous people came to dinner—from the worlds of politics, culture, or sports—the children "were always included in the conversation and [they] were expected to say something smart, not to be silly or stupid, but to participate." Kennedy observed, "I think that was really important in developing kids who had a broader view of the world. . . . The dinner table ritual was where we learned a lot about what was going on in the world, and about what was right and wrong, how to conduct ourselves and how to talk and how to speak, how to interact. I think it gave all of us very useful conversing skills." Kennedy tried to replicate these family dinners with his own children. "We make the kids turn off all the screens and sit through all of dinner, we bless our meal, we all eat at the same time, no one gets up without being excused, but it's really hard, and there are so many distractions. It's a struggle oftentimes to hold them there. But you've got to do it."[91]

CNN correspondent Soledad O'Brien said that at her childhood family dinners, she learned how to listen to many points of view and to defend her own position in an argument. When she and her husband realized that they were traveling nonstop and dinner with their four kids had become "a crazy countertop affair," they instituted a ritual Sunday dinner.

> My husband cooks, and the kids have gotten completely involved in helping him with the meal. The results have been incredible. First of all, we have gotten them to eat better. My daughter, who never met anything healthy that she likes, is now in love with salad. My nine-year-old said to me the other day, "You know I've really gotten close to Daddy helping him make dinner." Our five-year-olds clear the table; I fill and empty the dishwasher. They sit, we all talk. They've learned manners, too; they now know where their napkins go.
>
> It is so important to carve out family time as a way of remaining close to your roots and sharing them with your kids. Family dinner is one way to do that. My parents understood that. As parents we see it now, too. When I was growing up, my family had dinner together every night. I think part of that was there wasn't gymnastics practice that went until 7 p.m. like my daughter has. There was no swim team across the city. That didn't exist. People did everything at school and then there was a five thirty bus that brought you home in time for dinner. My dinners growing up had a huge impact on me because it forced us to spend so much time with each other. We discussed everything at dinner. I remember when I was in high school and my brothers and sisters would come home from college and we would sit at dinner and argue about law cases (they were all pre-law). We'd argue over movies. There was an unwritten rule in my big family that you had to defend your position. You had to argue your point of view. That was great life training.[92]

Conversational skills are a form of cultural capital, a resource contributing to success at school and work.[93] The elite have always known this and have made a point of developing the conversational skills of their children, both at the dinner table and at elite educational institutions. But a robust democracy needs these skills to be widely distributed. Having dinner with people who expand our horizons is one way to build the cultural capital of the nation as a whole. A parent I interviewed spoke eloquently about the dangers of class inequalities in conversational skills, the importance of learning these skills at the table, and her own experience conversing civilly over dinner with a person with fundamentally different political views.

How often do American families invite others over for dinner? I see a gap between the elite and the majority of Americans. The elite and the politicians think conversation is important, opinions are important, we need to discuss things, we need to bounce ideas one to another, we need to have conflicts. The high class has been cultivating that, but it has been lost by the majority of the people. It is not only the vocabulary but also the connections—who do you invite? After the recent presidential election, a friend of my son sent me this quote by Thomas Jefferson: "I never considered a difference of opinion in politics, in religion, in philosophy, as cause for withdrawing from a friend." You can be my friend with different political and religious beliefs.

I recently went back to school, and we did a dinner for seven. I have a woman partner, and we have two kids. The other student was in the army, and we were invited to an army base. He had five children, very religious. We couldn't be more opposite as far as way of life, culture, religion; yet we had a lot in common in certain values. We were able to share these values through school, but the physicality of getting together for that dinner sealed it. We have been on Facebook together and it's been difficult to see some of his postings that I could very well have taken personally about gay marriage, women's issues, and abortion.

Whether it's the meal or acknowledging that we have common values, he is a friend the way Jefferson talked about. I think it makes my experience richer—it's very important in a way for me to understand. It is about trying to keep the essence of, yes, we can have very different opinions on these things, but let's keep it leveled. To be honest, I don't think that the meal was the reason. I think it was more the ethics class that we took together, and the way we referred to us staying friends. The way we connect now, he is telling me, "You have been to my house. You are a welcoming friend and you will always be so. Our children have played together."

There is some type of bond, honor, experience that cannot be taken away that is much more concrete. There is something very concrete about stepping into somebody's house that is much easier to put into words than the discussions that we had on specific issues. I was struck with his very formal way of inviting his classmates. "My wife and I are so honored to have you come to our house." In a way that felt almost a little cheesy, but I could sense there was a lot of value in that—the sacredness of somebody's house because so much is happening, their souls are there.[94]

This woman articulates how table talk is civic training: conversational skills need to be democratized, not confined to elites; differences of opinion should not drive friends apart; the physical act of sharing a table forms a social bond and facilitates finding common values, even when conversants have deeply held differences of opinion; and polite behavior during difficult conversations can enrich human experience and broaden understanding. There seemed to be a fundamental sense of respect that got communicated during their dinner and lasted after it.

A teenager I interviewed agreed that conversational skills foster respect and social trust. "Family meals have helped me to become very sociable and articulate. They have allowed me to present myself in social situations that certain people do not have the skills to do. It is important to be able to present yourself in a way that is respectable but not feared. I feel that when people are afraid of me, that it is not necessarily a good thing. I think that what family dinners have brought me is a way to improve my social skills to a point where I can successfully be a contributing member of society."[95]

It is interesting how this student associated being sociable with being articulate. Expanding one's vocabulary is crucial to the development of conversational skills, civility, and social trust. A study of how children learned new and rare words during mealtime conversations found that parents used a variety of approaches. Sometimes the conversational context provided enough information for children to learn what a rare word meant. Mothers provided most of the informative uses of rare words; fathers tended to provide less support for word learning. Preschool-age children sometimes used rare words, "suggesting that they already knew some of the words, or that they were trying out their understanding from hearing the word in conversation. But, these children seldom asked directly for the meaning of rare words use by other speakers. . . . Discourse that engages children in extended discussion around a topic offers many opportunities for the child to hear unusual words being used by a more knowledgeable speaker, and perhaps to make the appropriate semantic connections with what they already know."[96]

How much learning takes place at a table depends in part on a caregiver's style of teaching. The two extremes of permissive (anything goes) and authoritarian (do as I say) approaches are not as optimal for creating a democratic table as is an *authoritative style* (I am knowledgeable, willing to explain my thinking, and open to hear what you think). Caregivers adopt one or more of these teaching styles on a daily basis with respect to their children's food choices. There is a consensus among nutritionists that an authoritative approach is best, since it gives the child food options, and practice making choices from these options helps build a child's sense of agency and purposive decision making. Permissive feeding amounts to "nutritional neglect," whereby children are allowed to eat whatever they want. Authoritarian behaviors, such as restricting or forcing children to eat certain foods, shows little regard for their choices and preferences. "Feeding styles have been associated with dietary intake. Authoritarian feeding has been associated with lower intake of fruit, juices, and vegetables, whereas authoritative feeding has been associated with greater fruit and vegetable availability, higher intake of fruit and vegetables, and lower intake of junk food. Additionally, when parents restricted their child's consumption of foods high in fat and sugar (a form of authoritarian control), children were more likely to fixate on those items and consume more of these 'forbidden foods' even when they were satiated."[97]

Caregivers use dinner tables not only to train their children in vocabulary development and food choice but also to prepare them for life's slings and arrows. For example, in anticipation of the emotional damage caused by societal racism, parents emphasize racism awareness (reactive socialization) and teach racial pride (proactive socialization) to help their children cope with discriminatory practices and negative stereotypes. A study of adolescent discrimination distress found that teenagers who were socialized to be aware of and respond proactively to racism had a greater sense of personal efficacy and self-esteem.[98] Training tables have many social purposes, but they are all meant to equip people to deal with both opportunities and challenges.

Dinner Parties

Dinner parties are a great way to reach beyond comfort zones and brush up on conversational skills. Interestingly, most studies and stories emphasize how hosts place a very high value on making guests feel comfortable. In her research about dinner parties, sociologist Alice P. Julier was struck with how the people she interviewed evoked a sense of family rather than "the formal welcoming of strangers and non-intimates." One woman preferred "putting people completely at ease and making them feel like they are at home" to "that really stuffy attitude where it would be a real success if it was really fancy and formal and everybody was afraid about dropping something on the rug." Julier saw this concern with comfort as a desire to set the stage for greater intimacy between people. When it came to conversations, women, "both those who cooked and those whose partners were the main cook, tended to evaluate social events based on the quality of the conversation, whereas the men spoke of the food and how well the food itself went over."[99]

Stories about elite dinner parties underscore the themes of comfort and conversations. Novelist Nora Ephron wrote about what made cookbook author Lee Bailey's get-togethers so memorable. There was the sense that having people to dinner wasn't that big a deal. The food was honest, simple, and delicious. And there was the conversation.

> Somehow, the greatest conversation, the hugest laughs, and the most hilarious stories were at Lee's. The party never left the table, and lasted well beyond the time anyone intended to stay. Why? Simple: there was a round table. . . . If you have people to dinner and make good food and then put your guests at a long rectangular table where people at one end can't hear what's going on at the other end and are pretty much trapped talking to the person on either side of themselves—well, what's the point? But put them at a round table, and at some point in the evening you can have one conversation. With any luck at all, the funniest person in the room will tell a great story and everyone will fall on the floor laughing and go home believing they've gone to the best dinner party of their lives. . . . Amy Gross once said that eating at Lee's was like going home; I hope someday somebody who doesn't actually live in my house will say that about me.[100]

Some in New York's high society have lamented the decline of civilized dinner parties, which are imperiled by trendy, anything-goes restaurants, hosts' status-seeking perfectionism, the demands of business entertaining, and an obsession with time. They longed for the days of simple home-cooked meals and good conversation, where one could hear and be heard. William Norwich laments dinner parties where guests spoke in "decibels one is conditioned to expect in trendy restaurants. How can anyone know better? Very little in modern public life reinforces the civilities of private life. . . . Thanks to trendy restaurant dining, anything goes. You can arrive late to dinner, leave early, talk on your cell phone, act outrageously, dance on the tables, smoke at the bar and order whatever you want." He interviewed a seasoned host who said,

> I think the greatest luxury nowadays is to have a delicious spaghetti and salad at someone's home rather than go to La Grenouille, or wherever. And one mustn't think it is about the money. Surely, that spaghetti and good bottle of wine is less expensive than dinner in a fancy restaurant. I remember years ago, in Paris, how well Françoise de la Renta entertained at home even before she married Oscar. Maybe, some nights, she had one maid in the kitchen who helped. Françoise always served something simple and delicious, and all the grand and interesting people came because it was so cozy and easy."[101]

A caterer blamed what he called the "New York syndrome." "There's so much perfectionism in New York that when someone entertains at home, no matter how rich or secure, it is still like an opening night," he said. "The host knows that critics will be giving their reviews the next morning." He added, "There's so much business entertaining during the cocktail hour, two or three pit stops a night, if you'll excuse the expression, that by the time people get to dinner, they are exhausted and grumpy." Another New Yorker observed, "In Seattle, I don't think they have this problem. In L.A., they don't go to dinner parties during the week for fear that someone might think they are not working. But here, in New York, people are inundated with business entertaining, and they're exhausted by it. Still, that doesn't excuse poor behavior. If you commit to going to someone's dinner, make an effort. Comb your hair. Look pretty. Talk to someone you don't know."[102]

Margaret Visser, in her classic work *The Rituals of Dinner*, equates our disdain for formality with our obsession with time.

> She believes that "all we feel we can manage in our rushed and exhausted state" is "casual manners." "Eating a homemade meal with invited guests, or even with one's family, cannot be entirely 'causal,' at least in the accidental aspect of the word," Visser explained, "because preparations and forethought are necessary, and all those present have had to turn down competing events and commit themselves in advance to appearing on a certain date. They have to sit down, face each other and not get up and leave before everyone else is ready to do so." Eating together with friends can "come to seem a formal, implacably structured and time-consuming event," writes Visser, "even for those who do not have to cook. We are conditioned to think that even a low level of formality is a constraint just because it entails participation with other people, whereas being in one's own personal hurry must be free and preferable."[103]

Notice how the "pressed for time" theme is developed here. Up to this point, we have focused on the time pressures on the working and middle classes. Wealthy people are harried in different ways. Manhattan's elite find it hard to have civilized conversations because they go to noisy, trendy restaurants to save time and to be seen, not heard. Business entertaining requires so many early-evening pit stops that people are exhausted by dinnertime. Even if they do manage to entertain at home, they are paralyzed about how their performance will be judged by the cognoscenti. Visser elaborates on the theme of "table obligation": someone has planned and prepared a meal, and participants have agreed to turn down other uses of their time to attend a dinner. There is an obligation to the meal preparer and the group to stay seated, face each other, and not leave until everyone is done. Our time-obsessed culture encourages us to think of such obligations as a constraint on our freedom—it is a drag to have to participate with other people and preferable to be in our personal hurries.

Other members of high society have bemoaned the decline of dinner parties as enjoyable occasions for networking, which is not only about social climbing but also about camaraderie and good will. Admittedly they have ample resources with which to entertain, but they also appreciate dinner parties for their fun mix of people and face-to-face conversations. Guy Trebay notes that New Yorkers have always prided themselves on their tables, "competing to populate them with lively strivers who do their social networking not on tiny, glowing screens but cheek by jowl. Increasingly, such gatherings seem outmoded, squeezed out by overcrowded schedules, the phony urgency of affinity sites, restaurants cultism and overall tectonic shifts in how New Yorkers congregate." Judith Martin, also known as Miss Manners, told Trebay that she thought that cooking for others was not going to disappear, but that the etiquette of dinner parties had run into problems. "Conversation is in trouble," she said. "People have been brought up to express themselves rather than to exchange ideas." Hand-held devices had disrupted the social contract. "People don't even respond to dinner invitations anymore," she said. "They consider it too difficult a commitment to say, 'I'll come to dinner a week from Saturday.' Not only do they cancel at the last minute, they do it by text message."[104]

Why bother with dinner parties when it is easier and more convenient to meet friends in restaurants? Trebay maintains that even the best restaurants do not approximate the intimacy of eating at home. Karen Mordechai was a Brooklyn photographer who developed "Sunday Suppers" to relive the camaraderie she remembered from Sabbath dinners in her childhood. "My favorite part of the dinner is just sitting at the table and talking for hours, and that doesn't exist when you are at a restaurant," Mordechai told Trebay. "I was born in Israel and grew up in a big, Jewish, Middle Eastern family. We think there's nothing better than sitting around the table with family and friends." She had not intended to turn her dinner parties into a business, but after she posted photos of the first one on her blog, she got emails from strangers who "wanted that old-school dinner-party feel." Sunday Suppers, for which subscribers pay $150, sell out quickly. Mordechai said that it was "basically about making friends and hanging out," eating good, simple food, and providing a far less geeky way of networking than a Meetup.[105]

Cookbook author Alex Hitz told Trebay that dinner parties were great social equalizers. "What they had in common was a sense of fun and community and gathering people together for good simple food. There is no leveler quite like a dinner table." Dinners at his California home were populated by a wide variety of Hollywood types. "The 20-year-olds enjoy the 90-year-olds," he said. "And I can assure you the 90-year-olds enjoy the 20-year-olds." First lady Nancy Reagan, widow of Ronald Reagan, was a frequent guest, and her favorite dish was a simple chicken potpie. "If anyone tells me, 'I'm freaking out, I have six people coming for dinner, what do I do?'" Mr. Hitz said, "I say serve chicken potpie and a salad, make sure there's plenty of wine and keep the lights low. How can it go wrong?"[106]

Trebay fears that hosts' skills in orchestrating conversations are in danger of disappearing.

> Trained from birth or on the job, the best hosts of another era commanded their tables as though part of the European Theater of Operations, emplacing and deploying and juxtaposing guests in charged combinations, going to the rescue when conversation flagged and a combatant went down. Of course, they made sure the blowhard mogul was seated beside the lissome ingénue. What else is a dinner party besides a comic operetta without a score? But they also orchestrated every element of the evening, arrival to departure, most crucially, directing the conversation, which they either allowed to follow a traditional serve-and-volley pattern (20 minutes right, 20 minutes left), or else commandeered for so-called "general discussion" as provocateur hosts like the television journalist Barbara Walters still do.[107]

There is an art to hosting a dinner party: juxtaposing guests in combinations, going to the rescue when conversation flags, and orchestrating conversations either in small groups or as one. In spite of the best efforts of hosts, guests often fail to do their part to make the communal enterprise work. How can they engage in conversation when they have been brought up to express themselves rather than to exchange ideas, and when hand-held devices rupture the social contract? Many invitees fail to respond to invitations because they value flexibility over making a social commitment. Those who do not see connecting with others as impinging on their freedom are creating hybrid forms of dinner parties. Sunday Suppers filled a need for commensality among strangers who were willing to pay $150. Many people with means enjoy making friends, hanging out, and eating comfort food like chicken potpie.

The operations of high society were in full display at the San Francisco home kitchen of Ann and Gordon Getty, whose dinner party rituals included a veritable moveable feast of guests at Ann's Super Supper Sunday. This informal weekly get-together began when Ann's closest friend, who had been living at the Getty home, was housebound the night before surgery. "Getty called in a few intimates for a cozy meal of leftovers in the kitchen, Sunday being the cook's night off. Everyone had such fun that the next week they all did it again, and again the following week, until Getty decided she would put on an apron and whip up a hot meal for her guests." It became so popular that Getty said she was "condemned to cook for the rest of [her] life." So except when she leaves town, "the woman universally recognized as the queen of San Francisco society dependably cooks every Sunday for whichever 40 or 50 friends happen to claim a seat around the long pine table in the middle of her kitchen." Getty, whose formal dinners have included such family friends as the king of Spain and the Prince of Wales, does not bother with invitations. "People come from all over. It's quite diverse. I actually don't know everybody."

> One night, she recalls, neither she nor her husband said hello to one bewildered stranger until a secretary pointed out that he was a Russian conductor and was, unbeknownst to anyone but the staff, installed in a guest room at Gordon's long-forgotten invitation. The man's arrival had gone unnoticed by his hosts in the comings and goings of the more than 30,000-square-foot house, which has, among other amenities, a recording studio for Gordon and a private Montessori nursery school for the Getty grandchildren and other lucky neighborhood tots. "Anyone could move in here, I swear," jokes Getty, as she thinks back on the conductor's unheralded arrival. "They could just show up and say they were expected!"[108]

At one Super Supper Sunday dinner, Gordon Getty sat at the head of the table, joined by guests who included weekly regular California senator Dianne Feinstein, a Berkeley professor and his wife, and director Philip Kaufman.

> As dinner winds down, the murmur of conversation is interrupted by a sonorous bass voice. It's Gordon, robustly singing an aria from one of the several operas he has composed. The performance elicits applause, and then a young man at the table, the guest of a regular, asks if he might have the honor of singing for his supper as well. Gordon assents and the guest proves to have a trained operatic voice. Gordon looks transported, clinching his eyes tight during a particularly expressive phrase. "Schumann, *Dichterliebe*," Gordon announces at the song's end. He responds by singing a heartfelt if somewhat shaky version of "Danny Boy," which the visitor takes over in the final verse to finish in high and haunting falsetto. Gordon loves it: He offers a hearty hand of applause, then drains his final glass and disappears into the bowels of the mansion. . . . San Francisco may well be the last place in America where . . . leaders from the worlds of business, philanthropy, culture and politics still mingle around the tables of the town's most illustrious families.[109]

In order for a dinner party to be successful, not only do guests have to commit to attending and being open to meet a wide range of people, but they also must be prepared to say something. One New York restaurateur thought that both hosts and guests should come to dinner parties prepared to talk about three things. As a child, she worked at her parents' hotel in Brittany, and when she entertains at home, she pretends she is back there and tries to forget all the new things she has learned. She thinks that the biggest mistake people make when inviting friends for dinner is that they try to do too much. "They try to create a restaurant for one day. They choose complicated recipes. Experiment on your family. It is better to stay with dishes you are most comfortable with, ones you grew up with or at least the ones that make you feel good that you are at home. The foods you can't get in a restaurant. Otherwise, why not take everybody out to eat?" She can't understand why Americans seat couples together at dinner parties. Seating them apart stimulates conversation and prevents them from trading secrets all night. "Couples can talk all they like when they get home. Besides, I think separation gives strength to a man and a woman," she asserts. "However, you should always introduce people to each other before they are seated. . . . I am always in a good mood when people come over, but then you have to be. Otherwise, there's no point in doing this. Friends aren't really coming for the food. And you should be ready with three things to talk about. Guests should come prepared as well, though they almost never do."[110]

Democracy is strengthened by vibrant dinner-party conversations, where fun and pleasure are combined with open minds and respectful talk. Paul Saffo thinks we should arrange dinner parties for the express purpose of having civil political discussions. He thinks that Americans do not talk enough about politics and have "outsourced the conversation to quarrelsome politicians and talk show celebrities." We are shirking our civic responsibility to be informed citizens. He contrasts "our aversion to politics at mealtime with attitudes" in most other countries. He recalls, "I remember the first time I was a guest at a dinner in Paris where most of the evening was occupied by a vigorous debate over European Union policy and politics. At the end of the evening, everyone warmly air-kissed all around, promising to continue the discussion at the next gathering." He admits that one reason why political conversations are not popular at American dinner tables is because many Americans are clueless about politics. He cited a poll showing that "38 percent of Americans would fail the U.S. citizenship test, and . . . 73 percent couldn't explain why we fought the Cold War." But he thinks we can lessen this ignorance at dinners where the host picks a discussion topic and asks guests to read up on it in advance. It is important to invite guests with the right mix of viewpoints: too much agreement results in a dull conversation, and too much variation makes it "difficult to find common ground." The goal of the dinners is to learn to converse about controversial issues and to explore ideas. The point is not to persuade others, but it would be "a sign of success if guests actually change their minds." Saffo asserts, "We must question our opinions and listen to the insights of others, and I can think of no better place to do it than over dinner."[111]

Express Yourself

It is commendable to make a concerted effort to discuss politics at dinner parties. But there are many ways to build a sense of connectedness at a table, where people inevitably express themselves in different ways. Gordon Getty was not the only one who sang for family and friends at the table. As a child, Nancy Wilson, member of the rock band Heart, did so too.

> At dinner we talked a lot, about our day, about politics, history, philosophy, spirituality, and people we knew. We often had a lot of our extended family and friends over for dinner. Our mom was an avid family historian and she liked to tell long tales about the history of our relatives, stories that dated back to the covered wagons and even earlier. Some of our relatives were the first settlers that came over in the 1600s! It gave us kids a deep sense of connectedness to history. On Sunday mornings, our mom and dad started another great food ritual. It was amazing. Opera and pancakes! My parents would put on *The Mikado* or *Madame Butterfly* and we would have eggs, fruit, pancakes, sausage, and syrup, and make a big occasion out of it. Singing at the table was obviously *allowed*. . . . It's a great gift to my twin boys to make sure we have some of that ritual still in place around our dinner table. We take time for talking by candlelight and music. We share stories about our day and our lives, tell jokes. At the family table, they come to know they can share anything that's in their hearts. It's a safety zone. I want to give them what I was so lucky to have and I cherish the solid family I came from.[112]

For some, poetry is a powerful way to express oneself at the table, using evocative rather than literal language. At one time, children were expected to memorize and recite poetry at the dinner table, but we no longer have a culture of memorization. America's Children's Poet Laureate urged everyone to commit a poem to memory. "When you memorize a poem, it truly becomes 'yours.' Nothing is more satisfying than 'getting it by heart' and you will know that poem far more deeply and completely when you have read it out loud a number of times." Poetry at the dinner table is a way to recapture this confidence-building tradition. A school headmaster noted, "Poetry is important because it teaches children the magical qualities of language. It shows you that words do more than give information; they transport us over the tops of mountains and across wide seas."[113]

In Kevin Young's anthology of poetry about food and drink, his dedication reads: "for my mother/ who taught me how/ to cook & to listen." He thinks that the connecting power of food is best expressed through poetry, and he has written food odes about healing after loss. "It is a tradition I know best from the African-American repast," he explains, "but it can easily be seen in many others: from the Midwestern casserole or Southern collard greens brought to the house of mourning to an Irish wake, toasting those gone. Such meals and drink, whether sweet tea or hard cider, remind us we're alive, while making us realize: what else can we do but provide some sustenance for those whose only meal otherwise may be sorrow?"[114]

Dancing in the kitchen was an inspiration for choreographer Michael Smuin, director of San Francisco–based Smuin Ballet. His "Fly Me to the Moon" was set to nine recordings by Frank Sinatra. When asked why he chose these songs, he replied: "When I was a child, my mother would get home from her job around 5 or so, and my dad wouldn't get home until about 6:30. So we ate dinner relatively late. And my mom and dad were always in the kitchen. He'd come in and help her. And if a Sinatra tune came on the radio, my dad would grab my mom, and they would dance in the kitchen. Every time it happened, it was just thrilling. And they were very good dancers. So I think way in the back of my little pea brain that sort of struck a chord."[115]

Designers use tables and seating to promote creativity, trying to capture the intellectual charge from sharing ideas in personal conversations. In one study of workplace creativity, participants felt most creative on days spent in motion meeting people, not working for long stretches at their desks. Also, employees who ate at cafeteria tables designed for twelve were more productive than those at tables for four, thanks to more chance conversations and larger social networks. Having company-wide lunch hours and cafes boosted individual productivity by as much as 25 percent. "If you just think of serendipity as an interaction with an unintended outcome, you can orchestrate pleasant surprises," said one designer, who positioned couches near doorways and stocked rooms with multiple types of seating to encourage lingering conversations.[116]

There is even some evidence that democratic tables can energize and empower young musicians. A journalist visited Marlboro College in Vermont to report on the sixtieth anniversary of the Marlboro Music School and Festival. Young performers were paired with established players and worked for seven weeks on chamber repertory of their choosing. She described the dining room as resembling "that of a rambunctious boarding school, as scruffily dressed musicians of all ages energetically tossed paper napkin balls at one another across long tables," adding that such informality belied the disciplined intensity of rehearsals between mealtimes. Two young women said that it was initially intimidating to work with their musical idols, but they quickly overcame their apprehension in the collegial, egalitarian atmosphere. Everyone participated in dining-hall duties, and the young performers spoke of being startled to have famous musicians serving them drinks at dinner. Musicians of all ages hung out late into the night talking in the coffee shop.[117]

This pleasurable sequencing of food and drink—from first course through coffee—can entice people to linger at tables long enough to express themselves and enjoy the excitement of one another's company. One parent I interviewed described how a French tradition kept people at tables and facilitated conversations. "There is a great pleasure in having bread, cheese, and wine after the main dish. These three ingredients really fit so well together and extend the meal. We are not hungry anymore, so now there is a sense of relaxing. The same thing with a small cup of coffee as a closure of a meal—it's almost a kind of desperate, 'I want to continue with this. We are not quite done yet. Let's just extend it for a little bit.'"[118]

Transition Tables

Pleasurable table connections can ground us during difficult transitions in our lives, as was the case for Gillian Clark when she was a "latchkey child": "At lunchtime during the week, I found the table set for one and a note from my father. 'It's tuna today. Pour yourself a glass of milk. There's fruit in the refrigerator. Love, Daddy.' I didn't feel so 'home alone' now. . . . There was love and thoughtfulness on the table. Food was the most perfect form of love, I thought. It could be reliable, comforting, satisfying. Sometimes there was too much mayonnaise on the bologna or too many brown spots on the banana. That was okay. My waiting lunch meant I was not forgotten. Though they were not there, Daddy and Mommy would take care of me."[119]

For Kim Severson, the transition of moving from a family home to smaller quarters highlighted the emotional significance of family tables. When her parents moved into a small condominium, they planned to sell the family dining-room table and the old oak kitchen table. Instead, Severson shipped the kitchen table to her brother and the dining-room table to her Brooklyn brownstone. It was a bit too big, but it was where "special meals were served."

She had "eaten hundreds of plates of spaghetti on it" and "[felt] the need to keep it, to pass it on to [her] children." She wanted to tell them that it was their grandmother's table and to let them know what she had learned when she was home: "That we are a people who can always make do, no matter what. And that you can never really know who you are until you know where you came from. And then I will make them sit down and eat spaghetti."[120]

As children grow up and spend more time with friends, there are fewer opportunities for family meals. This realization caused a student I interviewed to want to linger a little longer at the table.

> As I grow older, I have more homework, I am more engaged, and I am more away from my parents and my sister. I don't have as much free time to talk with them, so I look forward to dinner even more. I feel like when I was younger, I might be like, "Hey, can we finish dinner? I want to go watch TV or something." But now I look forward to dinner, and I almost don't want to leave the table because of the great conversations we have. It's mostly about time spent with my family. When I get up early, my mom sits with me at breakfast. My sister is still asleep, so I guess you could say I am never alone at a meal, and that's something I really enjoy. No topic is off limits at home. Sometimes we have rather serious conversations. Just the other day actually we were eating, and I was talking about college with my parents. That was something that I wanted to talk about, and I felt like I could talk about it at dinner because I feel safe talking about whatever I want at dinner. It's with my family, it's with people I love, and I know that they are okay with talking about anything as well.[121]

Table rituals can provide an emotional lifeline for children reeling from the death of a parent. One student I interviewed had a moving story about a tradition that honored her father.

> The birthday dinners started in 1977 by my dad, who was dating my mom in graduate school. It became a ritual for them. My birthday is close to my mom's, so I remember the dinners from childhood. It was like a dinner for both of us. Dad made dinner for a change, and we shared it with neighbors and friends. When dad died, my brother took over. There was no question that we would continue it. He was about twelve years old, so neighbors helped him. He made the dinners throughout high school. When he went off to college, I took over at age fourteen. I had help. My mom remarried, and my stepdad, Joe, helped with dinners and still does. I have been doing them for the last four to five years. When I go to college, Joe will take over. My brother and I will help. My brother comes back for the dinner every year even though he lives in New York now. The structure of the dinner is that the main chef picks a cookbook, and the cuisine is a secret.

With each dish, guests guess what the cuisine is. At the end, the chef presents the cookbook to Mom, and everyone there signs it.

After my dad died, it was important to have something normal for us, and that dinner ritual was definitely normal. We needed stability and ritual, so that not everything had changed. I think that was really important to for us. Friends and neighbors really liked coming over for these dinners. I was close friends with one neighbor whose family was not really big on family meals. They did not have family meals every night like we do, but they definitely helped out during that transitional period.

After my mom remarried, food has been important in blending together the two different food traditions. For example, we make Christmas Eve duck dinner here, then on Christmas day we go to Joe's house to have the Yorkshire pudding and roast that he traditionally makes for Christmas. Every night we try to blend what Joe is used to making with what we are used to making. We have a family cookbook with all of our family's recipes. And we add new things like foods we discover when we are on vacations. We just went to Spain, so now we make *peppers de padrone*, and we fry them like in Spain. So we add our shared experiences with food to the cookbook. I enjoy eating what I am used to and also new things. At home I sometimes try to push my mom to make things from our family recipes because mostly Joe cooks from his recipes and I miss what we used to make. But it is not tension, just reminding my mom, "Hey let's have lasagna or beef stroganoff or something like that."[122]

The transition of going off to college causes some teenagers to compare home tables and college tables. Here is how a student I interviewed thought about it.

I think it's important to have a family meal at least a few times a week. In addition to providing a nice break in the day, to relax and kind of just enjoy sensory pleasure, it's nice to be able to catch up with your family. We have recently decided to clean up the house and start moving rooms to get ready for me to go away to college. We got this new dining-room table and new chairs, and we have been really enjoying our food lately. We got an ice cream maker and a couple Dutch ovens for so much delicious food—braised chicken, braised beef, and chicken cacciatore. We have been trying to make the most of these last few years before I move to college. And that's not to say that I won't move back to this area, but I think it's definitely going to be a new period in my life where I am not necessarily dependent on my parents anymore. We've always talked about the advantages of knowing how to cook. My parents joke with me that in college I'll never have to do any dishes because I'll be the one that cooks. I'm not sure if that's entirely true, but it's something that I enjoy so I like to do it as well.[123]

For their part, parents also have to prepare for the transition to an empty nest. In reflecting on table rituals, some of them compare their mealtime practices before and after their children moved out. A librarian I interviewed had a group of friends who shared holiday potlucks together. One person kept track of what people brought each year; another always brought the same rum cake. "It is all very ritualized," she recounted. "It is always the same. We have been doing this since our kids were little, and none of us really have kids at home anymore. It's very sad. Now it is just the adults getting together without the kids. We don't do Shabbat every Friday night anymore, but when our kids were little we always had Friday night dinner."[124]

Parents make special use of table time to help their children cope with the disruption of divorce. Gillian Clark thought it was important for her daughters to feel like part of a team. She warned them that there would be disappointments, and they made a pact to be flexible. "As corny as it sounded, we would always try to look on the bright side. The talk yielded results. I got them to take care of their personal hygiene without being hounded. They agreed to take turns setting the table and letting me know when we were out of milk. Our lives were different now, and no matter how young they were, we could not hide from it or pretend things hadn't changed." She thought that it was better to get difficult conversations on the table as soon as possible, and that included the one about their absentee father.[125]

Some divorced parents practice nesting: moving in and out of a shared house so that the children do not have to. This was Laurie David's arrangement, and she believed that it created an opportunity for maintaining old table rituals and introducing new ones. Her husband got an apartment, but he ate dinner with his daughters and stayed at the family house two nights a week, during which time David left before dinner and stayed at her sister's house. On her nights with the kids, she remembered brooding meals with forced conversations and begging friends to come to dinner to relieve the tension.

> Skipping organized dinners and letting everyone do their own thing would have taken some of the pressure off the kids and me, but only temporarily. I was desperate to get back to feeling "normal" as soon as possible, and the fewer things that changed, the better off we would all be. . . . If family dinner had stopped, the lesson to my kids (and to myself) would be that we weren't whole anymore, that something was broken forever. I honestly didn't believe that to be true. The message I did believe, and the one our continuing dinners provided was—this family is not changing, we are in a transition, but we are still a family![126]

She was determined that her family would "get through this and come out strong and connected. . . . When things got uncomfortable and no one was talking," she dipped into her toolbox of table games.[127]

Some parents in blended families involve children in creating menus to invent rituals to cohere the new social unit. Family therapists point out the benefits of letting the two sets of children plan dinners. They recommend serving foods that the kids from one family like on one night and the foods that the kids from the other family like on the next. On another night, plan a menu with "foods that both sets of kids enjoy." They acknowledge the emotional fragility of the situation. When children talk about cooking because they cannot say the words, "I miss my mother, I wish things were different," they complain about the food. Even so, food rituals maintain and create social cohesion. When people are expected to do something together regularly, they will begin to see themselves as part of a newly configured group.[128]

In addition to strengthening this identity, asking children in blended families to be responsible for getting dinner on the table during the workweek relieves harried parents. Some children use the occasion for novelty, others for repetition. One couple raised five daughters in their blended family. When the girls were teenagers and both parents were working, each daughter made dinner one weekday night. While some of the girls produced ambitious and varied meals, one of them made tacos exactly the same way every Tuesday night for years. Because the parents "wanted this enterprise to succeed" and needed to depend on their girls, they enjoyed their weekly tacos without complaint.[129]

After a divorce, family therapists tend to focus on children's need for table rituals, but parents also benefit from them, as was the case for Gillian Clark. The ritual of family dinner shaped her during her childhood. Everyone ate around a big table every night "unless someone had a game or was in the school play." Her New York siblings still "can't resist [her] father's cooking and the familiar talk and humor at that table. Sunday brunch is pretty well attended." As a parent, she tried to re-create this ritual while helping Magalee with her homework and reading to Sian. With her busy schedule, dinner had to be easy to prepare. They ate out on Sunday nights. Over dinner, they would unwind and talk about the day. The food "[settled them] into a comfortable" place where they could talk about anything. Cooking for a living took her away from her daughters, but cooking also brought them together as a family.

The truth is I needed my kids. Having their help eased my panic during those days when I found myself alone in a kitchen except for Magalee singing and peeling five potatoes, or Sian asking me what the eggs do and why she can't just put them in all at once. . . . They are too young to remember and I did my best to hide how hard it was. . . . The unfailing cheerfulness of my daughters may have been ignorance. Perhaps they were simply too young to understand the gravity of our situation, when I lost my job, couldn't cash my checks, or there was no support from their father. But it buoyed me.[130]

Death marks another important transition, and people struggle to find the best way to express their sympathy. For many, sharing food is a respected way to show concern and support. Molly Wizenberg described how food rituals figured prominently in her grieving process when her father died. She noticed that many people did not know what to do when someone is dying. The brave ones came by and visited. Others expressed their sympathies by phone. And many cooked. There was a "constant influx of soups, stews, roasts, cookies, and pies. I never knew how many friends my parents had until the food started arriving. The neighbors walked over with a tureen of beef stew. A bag of sugar cookies showed up, propped against the side door. A friend arrived with a car full of aluminum pans and cake boxes, enough to line the entire kitchen counter. I've never seen so much food outside of a college dining hall." She enrolled in a grieving group at a local hospital. She was by far the youngest person in the group, and she "cried the hardest." The main thing she remembered about the sessions was the baking. She made brownies, cookies, and strawberry tartlets for the group. She even made a pot of Italian vegetable soup, "and forced [her] fellow group members to sip it from Dixie cups at ten o'clock in the morning." She recalls, "When I called my mother to tell her, she laughed so hard that she actually hooted like an owl. My eyes were swollen from crying all the time, but I was the Official Grieving Group Food Pusher. I am *so* my father's daughter. Whatever you love, oh yes, you are."[131]

For some, the shock of the sudden loss of a family member is best absorbed by cooking and table rituals. Three days after Mai Pham's mother was hit by a car and killed on her daily morning walk, she gathered with her father and siblings in the kitchen of their family home to cook a meal in her honor. Her father awkwardly tried to peel the ginger, a task he had never done before since her mother had cooked every meal for twenty years. "It was she who would peel the ginger, plan the sumptuous reunion meals, and convince my father to drive from market to market in search of the sweetest orange, the freshest bluefish and the most fragrant batch of jasmine rice." In their grief, Pham thought that preparing a meal was probably the only thing they wanted to do, and she wondered why it had taken this tragedy for them to make the time to cook together. She was sure that behind all the chopping and cooking, they were all overcome by similar emotions, which she could hear in the voice of her older brother, who had just flown in from his job in France. In the Vietnamese tradition, her mother always treated him with reverence because he was the eldest son. When the meal was ready, they observed the Vietnamese custom of placing food on an altar they had made to honor her mother's memory and to share their lives and meals with her. "At the table, the food looked warm and inviting. The aroma of just-cooked rice soup wafted into the dining room and made it seem cozy and normal, if only just for a moment. . . . Throughout the meal we told wonderful stories about Mother, joking and laughing. We knew if she were here with us, she would make us all sit down while she served and watched over us." For the next two weeks, they cooked and ate together, using their mother's favorite recipes. Pham thought that although the meals were comforting and satisfying, it was the rhythm of peeling, chopping, and being in the kitchen together that most eased their pain and allowed them to express their love through food.[132]

Another emotionally demanding transition is immigration. When people are uprooted from their homeland, the disruption is often smoothed by table rituals with fictive kin in their new country. Fictive kin are a form of social capital in new immigrant enclaves. For example, in many Asian communities, it has been common for single males to migrate to the United States first and to send for their families after they have found jobs. These men are usually befriended by families in the immigrant community that are already reunited and came from the same locality back home. As one Vietnamese woman described it, "My grandparents were among the first Vietnamese to come to Houston in the 1970s. On any given Sunday, we would have three or four bachelor men at our table. After a while, we children would begin calling them uncle and they would play with us, teach us about our Vietnamese culture, and help us find part-time jobs when we got to be teenagers." When these men brought their wives and children to Houston, they were also incorporated into the host family as fictive aunts and cousins. Among the African Yoruba, household members were expected to take care of each other financially as well as spiritually. A principal method of economic cooperation was the fund raiser, most often in the form of selling dinners. "One's god-brothers and god-sisters distribute notices that a sale is taking place and may also take dinner orders. The proceeds from the sale are used to provide material necessities or provisions for an initiation ceremony for oneself or someone in need." When immigrants identified family networks as their most important source of help on arriving in Houston, they almost always included fictive kin as well as blood relatives among "family" who helped them.[133]

Aging is a universal kind of transition. As people age, they experience changes in commensality, but they continue to value conversation and fellowship as sources of happiness and appetite, as illustrated in a case study of elderly women in Sweden. Their favorite meal was the one eaten with family members or friends together at one table, eating and talking about everyday events. "The conversation and fellowship gave, according to the interviews, happiness and appetite. It was also an opportunity for the woman to obtain direct feedback and to be shown gratitude for her gift, the meal. She felt her planning, preparation, and presentation were successful when her guests praised her dishes and the laying of the table and enjoyed the fellowship. The commensality arose from her efforts, thereby giving her work meaning." Women living with their husbands enjoyed fellowship at everyday meals.[134]

Women living alone who had earlier lived with another person compared eating alone and sharing a meal. Some said that it was not fun to cook for one person and eat alone, and some had lost their appetite. Women adopted several strategies to deal with mealtime loneliness. One listened to a radio program in her kitchen, lighting a candle "to make it nice and cozy." Some women ate in the living room while watching TV. Others decorated their kitchen table or the window beside the table with flowers, or placed a bird table outside the window, or ate at the same time as their pets, or kept photographs of family members near their dining space. Most women did not enjoy eating in restaurants. They "found it depressing to dine with sick and disabled persons" and difficult to talk with unknown table mates.

> Several women had different types of social networks, such as friends, clubs, pensioners' associations, or church programs and found that to be a good solution to loneliness and a possibility to have lunch or dinner in commensality. "There are a few of us who are widows, who have remained together since 10 years ago. We visit each other . . ." One woman had dinners together with another woman in her apartment building. Another woman proposed living where a number of flats were built around a common room where she could meet like-minded elderly people and also have dinner with them.[135]

To summarize our discussion of tables at home, there is much evidence from linguists, developmental psychologists, cognitive psychologists, anthropologists, and sociologists that domestic tables are places where we learn rules about sharing, participating, and speaking. Inclusion in domestic table conversation fosters self-esteem, resiliency, and a sense of belonging to something larger than oneself. Scholars, along with writers and poets, foreground the powerful emotions associated with household tables: inclusion and exclusion, domination and comfort, expression and repression, selfishness and generosity. Domestic tables prepare us for difficult conversations outside the home, where we inevitably learn about other people's rules about sharing, participating, and speaking, along with their opinions and values, which are bound to challenge ours.

Chapter Four

Tables Away from Home

School Tables

Commensality and conversation are found not only at domestic tables but also at tables outside households. We begin with a look at school tables. When I interviewed Renee O'Harran, chef at the Northwest School, in Seattle, Washington, she described many practices that exemplified the democratizing potential of school tables. For starters, schools have to decide when to introduce children to adult food and how much explanation to provide. Broadening tastes and providing the courtesy of explanations are civilizing and democratizing table activities. O'Harran said that in the early days, she was on a very tight budget and the menus were very kid-driven. She surveyed students, trying to figure out how to get them away from kid food. Then she read about Chef Bobo at the Calhoun School in New York, who was serving adult food. She spent a week as a cook in his kitchen and noticed that he talked to the kids as they came through the line, explaining the food to them.

> I got a huge inspiration from that and came home and started turning it around: serving fish, chicken on the bone, a lot more veggies and beans. Not just generic, plain kid food. We cooked from scratch and used excellent ingredients, but we weren't putting the bold flavors out there. What we found is that kids loved the curries, pad thai, those are some of our favorite dishes. We interacted with the kids more. I was not just that person that you don't see. We started fostering relationships with the kids. I got that customer thing going, that family thing going, so they will be comfortable talking with us. Sometimes kids will not eat something you are trying to get them to eat because they want that control. I think food is one of the only things that they can truly control in their lives. You have to get them to think that you are not the enemy, the broccoli police. I try to talk to them like I would be talking to you. I don't have to talk down to them; I just say, "Hey,

this is really good." I might put a little lemon zest on it, tell them what I've done, and add, "Hey, it came from a farm over in Yakima." Just a little information that might spark their interest.[1]

O'Harran kept a watchful eye on students out of concern for their physical health. But she also used food to show respect for their choices, providing an opportunity for them to speak up for themselves and to participate in making rules that affected their lives—good training for democratic citizenship. It was important to create an enjoyable environment where kids could be comfortable and express themselves, just as they would around a family table. Keenly aware of the power of peer pressure, she used it in two very creative ways: welcoming students who felt awkward because of it, and exploiting it to get students to try new foods.

> I see some kids come in, get their lunch, and just stand there. "Where are my friends? Where am I going to sit?" There are many chairs available, and yet if I don't say anything to them, they may go over and sit in the corner. When I see that going on, I'll just walk up and say, "Hey, you know, there's a chair over there," or "Why don't you just sit right here by so-and-so, or a teacher?" It's always pretty easy to identify the kids that are struggling like that, so I try to tune into that and help them along. I do that just as I poke at them to eat more vegetables. They come up and maybe we are having pasta that day and they only want the pasta. They pass on the chicken, or they pass on the vegetable and I'll say something like, "Make sure you go over to the salad bar. Make sure you get a piece of fruit." I don't mind being like a mom. They are children, and my customers. I try to be very low-key about it. I don't want to draw attention to the fact that they might be standing there looking for someone to sit with, or that they might be eating just pasta.
>
> Sometimes a group of girls will come in, and maybe one of them will want the vegetable. So I will talk it up to her, and she'll say, "Yeah, I really like it." And it is always interesting to see them go and sit down and they will try it off her plate and then some will come back, not all, but some. Whenever I see the kids that are eating a lot of vegetables, I'll say, "Hey, right on. Good job," so they will recognize that someone is noticing that they are eating their vegetables. They are probably mostly told, "Eat your vegetables. You didn't eat this. You didn't eat that." I just try to get one to try it, or to notice one who already likes it.[2]

O'Harran constantly sought feedback from students about their likes and dislikes, sending a message that their opinions mattered in the dining room as much as they did in the classroom. And she thought that when they ate adult food, they were more inclined to engage in adult conversation. At the cafeteria, not only did sixth graders talk to twelfth graders, but all students mixed with faculty and staff, who were also referred to as faculty at this school.

> When students eat with adults and eat more adult-like food, they just feel more mature and older. They enjoy sitting and talking with the teachers, and the sixth graders like talking with the twelfth graders. We present food in a family style. I call them my customers because I always want them to know that their needs, wants, and likes are extremely important to me. You start to get a little feedback from kids, you know, eggplant moussaka is not very popular. They're very comfortable asking me for a variety of things, or letting me know that they really don't like a dish.
>
> I think because we do this community mealtime, they are more comfortable in speaking with me than they would be if we had a separate cafeteria for the students and the faculty ate in the faculty lounge. We include faculty in the meal program, so it's a benefit to them, fostering the whole feeling of the family table, the community table. Everyone is getting a hot lunch, not a bunch of processed food. It's prepared from scratch and portions of it are organic. We try to follow the environmental philosophy of the school, and they know that we are interested in sustainability.
>
> Sometimes the student feedback is right there in the food line, "I don't like black beans," and I try to help them. Often it might be a younger student, so I'll try to help them find something that they can eat. Especially the sixth graders coming in at the beginning of the year, they feel intimidated, they aren't sure where everything is, so I always try to walk them through some different scenarios.
>
> We have a number of students that have special diet needs, and we're very attuned to not making them feel excluded or special. We try to mirror what we are serving the mass with what they get every day. We make sure that we don't point them out because adolescents don't want to be different from anyone else. I've actually been at another school where they had a table for kids with peanut allergies; it was up against a wall, and the two little girls had to sit there facing the wall.[3]

O'Harran saw the cafeteria as reflecting two of the school's founding principles: shared faculty-student participation and environmental sustainability. Tables were used to draw attention to civic purposes. "At the beginning, both the students and the faculty participated in making the food. There were one or two cooks. Involving the kids in food preparation was one of the founding principles of the school. The kids put out the bowl of apples and the peanut butter. They participated. They chopped vegetables. Work-study kids gave back to the school by helping with dishes. The school started vegetarian, and it was because of pressure from the parents of international students that we introduced meat."[4]

She was aware that at the table, children learned habits that they would take with them into adulthood, even if they were resistant at certain stages in their development. She explained, "The sixth graders are so open to everything. But in seventh and eighth grade they kind of go away. Ninth graders are more interested in their social interactions. By about tenth grade they are coming back around, and I think they are really starting to set their likes and dislikes—pretty much how they are going to eat the rest of their lives. By the time they are seniors, they are eating really well I think."[5]

When I visited the school, I spoke with several students and faculty in the cafeteria. Some students enjoyed sitting and talking with faculty, but most clustered by age group. And the faculty tended to sit together as well. But the cafeteria did have a welcoming feel and conversations were lively. One student I interviewed liked talking to faculty.

> Something I enjoy about this school is that we have a general lunchroom where we get to sit down and have conversations. It reminds me of home when I am eating with my friends. Usually I sit next to my friends, but that's because there are a lot of us and the tables get filled up easily. But I have no problem sitting next to faculty. They have engaging, fun stuff to talk about, and often it's interesting. In the classroom they are the teacher and I have to listen to them, and I can't really object to that, but at lunch I can sit down and talk to them as just another person who has stuff to tell. I do have to hurry back to class, but it's still a lot of fun. We get forty-five minutes for lunch, and sometimes I spend thirty of those minutes sitting at a table eating and talking because it's engaging, it's interesting, it's fun.[6]

The school's librarian also thought that the common lunchroom was a fun place to connect with teachers. She enjoyed the delicious food and the interesting conversations.

> The food is absolutely fabulous, and I love talking to the teachers. The stuff we talk about at lunch is very interesting. Just yesterday, somebody sat down as we were talking, and she said, "I can't believe I'm sitting down in the middle of this conversation." It was just funny and off the wall. Sometimes we have very political conversations, sometimes they are a bit tense, and other times it's just casual conversation over a good meal. And it's always hard to come back to work. It's nice to just sit around and chat because we have really interesting people who work here. So it is just fun to find out what people are doing on the weekend, or where they went on vacation. We talk about all kinds of things. Lunch five days a week is included in our contracts. It's definitely a huge fringe benefit. The lunches here are a way to talk to faculty members that I don't normally see and to get to know the new faculty members.[7]

Some parents at the school also took the initiative to connect with others over tables. Parents of incoming sixth graders thought that it would be fun to get together to ease transition anxiety—theirs as well as their children's, as one parent candidly admitted.

We started what we call "A Dinner for Three." Sixth graders are hungry to know other people since they are new to the school. Families can decide if they want to join or not, and every quint [a unit of the school year] three families are randomly put together. One is assigned to be the facilitator. They can be a host or they can do something else, and basically these three families have dinner together for that quint. We have had it for one quint now, and our personal experience when we had people over was really neat, particularly because the kids are at an age where it's not anymore only about, "Sit down, eat your food." They understood a little bit about civility, so the conversation is not overwhelmingly around manners or logistics. It was a really great experience from the feedback I've gotten from other families. I think people have truly enjoyed it.

It is not often that we have opportunities to spend a substantial amount of time in these smaller settings. It's not too intense. When it's just two families, if you don't have anything to talk about, then the dinner gets a little long, but with three, there is a little bit of flexibility. Yet it is not so big that it's going to be this gigantic potluck, where you have a hard time really making connections with other people. This is more to help with the anxiety of the parents. The school does a great job taking care of the anxiety of the kids. There is also that preteen window where we are still cool and it is okay to invite that person's parents over. In two years, it will be more awkward. But we've had that meal with that family, so, "What do you mean I cannot call X, Y, and Z? I know them. We had dinner together." So there is a level of comfort.[8]

School cafeteria dynamics, especially the challenging ones, are an important topic of conversation with children. Gillian Clark observed that what is on the cafeteria table symbolizes status, identity, and meaning. Her children talked to her about school meals. Sian noticed that some kids in her class did not know that you could eat squid. Magalee said the whole cafeteria laughed at her because the bread in her sandwich was shaped funny (it was challah). For her daughters, school food "was a status symbol, a way to relate to others, a form of socialization, a glimpse and clue to who they are. [It] provided a window into the life of a schoolmate worth hundreds of questions and thousands of playdates. Was your mother generous? Did she let you eat candy? Did she take the time to make your lunch or were you the one with the Lunchables every day? Did you eat weird stuff out of Tupperware?

In Affton, Missouri, this middle school student drew a card that meant he could not sit with his usual lunch table friends. "No One Eats Alone Day" encouraged students to talk to kids outside their immediate social circle by switching lunch seating. School tables are important places to learn the art of conversation.
Credit: Laurie Skrivan, *St. Louis Post Dispatch*.

Was there nothing but vegetables and sensible things? Or did she throw in a surprise every now and then—a piece of cake or some Hershey's Kisses?" Clark recalled having to explain to the kids in her cafeteria at school why she recycled her brown paper lunch bags. Her father said that five lunch-sized brown paper bags were hard to come by, so she should tell classmates that she was a conservationist.[9]

Camp Conversations

Children also share enjoyable and excruciating times at camp tables, with new food rules that they have little say in creating. In recent years, some camp counselors have noticed two disturbing trends: a sense of entitlement to individualized meals, and an inability to share a meal with others at the same table. A professor of family social science thought that these trends were due to overindulgent middle-class parenting that treated children as customers who needed to be pleased. Parents allowed dinner to be an individual improvisation with no routine or rules, the television on, everyone eating what she or he wanted, and teenagers taking a plate to their room so they can keep IMing their friends. He said that this "food-court mentality" came at a high social cost. Meals together send a message that citizenship in a family entails certain standards beyond individual whims. A meal should be about sharing and compromise: "Not everyone gets their ideal menu every night." He heard from a camp counselor about a number of kids who arrived with a list of foods they would not eat and who required basic instructions from counselors on how to share a meal. "They have to teach them how to pass food around and serve each other. The kids have to learn how to eat what's there. And they have to learn how to remain seated until everyone is done."[10] It is interesting to compare his views with those of Renee O'Harran, who defended treating kids as customers. She did it for what I see as civic reasons: to show respect for their views, to give them a measure of control, and to hear their voices. This worked as a democratic project because it was done in a context of routines and rules that fostered civility: common tables with people of diverse ages and occupations who had the time to engage in conversation over a delicious meal. Most schools and camps do not give children this kind of voice.

As mentioned earlier, Barbara Scheifler had to teach children at camp how to sit at a table, share food, and converse, with adults and counselors modeling what affectionately came to be known as "the pleasant dinner conversation."[11]

> The kids knew they couldn't leave the table, so they were sort of captive—they could either sit there in silence or participate. In some ways it was a bit artificial because they had nowhere else to go. Initially it was the counselor and the adult chatting with each other. Counselors were trained ahead of time to role-play, asking questions like: "How was your day?" "What did you learn today?" "What is a typical dinner like for you?" "What do you do when you go home after school?" "Why did you come on the trip?" "Is this the first time you have been away from home?" "What did your parents think about your coming?" "Your brother or sister came two years ago. Is that the reason you came?"[12]

Scheifler came up with the idea of the pleasant dinner conversation the first year she ran the camp, when she was shocked to learn that the children had no idea what she was talking about. They wanted to eat and run. So she made it an official activity. "When we sat down the first year and they popped up and down I thought, 'No, we are going to stay here.' It was also a lesson in how to eat in public, how not to gobble your food, and how to take your time and slow down and review the day. It was one of the activities—not a path through to the next activity. It was a valid activity in itself—as important as the centers or the gathering time or the fireside."[13]

Even though none of the children had cooked at home, they all learned how to prepare dinners at camp. It was a challenge to model slowing down to eat and converse, especially since both the children and the teachers were used to rushed lunches at school.

At camp, they all had different chores, so they learned how hard it was to prepare food. It was the first time any of them had done any cooking. They said they cooked at home, but it was those cup of soups that you put hot water in or cereals. It was the first time they had chopped, sautéed and put a salad together. They took an hour to prepare the food, so why eat it in two minutes? There was no prize for being the first one finished at the table. In fact, it was probably a detriment. Slow down, eat, and enjoy what you are doing because you are not going anywhere until we are all done anyway.

The adults at each table were all probably born in the late 1940s or early 1950s, and we grew up with pleasant dinner conversations. We'd seen the kids eat at lunchtime and knew they scarfed lunch down quickly to get out on the playground. They only had thirty minutes, and if they wanted to run around, they only had ten minutes to eat. And the younger teachers in the staff room were done in ten minutes, even though we had the same thirty minutes for lunch. And they weren't running out to play. It gave me indigestion just watching them. They had a sandwich and some chips and a piece of fruit. But at least they would sit there and make pleasant conversation.[14]

The high school counselors, who had previously attended the camp, remembered that "pleasant conversation time" had been a new experience for them. Scheifler thought that it was important for the conversations to be fun and to be based on stories. When the storyteller spoke, others had to listen. As we saw earlier, by the end of the week, there were more shared experiences, which made it easier for the children to initiate conversations.

It wasn't teasing; it wasn't silly; it was fun: "Oh I remember when José fell in the pond" and we would laugh. It was not serious things, but it was one person talking and everybody listening. While that one person was talking they obviously couldn't eat, so they had to slow down. The rest of us could eat while they were talking. By the end of the week, we did not have to initiate as much of the conversation. Because there was more to participate with, and we had modeled it earlier in the week, by the end of the week the kids knew this was going to be a pleasant dinner conversation. So *they* would start conversations. I know there was a lot of carryover from the camp into their lives. Parents told us the kids would go into the kitchen and help do some food prep. They were impressed with the kids' ability to take control over the whole camp and willingly help out and not complain and moan.[15]

She put into practice two of linguists' conversational lessons: facilitate turn taking and ask "wh-questions" instead of yes-or-no questions.

> Some were quieter than others. Some of the girls would speak so quietly it was hard to hear what they were saying. And I would ask them to speak up a little bit. It tended to be the girls, but not always. Initially we just went around the table asking, "How was your day?" "How did you like the stream?" They didn't have to go on and on if they didn't want to, especially at the beginning. A sentence or two, a few words was fine, and we would go around again. Once I made sure everybody said something, then there was always somebody at the table who would chatter more than others and that was fine. But the adult and the counselor monitored things so it did not become a monologue. "Thank you. Now, Pedro, how was your hike up the hill?" And it didn't make any difference what you asked. Everybody had something to say. It wasn't like a yes or no question, or a quiz. It wasn't "Who's the president?" It was "How was the pond?" "What did you like or dislike?" "I didn't like getting my feet all wet," and that was fine. It really did not make any difference what they said. It was that they shared with each other how their day was. I don't ever remember anybody not saying anything.[16]

Scheifler thought that the conversational potential of the table was enhanced by the family atmosphere of the camp: there were only five or six people at a table; the high school counselors were graduates of the school and neighbors; siblings had attended the camp; and children were encouraged to talk about their feelings. These conditions made the situation familiar, nonthreatening, and conducive to conversation.

> They all knew us and we were all going by our first names, so it wasn't like outsiders were running the camp. It was a family situation. It was the same faces all week—different faces at the tables—but it was the same group of fifty all week. The basis was the shared camp experience, but we would go into "Oh yeah, this reminded me of when I went to the Grand Canyon two summers ago, when I hiked up the hill and found that same rock." Sometimes the kids who had been traveling a lot would make these kinds of connections. There were kids who hadn't been traveling so they couldn't make those connections. Or we would ask them their feelings, "What is it like to be away from home?"[17]

College Tables

In addition to camps, colleges also provide many young people with important "away from home" table experiences. College students increasingly want a say in campus cuisine, and university food services are responding with greater variation in cafeteria menus. In colleges across the country, there is a trend of more home cooking, dinner parties, food clubs, and cooking classes. Students' seriousness about food is creating new opportunities for table talk. Yale's *Campus Cuisine*, broadcast on New Haven's public access TV channel, covered topics like grilling, spicing up dining-hall food, and even dating. It was aimed at the growing number of students "who would rather gather around a table for a gourmet meal than find themselves at another kegger."[18]

> Whether it is a "foodie" chat room at Wellesley, which is visited by hundreds of students; a personal food column with recipes in the University of Chicago's newspaper; or an "Iron Chef"–inspired competition at Bloomsburg University in central Pennsylvania that has drawn an audience of 500 students, today's undergraduates are taking serious interest in all things food-related. They give dinner parties and have wine tastings. When they eat in the cafeteria, they want sushi and pho, the Vietnamese noodle soup. And at an increasing number of schools, they want the vegetables in that pho not simply to be seasonal but organic. . . . Soon, a spokesman for Aramark [a food service company at over four hundred colleges] said, it will be adding full-fledged grocery stores to campuses for students who want to cook for themselves. Students at Reed College and Wellesley, among others, have organized cooperatives centered around cooking meals. . . . At the University of Virginia, [the organizer of a dining club said,] "I thought we could take the love of food and turn it into a cohesive club and share our love of food. And when you're in a forum like that, you get all sorts of new ideas, like what to cook and places to go." . . . At [some campuses], cooking classes offered by faculty members have been consistently sold out.[19]

Folklorist Andrea Graham's study of a student cooperative household illustrates how food—its procurement, preparation, service, and consumption—was central to maintaining group cohesion. Students devoted a lot of time and energy generating their own food rules and rituals, without parental input. Their efforts paid off with stimulating conversations. Not surprisingly, when students stopped putting in such efforts, group cohesion suffered. Dinner was important both culinarily and socially. "A person's cooking style was an integral part of his or her personality, . . . and culinary skill was part of being a 'good housemate.' During the meal, comments were nearly always made to let the cook know the food was appreciated; silence usually meant that not much good could be said. Etiquette, like service, was decidedly informal—salad served with the hands, occasional food fights. Conversations were wide-ranging." There were rules about frugality, the storage of leftovers, the disposal of waste, and leaving pots on the stove for latecomers.[20]

There were celebratory meals. Birthday honorees chose their own meals, which were more elaborate than usual, and they received "a huge birthday cake of interesting construction and personalized decoration." There were two-turkey Thanksgiving dinners with ten guests, Christmas dinners and gift-giving, and a Passover seder "that required the use of every pot, pan, dish, and utensil in the house." These events required "cooperative cooking . . . [and] the sharing of diverse cultural heritages and traditions, which often developed into new [culinary] traditions for the house. For example, . . . Thanksgiving turkeys were accompanied by rice, potatoes, and sweet potatoes as a result of disagreement over which was proper." Visiting parents were impressed with what a "nice group of people" their son or daughter lived with and noted how "wonderfully they got along." A student commented, "One visitor at Thanksgiving dinner observed this house 'spirit,' remarking on the air of 'affectionate tension' he sensed—a characterization that helped us understand ourselves more fully and that tended to reinforce our sense of group identity, which in turn gave additional impetus to cooperation."[21]

Late-night cookie baking became a tradition. A few housemates would gather in the kitchen for a study break, and "the smell of baking would bring everyone in" for discussions that often lasted for several hours. "These times were very important in the evolution of a community spirit. The rituals of arguing over what to bake, or feigning horror at the calories involved, and of cajoling someone into cleaning up are cherished memories among those who shared these experiences." Over the years, as membership in the household changed, the spirit of cooperation waned. People failed to sign up to cook, and the quality of the dinners declined. When residents withheld their time and effort, it eroded the collective spirit of reciprocity. Graham maintains that "food as a microcosm of a shared lifestyle [could] be applied to any number of people living together, from a married couple to a family to a monastery." The processes may be more complicated with a large group, "but the mutual respect of others' ways and the maintenance of flexibility and effort are common to all committed groups." The call to eat "connotes much more than just a call to consume foodstuffs; it anticipates a table full of smiling faces, ready to share in an offering of food and to offer a share of themselves in return."[22]

Some campuses held Slow Food dinners. Those at College of the Holy Cross emphasized commensality and engaging in meaningful conversations about fundamental questions.

"Turn your cell phones off and put them away!" "This dinner will take two hours to complete. You are here to sit around the table and enjoy the food and each other's company." These words . . . were met with raised eyebrows as the first group of 12 students (who were accustomed to grabbing a slice of pizza on the go) sat down at a table adorned with linen tablecloths, napkins and Holy Cross' best china to experience what has become one of the college's most successful dining programs and most popular "green" initiative—Slow Food. Developed by renowned food and wine writer Carlo Petrini in 1986 in response to the opening of fast-food franchises in Rome, Slow Food is a growing international movement dedicated to preserving and supporting traditional ways of growing, producing and preparing food. It's about respecting and protecting the land, appreciating the people who care for it, and accepting the responsibility to live sustainable lifestyles, "Because," as Petrini has famously said, "we all sit at the same table." His words have become a mantra at Holy Cross. As opposed to fast food and all it implies, Slow Food also emphasizes the value of sitting down, enjoying your meal with company and engaging in meaningful conversations about fundamental social, ethical and environmental questions—questions that are an integral part of the Holy Cross mission and its Jesuit tradition. . . . [The chef] thoroughly explains each course, educating participants on where the food was grown, and what ingredients and methods were used in preparing it.[23]

When researchers interviewed university students about "comfort food," they were told that it conveyed powerful reminders of social connections, especially during times of distress, such as homesickness. One woman's comfort food was blueberry muffins, which brought back memories of Saturday morning chats with her family. "If I'm feeling lonely or missing them too much, I can pull out a mix and memories of my family instantly comfort me." When one man got "depressed, sad, or just bored . . . fried pork skins" boosted his spirits. He remembered "sharing them with his dad while watching Saturday college football games" and joked that "it makes sense if you are watching pigskins on TV, you should eat [them] as well." For one woman, "dirt pudding" was her comfort food, since she associated it with Brownie troop outings. Many students were from other geographic areas and used food to alleviate their feelings of homesickness. When an Oregon woman was feeling homesick, she ate apples grown on the West Coast. Another homesick woman prepared Hamburger Helper, which her mother often cooked when she did not want to make a big dinner. For one woman, fudge was a comfort food because "the recipe had been passed down through several generations in her family" and she wanted to keep the tradition alive. Several people selected comfort foods that had been served at family gatherings, such as sweet potato casserole, Swedish meatballs, chicken wings, noodle dishes, hummus dishes, and soul food. For a man who had served in the military in Germany, "German salad . . . evoked memories of the good times he had spent with his buddies." And a woman who grew up in a poor household "derived a sense of comfort from eating pork chops because it reminded her of times in her life when her mother seemed under less stress and was better able to care for the family."[24]

Many individuals, mostly women, described nostalgic foods as those they prepared with mothers and siblings, such as fruit salads, breads, and cookies. They valued the "intimate social interactions" that "often took place with significant others in the kitchen." One woman remembered making fruit salad with her mother when she got home from school. "They would talk about her day at school, the latest town events, and upcoming events. She explained, 'This fifteen minutes of the day helped the bonding process between us. It was a time of sharing, listening, and getting to know each other more.'" Researchers commented,

> Intimate social exchanges occurring among close friends and family members while preparing and consuming foods might be viewed as "kitchen therapy." Indeed, such activities can be quite therapeutic as intimate conversations take place and daily stressors are diffused. In addition, the physical activity of preparing the food, such as chopping the fruit or kneading the dough can be therapeutic. For example, one woman described making cookie dough as a tremendous reliever of distress. She observed in making chocolate chip cookies from scratch that "there is something very therapeutic in getting your hands messy while mixing seemingly simple ingredients to form something so perfect."[25]

Religious Tables

Food and tables figure prominently in many religious traditions, setting the stage for virtuous behavior: sharing, connecting, empathy, solidarity, and gratitude. A Yale University chaplain was a firm believer in what she called "the ministry of gastronomy."

> I attribute to it more breakthroughs and holy moments—around the table, around a bowl of chili, around a thoughtfully assembled tostada bar—than the approach where we all go to the seminar room, and everybody cracks open a book and says what they think about this particular tenet in their faith. It's also a way for students and faculty and staff to disarm. We all need to eat. And there are ways to prepare meals, to have them ready so everyone can enjoy them. . . . It leads to wonderful moments of connection between people. . . . When at all possible, I still try to cook everything myself. It matters so much to be invited into someone's home and cross traditions. You are less likely to demonize when you have broken bread together. . . . The notion of how to serve others means physically serve them. Get up out of your chair, go bring someone a plate of food, give them a refill.[26]

Two scholars of religion describe food and table fellowship as central features of Judaism and Christianity.

Christianity inherited from Judaism an emphasis on table fellowships. The heritage of table fellowship reflected the background of harvest festivals that were eventually incorporated into Israelite religion. The central event in the mythic foundations of Judaism, the Exodus, demands a carefully prescribed meal for its celebration during Passover. The meal itself provides a context for retelling the story and its implications for the covenant community. Christianity incorporated the practice of Passover in its telling of the story of Jesus in the gospels. In the gospel of John, Jesus' ministry begins with the miracle at a wedding feast and ends with the celebration of Passover. . . .

[In African American churches,] permanent committees are formed to ensure that food is provided by the church at appropriate times—receptions for new ministers, funerals, homecomings, watch nights, and visits from sister churches. Indeed, it is not unusual for congregations and visitors to purchase dinners from a church auxiliary or club after morning worship service. The dinners provide a source of income for the church and at the same time, onsite diners take an opportunity to sit and share while reconstituting community or portions of it. . . .

The importance of eating in re-membering the community as a national body came through in the fieldwork of one of the authors at a Women's Convention of the Church of God in Christ. The convention package included two meals each day, and the approximately five thousand women in attendance ate these meals in common. . . . While not the only expressions of national solidarity, the mealtimes were one of the few points in the proceedings when the participants were gathered and "of one accord." All were served at their tables but only after the approximately five thousand were served was grace said. Only then could they begin to eat.[27]

Most religious traditions emphasize the virtue of gratitude—giving thanks for life's blessings. Of course, religious people thank God, but there is also an important secular and civic function in expressing gratitude to others and in recognizing a common good. Olivia Wu interviewed residents of the San Francisco Bay Area to shed light on the various ways in which saying grace and expressing gratitude were important mealtime rituals. She cites a 1998 Gallup poll in which 64 percent of Americans said they expressed gratitude by saying grace at meals. The numbers have stayed constant since the 1960s, suggesting to Wu that people both rely on tradition and express thanks "in creative, ecumenical ways." One professor told her that grace can be many things—a pause at the beginning of a meal, not eating before everyone is served, a toast, a salute, or "a moment of reflection and appreciation."[28]

Wu spoke to the mother in a blended family that included "her 22-year-old son, his 19-year-old girlfriend and three younger children." She said that after they shared a blessing, they each talked about their day, what they were grateful for, and the positive things that had happened to them. An immigrant from Peru, who was raising two young children, said that prayer was how he kept his childhood tradition alive, especially at dinner, because that was when they were together and had time for meaningful conversations. He and his wife shopped and cooked with their children so that they would "understand the whole circle of food," he says. A single father said that a moment of stillness in the blessing with his seven-year-old son was a conduit to talk about his upbringing in England. His son recently surprised him by setting aside some of the food he ordered at a restaurant to give to the homeless. "Through giving and prayers, he's not thinking of food for himself. . . . He knows we live in a world (of hunger), not just in America." One couple celebrated the Sabbath dinner every Friday with their three sons. The father saw it as a time set aside for the family as a group and as individuals, taking them "out of the rush of the everyday world." They frequently invited friends—Jews and non-Jews—to join them. They had "theme nights" when they invited the boys' teachers and sports teams. He said they were doing it not "to be evangelical" but rather to expose people to different traditions. He thought that sharing food broke down barriers and was life-affirming.[29]

A Baptist pastor thought that the story of African American food was "slipping through the fingers of the hip-hop generation." There has been an erosion in the southern tradition of having a conversation with God about gratitude and quoting a passage from the Bible. "The hip-hops feast on junk food, and there's no table around a mom and dad or aunt. There's no community, family or meal." So he created a Friday-night gathering of a youth group for basketball and dinner. "When African Americans were able to gather, their meals were steeped in stories and emotions. . . . Soul food was indeed for the soul and not the senses. 'Black folks got the leftovers, the fatback and chitterlings that the masters didn't want. So giving thanks at mealtime was always bittersweet.'"[30]

For the Muslims Wu interviewed, dates and pomegranates, foods eaten by the Prophet Muhammad, were especially important. Ramadan, the annual month-long season of fasting, taught the lessons of hunger and gratitude for food. Muslims thanked God silently before a meal with words reminding one "not to be wasteful and to remember the poor." Some people Wu spoke with fused food blessings from different traditions and gave "inspirational, in-the-moment expressions of thanks." One woman who was raised in a secular Jewish family and converted to Buddhism drew from a variety of religions for her blessings and saw the pause before a meal as a magical moment of prayer, awe, and praise. Since we no longer hunt and gather our food, "prayer and grace can remind us of that connection." Her community's mealtime prayer was open-ended, with one person leading off and others picking up on the theme.[31]

For some, the expression of gratitude was accompanied by a sense of openness, compassion, peace, and justice. For one young man, living with the Luya in Kenya transformed his relation to food. Despite the hunger and the constant threat of drought he witnessed, he heard his hosts' heartfelt prayers thanking "God and the earth for the food." He left with a respect for food and water and a vow to eat less. A woman who was a member of Overeaters Anonymous began her meal with the thought that one plateful was enough. She said that praying before a meal "slows down the chatter in [her] head that says it's not enough." The director of a Buddhist monastery said, "'We make our most intimate connection every day through the mouth.' The practice of offering food affirms that 'I do participate and I am of this fabric,' so that the act of eating turns into an act of compassion." As Wu observes, "In much religious thought—the Christian eucharist, the Hindi prasad, among others—the transformational force of food has engendered dense theological discourse for thousands of years."[32]

Many Christians saw table fellowship as central to Jesus's social message. The common table symbolized the elimination social distinctions, and food was a language that communicated this acceptance of all types of people.[33] For Christians who believed that people were the church, household meals and table rituals played a foundational role. This was the view of a Catholic theologian who thought that homes were where the church lived every single day. He was impressed by the power of home meals when he was a graduate student living in a household of Jesuits, who ate dinner together every night, getting out the candles and tablecloths and arguing all matters of politics and theology. He thought it was important to linger over a meal, talking and giving people space to breathe. In his view, the events of the day, the meal, and even one's breath were all gifts. He noted that Christ's life milestones depicted in the Gospel of Luke all took place at meals. Tables were places to build tolerance and peace.

> Anyone who has lost a spouse to death, or sometimes even to divorce, will tell you that they miss those meals, the shopping they did for them, the cooking, even the cleanup afterward. . . . Even in homes where love has gone cold, where

there is a violent or dark temper dominating the household—even there, meals are important. Sometimes those meals explode in rage and sometimes they are times of peace, but they remain important. . . . Things work out when you cook and wash dishes together. It's hard to sit down to table with someone you haven't forgiven. . . . I think at the root of this is a possibility for building a much more tolerant, peaceful society. Supper can be a small spot of peace, fellowship, and sanctity for us all.[34]

For some Jewish families, expressing gratitude and compassion for those in need are regular features of the Shabbat dinner. A woman with teenaged children said that when everyone says what they are grateful for, children can see their parents' priorities. When candles are lit, they offer a blessing to someone who seems to be having a hard time. This woman said, "One traditional Jewish expression for home is the same as the word for a house of worship: *mikdash me'at*, or 'little holy place.' Our dining table with our children is an altar. It has the potential to be the holiest spot on the planet."[35]

Kim Severson maintains that even if you do not believe in a transcendent God, putting meals on the table involves faith, trust, mystery, and magic. Cooking and eating are "the most consistent daily acts of faith of any activity, short of going to sleep and believing you'll wake up in the morning." We believe that recipes will work because we take someone's word on faith. And when they work, we become "believers even though we [have] no idea how they worked," and "we spread the word to others who then [try] them on faith," and in turn become believers. "Entire culinary cultures have been built on this kind of faith and trust." Severson thinks that science cannot explain certain magical moments at the table—when everyone has just settled into eating, or "when the delicious rush of sharing a good meal has ended." People laugh and glow. "Out of nowhere, you have compassion for the jerk who was bugging you before dinner, so you ask if he'd like seconds on the braised artichokes. You belong to everyone else at the table and they belong to you. You can't create that kind of communion alone, and you can't create it without food. That one moment ought to be proof to anyone that something greater than us is at work."[36]

Some people are born into families of great wealth and privilege. At democratic tables, it is a good thing when, instead of gloating at their entitlement, they express gratitude for their good fortune and a sense of obligation to the less fortunate. Robert Kennedy Jr. said that when he was growing up, his family always said grace before and after meals, not only as part of a religious tradition but also to be grateful for their privileges.[37]

Male Tables

Just like religious tables, male tables create distinctive forms of fellowship. An American studies scholar who researched how Boy Scouts bonded over "the manly art of cooking" called attention to its democratic characteristics, even if it did not meet standard (female) definitions of manners and civility. Boys and men enjoyed sharing meals in the great outdoors. The process of preparing, serving, and eating food together, face-to-face, made Scout camp meals a male-bonding ritual. Jay Mechling describes the dynamics of such camp meals.

> I know from my fieldwork that a good deal of the talk at a camp meal is about the food itself. One sort of bonding takes place with the general consensus that camp food is awful, though boys often will volunteer that they like one meal over another. The issue of cooking competence arises, naturally, and the boys and adults praise the well-prepared meal and tease, or otherwise show displeasure with, the failed meal provided by a boy cook. I never saw teasing that the boy couldn't take. . . .
>
> The grins on the faces of the boy cooks who accomplished the competent meal showed me that they understood the value of the pride in performing this act of service. And, of course, there is lots of other talk around the camp table, including the gossip, complaints, bragging, and ritualized insulting one finds in most male adolescent friendship groups. The adults in camp took turns as the dining guests at each patrol, and they sometimes would take part in the patter, but the adults also had their own eating and drinking rituals later each evening around the staff campfire, where their informal staff meeting was lubricated by snacks, beer, and wine. From the eleven-year-olds to the adults, these boys and men associated the sharing of food with strong experiences of male group bonding. . . .
>
> Boys are attracted to the disorderliness and transgressive nature of [playing with food]. Food is such a powerful symbolic substance that kids learn early how to take what little power is available to them by controlling what they eat or won't eat. Food is the perfect substance for resisting adult rules. Moreover, boys come to see girls' vocal judgment of boys' behavior as "gross" as a defining quality in the performance of masculinity. The more girls (and mothers and female teachers, I should add) declare that boys are "gross," the more pleasure the boys take in engaging in the gross behavior. . . .
>
> Food play takes no special skills; anyone can do it. Unlike other social hierarchies of abilities the boys experience at Boy Scout camp, even the least talented boy can make a "P, B, & P" (peanut butter and "pus," really peanut butter and mayonnaise) sandwich, or throw a can of beans in the fire, or flick a spoonful

of pudding at another boy. Food play is very democratic that way. . . . Food play has the same potential as other framed play to signal to the participants their close relationships with one another. A food fight, like verbal dueling, requires a "license to play," a tacit agreement that the "fight" is framed play and should not be interpreted as real aggression (though the play frame can be used to mask aggression in some cases).[38]

Many firehouses are still all male, and just like Boy Scouts, firemen create special bonds at their tables. Jonathan Deutsch spent a year doing fieldwork at an urban firehouse where men shopped and cooked two or three times a day to feed the group, which included African, Irish, and Italian Americans. They brought their distinctive value systems and ethnic heritages to the kitchen table. And the metaphor of "family" loomed large in their bonding. Deutsch notes that most fire departments do not financially support firehouse cooking. Firefighters have to "negotiate the menu among themselves, shop together for food with the fire trucks, so that if they receive a call, they will be ready to abandon their carts at the market and go to the emergency, and divide the cost for each meal among those present." They also "contribute to a commissary fund to provide staple ingredients" and to pay for kitchen equipment maintenance. The firefighters he interviewed were not formally trained cooks, but they prepared elaborate meals together in a "raucous and convivial atmosphere." They had an "underlying sense of urgency," not knowing which meal might be their last. They valued the "family atmosphere" within the firehouse and placed great importance on their own biological and/or legal family. One firefighter claimed that the draw to becoming a firefighter was the family atmosphere in the firehouse. Deutsch thought that cooking together was even more of a family act for the firehouse "family" than eating together, and that "not allowing outsiders to participate in the cooking process and inviting them to eat as guests [preserved] the integrity of this workplace family."[39]

Deutsch argues that the "brotherhood of the firehouse . . . [resembles] a familial brotherhood." As one firefighter put it, "Just like real life, you'd die for your brother, but usually, you want to kick his friggin' ass too." But these "brothers" come from a variety of ethnic and family backgrounds. "A heated discussion about the edibility of the trim from a chicken among an African-American and Italian-American firefighter, for example, is just one of many manifestations of differences in individual and ethnic orientation, causing misunderstanding, tension, disagreement, or outright fights that comes up during my fieldwork—when to add the basil in tomato sauce . . . which pans are most appropriate . . . whether quantities of ingredients are adequate . . . which foods are 'healthy,' or whether it is sanitary to spit in oil to determine its temperature."⁴⁰

"Linked to the metaphor of family [was] the construction and expression of masculinity, which figure[d] prominently in the kitchen and at the table." While cooking, they used off-color, sexist language. By contrast, they used mild and professional language while exercising, doing firehouse chores, or engaging in leisure activities. Deutsch attributes the fact that he heard little profanity outside the kitchen to their need to "'masculinize' the 'women's' work that they [did] in the kitchen." "Food and cooking brought about highly sexualized, heterosexual, and homosexual talk and play, with food, about food, and around food. . . . It appears that these supposedly macho, virile firefighters cook very much in a way that is often identified as domestic, feminine, or womanly . . . [including] domestic discussion [about] friendly and instructive butchers, double coupons, and buying in bulk to save money."⁴¹

Prior to each meal, they discussed what to make that would appeal to most of the men on each shift. They tried to provide "home cooking" for the firehouse "family," for a "family type" meal "eaten communally, starting and ending together around a table, representing a balanced proportion of major food groups, and culminating in a sweet." There were some food rules: someone who didn't eat one or more of the menu items could nonetheless join in the meal, and those who didn't want to eat a meal could pass on it. Once, a firefighter who announced that he wouldn't be eating because he had "the runs" ended up just nibbling on some bread, but he still paid his share at the end of the meal. "Even though he [was] sick, he [didn't] exclude himself from table but rather [sat], noticeably uncomfortably, with the 'family' and engage[d] in the conversations. The balanced meal has something for everyone, nutritionally and socially."⁴²

In contrast to the popular cultural stereotype that men cook over flames and women cook in vessels, the firefighters cooked mostly indoors using pots and pans. They had a grill but seldom used it, preferring to avoid the hassle of a charcoal fire and cleaning up afterward.

In all, the absence of women and the presence of everyday home-style cooking in Engine 3000 creates an interesting tension. The frequency and practical issues associated with the cooking process demand concern with domestic cooking attributes—economy, health, pleasing the group, and cooking with efficiency. But at the same time, these are men who self-identify as largely conservative, working-class men who enact distinctive gender roles at home. . . . This multiplicity suggests that the relationship between gender and cooking is complicated by particular contexts where people construct their work identities and their domestic lives.[43]

Addiction Recovery

Table talk can help people bond in a way that builds self-worth and identity. Recovering addicts are a case in point. Many have found that sharing their stories at meetings of Alcoholics Anonymous (AA), typically over a cup of coffee, creates a healing fellowship. Here is one researcher's account of an AA meeting.

> The formal presentation of AA found in numerous pamphlets and books says: "Alcoholics Anonymous is a fellowship of men and women who share their experience, strength and hope with each other [so] that they may solve their common problem and help others to recover from alcoholism." The term *sharing* is crucial for what goes on in AA. Whenever any two or three alcoholics are gathered for sobriety—sharing their experiences usually over a cup of coffee—they may call themselves an AA group, provided that, as a group, they have no other affiliation. . . . Communication is regulated by few and simple rules: no one should be interrupted when speaking, and all should confine themselves to reflections on their own personal experiences. Thus speaking is characterized by monologues instead of dialogues, and the only correct way to comment on other peoples experiences is to tell a parallel or comparable experience of your own. . . .
>
> [At the AA meeting I attended], at eight o'clock about 30 people are seated around a couple of tables put together in a row and lit with candles. Some sit by the table drinking coffee and smoking cigarettes—other have placed themselves in the background along the walls, their faces only dimly seen in the sparse light from the candles. . . . Stories . . . cultivate a certain degree of impersonality so that the experiences of the author are made available to others who can discover in them meanings of their own. A story is thus suggestive rather than definitive of meaning. . . . Anecdotes are often told as small pedagogical tales with an implicit moral, and may function as discreet efforts to adjust or even correct other life stories in a more appropriate direction.[44]

Conversations at Alcoholics Anonymous meetings are nonjudgmental and plainspoken, which helps working-class participants feel more comfortable than in therapeutic settings where professionals tend to use off-putting technical terms.

> AA groups work partly because potentially hurtful opinions about other members are firmly repressed. If any newcomer is tempted to make judgmental remarks

on other people's comments, he/she is told that "cross-talk"—editorializing or judging—is not allowed. . . . [The meeting] tolerates an extremely wide range of speech forms and emotional contents, and judgmental comments about others are kept to a minimum. . . . The prohibition on judging others may be particularly crucial in attracting to the organisation older working class [males]. . . . Men who have in the past felt judged by doctors, or who for class-specific reasons reject "psychobabble" will generally find that AA does not expect newcomers to have the sort of middle-class cultural capital that is routinely assumed in therapy groups and in feminist or left-wing organisations. . . .

AA encourages the sort of "plain" English—peppered with homespun folk sayings, somewhat trite metaphors, and the occasional four-letter word—that working-class males would formerly have found in a bar. Unlike most voluntary organisations in civil society, which tend to level upwards and systematically privilege those with professional backgrounds, AA tends to level downwards. . . . [Personal stories can] . . . solicit individual uniqueness, . . . create group solidarity, . . . validate the authority of the analyst, . . . replace analysts with self-help groups, . . . elicit sympathy for one's pain, . . . [and] gain approval for one's abilities as an entertainer.[45]

Even though meetings of Alcoholics Anonymous take place around the world, they always have the speaking rules of no cross talk or negative feedback. Some have circular seating arrangements, others have audience-type seating; some are closed, and others invite speakers. The flow of the discussion is determined by different turn-taking rules: in seating order, on request, by chair selection, or with the current speaker selecting the next speaker.[46]

Residential addiction treatment centers also have speaking rules. For example, at Twelve Willows, a talking stick is used in large groups to control communication, and on awards night, presenters can speak for as long as they want about the virtues of the recipients being commended for their sobriety.

The Talking Stick . . . serves to guarantee for its holder the ability to say whatever she would like, for as long as she would like. The holder of the Talking Stick may ask for feedback on her presentation, but those who offer feedback must listen and comment respectfully, no matter what is said by the resident with the Talking Stick. . . . After the resident who momentarily "owns" the stick has used it to her personal satisfaction, the stick is passed on to the next resident who expresses a desire to use it and thus make herself heard with the stick's form of "immunity." . . . A problematic aspect of the Talking Stick became apparent when "the stick was hogged" by [certain residents]. . . . More talkative members constantly held the group's attention, and others who wanted to speak may have been prevented from talking. . . .

Awards Night is a celebration of abstinence from drugs and alcohol held at Twelve Willows on the first Wednesday of each month. The ceremony lasts from 7:00 to 8:30 p.m., preceded by a simple potluck dinner. . . . The guests congregate in the dining room, where a simple dinner of soup, bread, and salad is arranged. A few guests bring food for the potluck dinner. Most guests who arrive late do not eat. . . . Certificates for length of sobriety are awarded to the residents, staff, and alumnae present. . . . One friend might come to the microphone, or an entire extended family of ten people. Presenters can go on at some length about the virtues of the recipient. Emotional embraces and tears often accompany presentations.[47]

Homies Dinners

Another group that has benefited from table talk is the urban gang. Although most people see gangs in a negative light and try to dismantle them, Cesar Cruz adopts an alternative approach. He thinks of them as fraternities (or sororities) of like-minded people looking for love and acceptance, and he invites them to dinner. He is director of Intervention Support Services at the East Oakland YMCA and cofounder of Homies Empowerment, a program that hosts Wednesday-night dinners to help educate Latino and African American youths about their history. His approach is controversial. He decries gang violence, but he thinks that efforts to destroy them altogether are misguided and wrong. "I'm sick and tired of gang prevention programs that don't' work," he said. "They're looking for acceptance, love—why not nurture that environment and make it healthier? It's about ownership, a community taking care of itself. . . . What I think is criminally violent is that we don't have a bookstore in East Oakland, but instead we have 150 liquor stores."[48]

Cruz believes that when sworn gang enemies cook and eat together, they are less likely to kill each other and more likely to be peaceful citizens who want to take care of their community. "Homies Empowerment members Adrian Arias and Nestor Ramirez discovered they could find common ground despite living in rival neighborhoods. Both have shared in the experience of grief from gang violence. 'We could relate to the things we go through but in a different way,' Arias said. 'They're gonna go through the same pain we go through,' Ramirez said. 'It's all the same thing. It's never going to stop until we stop ourselves.'" Cruz oversees more than two hundred people who are in or influenced by gangs. "I average six to ten funerals a year," he says. "Most are open casket. I'm tired of it." He teaches Latino history at the Homies Empowerment meetings and at an Oakland high school, where students say that learning about their history for the first time helps them dream big. "After you know that there are heroes in your race, it motivates

At a Homies Empowerment dinner in Oakland in 2011, Pocho-one took this photo of teenagers as he distributed food on paper plates. Teens watched a documentary and engaged in a free-for-all discussion about race and the criminal justice system. The founder of the Homies Empowerment Program, Cesar Cruz, said the goal of the weekly dinners was to get youth from different neighborhoods to meet face-to-face and to break bread.
Credit: Pocho-one.

you," a senior said. "Peace is happening in Oakland, and it's not just stories of murder and violence," Cruz said.[49]

A blogger who attended a Homies Empowerment Dinner at the Eastlake YMCA in Oakland, California, provided an account of youth from different neighborhoods breaking bread and discussing "divide and conquer" and police brutality. He saw event cofounder Pocho-one serving snacks on paper plates and taking photos. That week's dinner featured J. R. Valrey, an international journalist with local roots. The participants viewed Valrey's documentary *Operation Small Axe*, which presents the story of Oscar Grant, who was killed by Johannes Mehserle, a BART officer in Oakland, and addresses the larger issue of police brutality. "The young men and women enjoyed food, a special screening of a documentary, and an engaging discussion—all for free." The goal of the weekly dinner was to get youth from different neighborhoods together to share a meal. Much of the discussion at the dinner was guided toward getting past the concept of "divide and conquer." Jack Bryson, a friend of Oscar Grant, told the audience that Mehserle's two-year sentence had gotten him down. This was his first public appearance at an Oscar Grant–related event since the sentencing, but he said that this event had lifted his spirits. He concluded by asking why there was black versus black violence, brown versus brown violence, and black versus brown violence since the violence in Oakland that needed their attention was obviously blue versus black and brown. The meeting ended with a circle of teens shaking hands and hugging, a ceremony inspired by the United Farm Workers that expressed unity within the community.[50]

Military Meals

Sharing a table with fellow soldiers creates a bond, if for no other reason than to complain about the food. For some veterans who have fallen on hard times and are homeless, a chance to live with other homeless veterans is like living with family who have one another's backs, just as they did on active duty. Community kitchens and mess-hall-style seating help them reconnect and build new lives, which was the case for a group of veterans living in San Francisco. Mark Hedtke remembered sitting on the beach and guzzling beer after another depressing night in a homeless shelter. He considered killing himself, but then he recalled his years in the Air Force, when he earned two medals. "He and his buddies depended on each other. It was home. Maybe, he thought, he could have a home like that again. So instead of ending it all, Hedtke checked himself into an alcohol rehab program." After being sober for nearly a year and a half, longer than ever in his adult life, he moved into a supportive housing complex designed for homeless veterans. The new complex featured efficiency apartments with modern kitchen appliances, a game room, a community room, and two communal kitchens with mess-hall-style seating. "All of us here, we all have some damage, we can all relate," Hedtke said. "We can have each other's backs again. We can have new lives." "'I am alone in the world, and the military is really the only family I've got,' said incoming resident Ron Jones, 53, who served in the Army from 1977 to 1983. 'A whole lot has gone wrong in my life—crack, drinking, prison, living on the street, parents passed, you name it. But the fellowship I have from the military, vets understanding what vets go through—that is my family, man.'"[51]

A commander of the United States Navy's Medical Corps maintains that when you discuss military meals with war veterans, it inevitably brings back emotional memories. He encourages civilians to talk with vets about their wartime meals. It is the civic thing to do.

Food in war has been used to assess enemy forces as well as motivate our own. Most importantly, however, the binding ritual of sharing food that we experience in our own homes continues, even in the most adverse circumstances. . . . The feeding of warriors is more than simply providing a source of energy. There is an entire culture built around food in war. Meals are shared experiences and bonds are formed through these meals that many do not realize until many years later. Take the time to talk with a war veteran about their meals, but not until many years after the event. For the first few years too many memories are too fresh. As the years pass, some memories are pushed aside, and others fade away, but meals are always remembered.

Begin to discuss meals with a war veteran and you are likely to stir quite a bit of emotion. The conversation may start with how they had to use excessive condiments to make it palatable, or even about how the meals constipated them so, but this will lead to other memories and an understanding of what these heroes endured. Ten years from now, if you mention an MRE [Meal Ready to Eat] to a group of US veterans from the current war in Iraq, you are likely to get a few howls of laughter, and occasionally these will be followed by the knowing sighs of painful memories.[52]

Military officials who believed that sharing family dinners created resiliency in soldiers promulgated policies to encourage this ritual. One officer instructed soldiers stationed at Fort Hood, America's largest military base, to be home for dinner by six. "It does more than make everyone happy," he said. "It creates a more resilient soldier, one less likely to abuse drugs or alcohol, injure himself in a traffic accident, or fall to suicide." He maintained that since the policy was instituted in February 2009, the base had seen a noticeable reduction in traffic accidents and suicides.[53]

Civilians on the home front could connect with soldiers in the field through food, showing empathy, support, and patriotism, as illustrated by a poignant story narrated to the Kitchen Sisters by a Vietnam War veteran who received a pineapple upside-down cake intended for another soldier and tried to contact the parents in Connecticut who sent it. They received a flood of calls from many different kinds of people, including some with databases in Connecticut willing to search for the name of the family, veterans, mothers, and bakers. The Kitchen Sisters speculated about why this story resonated so deeply: "This simple, sweet act of baking, of strangers tending one another during hard times, of civilians supporting a soldier during an ambiguous war, and a soldier's wish to repay that kindness cuts deep into the fabric of who we are and who we want to be." They received a call from a soldier on active duty in the air force, on a runway monitoring F-16s. The story reminded him of his deployment in Bosnia in 1996, when he received an assortment of baked goods addressed "To any soldier." Touched by the anonymous gift, this man from Detroit became pen pals with the son of the New Jersey family who had sent it. The soldier said in his call that he could hear the emotion in the voice of the Vietnam War soldier and wanted the Kitchen Sisters to know that it had touched him. "The spirit and the inherent good nature of human beings will never cease to inspire me," he said."[54]

In conflict zones, food can be used both to humanize and to dehumanize the enemy. In Vietnam, when some Asian American Pacific Islander (AAPI) soldiers ate Vietnamese food, it reminded them of home, making it difficult for them to dehumanize the Viet Cong. "The similarities between Vietnam and 'home' reflected an important way in which some AAPI veterans experienced bicultural identification and conflict." One veteran said that he could eat their food because rice had always been a staple in his diet and he recognized their fruits and vegetables. Another recalled a time when he and his friends went to the PX and picked up some corned beef and onions to cook their own food. When some white GIs accused them of eating "gook food," they replied, "What do you mean gook food? This came out of the PX. What are you talking about?" Another AAPI veteran observed that from the moment he arrived in Vietnam, he heard "kill the gooks." "I remember the guys were on our truck, guys started throwing the c-rat [C ration] cans at the kids, busting their heads, busting their faces with the cans. I was like, oh man, that's what they meant, 'kill the gooks, kill the gooks.' Everybody is the enemy over here. Young, six, seven, eight, you know, young age."[55]

In Vietnam, some Asian American Pacific Islander soldiers attributed their ability to survive dangerous operations to the fact that they had shared meals with local Vietnamese personnel. One veteran recounted how he and another AAPI soldier worked well with Vietnamese Chieu Hoi (former North Vietnamese Army personnel who defected and worked for the South Vietnamese government) soldiers in his unit. They "walked point" together, keeping guard at the perimeter point nearest to the enemy. At the end of the day, they hung out together and prepared food. "So we get tired of eating c-rations and go with them. But the rest of the guys in our platoon . . . they would go, 'Hey, you fucking gooks, what are you guys fucking turning into gooks or what!' . . . They have the same food I like, you know. Rice and fish . . . we just go to share a meal with them. And the rest of the guys in the company talk to us, fucking calling us names, being like them." This hostility led the AAPI soldier to wonder whether, if they got into a firefight, the white GIs would fire at him. He was constantly looking over his shoulder. When he walked point, his Chieu Hoi friend watched his back, and he reciprocated when his friend walked point. "I don't know why they [white GIs] couldn't get along with the *Chieu Hoi* in the first place, you know. We could get along with them. Why couldn't they? . . . Because we from Hawai'i, we could relate to them. The people there is the same like us, you know, just trying to survive." Another AAPI veteran told of his delight when he would go into a village and see noodles and chopsticks. The white GIs would look at him and say, "Why is this guy with the Vietnamese eating their food?" "Don't touch that, man. They got booby trap or poison in there. You gonna get sick, they gonna kill you." He said he would "just grind [eat]," adding, "I don't care. Hey, I'm one of them."[56]

During the course of the Vietnam War, the Viet Cong occasionally blew up bars and restaurants frequented by American GIs. One group of Hawaiian veterans said that they owed their lives to the fact that they showed respect to the Vietnamese at a restaurant in Saigon, explaining, "Because of the way we were eating, you know, the local style with chopsticks, the people got to like us." During their fourth or fifth visit, a man wearing a khaki uniform with a red star emerged from the back of the near-empty restaurant. He was a Viet Cong. He sat down at their table and said, "You know, you guys are wrong to be here in this country." The Hawaiian soldiers at first just kept eating, but they finally replied, "Well, yeah, you're right. We are wrong to be in this country." When he said, "This is a war between us, and you guys are the invaders," they agreed. He asked where they were from and told them, "You guys are unusual. The way you eat. . . . You guys have respect, don't you?" "Yeah," they said. "We got local style. We go to other people's house, we take off our slippers. When you go to other people's house, you show people respect." He said, "You know, because you show respect, you can walk out of this place alive." People in the restaurant stared at them because they weren't afraid to come unarmed. But the soldiers just smiled at everybody, "Howzit! Good morning. How are you?" They were happy to be among the local people. "And we think with our stomach," one of the soldiers said. "The first thing we say is, 'Let's go eat!'" Because they usually wore slippers and joked and laughed a lot, the local people sensed they had nothing to fear from them. "And once, they tested us and found out that we talk honesty and respect," the Hawaiian soldier recounted. "That is it. Nobody [other GIs] from that day on could understand how we could drift in and out from those places and not get killed."[57]

To summarize our discussion of tables away from home, it is striking how many people gathered at them to emulate domestic tables by re-creating "family" or "comfort" or "safety," all of which are conducive to finding one's voice in conversations. And the same principles of civility and democracy apply: sharing, listening, taking people's needs seriously, expressing gratitude, and bonding. What is different, of course, is creating new food and conversation rules in unfamiliar environments: schools, camps, colleges, fire stations, addiction-recovery programs, gang intervention programs, and the military. Another important distinction is the enhanced levels of conflict: being ridiculed at school for what's in a lunchbox, alienating roommates by shirking food-preparation responsibilities, dealing with substance abuse, and living with violence in gangs and the military. It is hoped that democratic and civil practices at more comfortable tables provide the skills to deal with the difficult conversations at conflict tables, a topic to which we now turn.

Chapter Five

Tables and Conflict

Difficult Conversations

Of course, one does not have to be in a combat zone to experience conflict at a table. It is important to take a close look at table conflicts because democracy needs citizens who are willing and able to engage in difficult conversations. As mentioned earlier, difficult conversations are always three conversations: about facts, emotions, and identity. Skilled conversants need to be acutely aware of all three levels. Without a skilled conversant at the table, things can quickly degenerate as people beat a quick retreat to separate rooms to avoid conflict rather than deal with it in a constructive way.

When sociologist Samuel Vuchinich studied verbal conflicts at family dinners, he emphasized their positive functions: "clarification of rights and obligations, marking interpersonal boundaries, establishing and maintaining power hierarchies that streamline some group processes (such as decision making), providing a catharsis where important negative feelings are expressed, and promoting open communication. Good conflict management must allow for these benefits to be realized. The social value of these benefits partially explains why verbal conflict is a routine part of normal family interaction." All family members were equally likely to initiate conflict, mothers were the most active in closing them off, and most conflicts ended with no resolution. Dinners ranged from fifteen minutes to more than an hour, with about three conflict episodes per meal, usually about food, money, future plans, children's sexual behavior, or drugs. Families did not avoid disagreements once they were brought up. When someone initiated opposition, about one-third of the time conflict did not follow. Many of these cases involved corrections such as "Quit eating with your fingers," and others were simply ignored. Vuchinich thought that this "1/3 avoid–2/3 fight" ratio in moving from opposition to conflict allowed enough conflict to realize its benefits while preventing an excess that could be counterproductive.[1]

Conflict was ended in one of four ways: (1) submission, where one person gave in to another; (2) compromise, where disputants found a middle ground and each gave a little; (3) standoff, where people dropped the conflict without a resolution and tacitly agreed to disagree without winners or losers, and the conflict ended in a draw; and (4) withdrawal, where one party overtly left the interaction by refusing to talk or by leaving the room altogether. Withdrawals disrupted the flow of family interaction, while the other formats allowed for a smooth transition to other activities. Most frequently, conflicts ended in a standoff (61 percent), followed by submission (21 percent), compromise (14.2 percent), and withdrawal (3.8 percent). Vuchinich thought that a standoff probably occurred the most often because it was affectively and cognitively the simplest way to close a conflict. "In a submission the submitting person must 'lose face,' which is undesirable from a self-maintenance standpoint. The compromise requires rather complex cognitive work to create a position that allows each person to 'give a little.' The withdrawal disrupts the social occasion and carries negative implications about the ability of participants to sustain normal civil conversation. The standoff avoids all of these difficulties."[2]

Mothers were the most involved in compromise and standoff closings, creating twice as many compromises as all other family members combined and initiating nonconflict activities following standoffs most frequently. Children submitted three times more often than parents, displaying adults' social power. "Following standoffs, females (i.e., mothers and daughters) initiated nonconflict activities twice as often as males. This diversion away from conflict is a subtle yet very important conflict-management technique; first, because it occurs so frequently, and second, because it smooths the flow of interaction and encourages the disputants to leave the conflict behind. Overall, females were actively involved in twice as many closings. . . . These results suggest that females, and especially mothers, act as peacemakers in family conflict at dinner."[3]

Vuchinich's ideas are crucial to our understanding of everyday conflict resolution at the table. The first is that verbal conflict is healthy for the welfare of the group, since it helps clarify rights and obligations, mark interpersonal boundaries, facilitate decision making, provide a catharsis for the expression of negative feelings, and promote open communication—all constitutive features of democratic practices and difficult conversations. It takes skilled conflict management to allow for these benefits to be realized. The second is his "1/3 avoid–2/3 fight" ratio of moving from opposition to conflict, which is probably optimal to allow sufficient conflict to realize its benefits. The third is the expectation that most table conflicts will end in a standoff, without winners and losers. This is not only to be expected but probably the least costly to group cohesion. After all, submission means losing face, and withdrawal is quite disruptive. Although compromise is optimal in theory, it takes a lot of work and skill to realize in practice. We should not be hard on ourselves if we cannot achieve a brilliantly crafted compromise every time we experience table conflict. Finally, females are the peacemakers at the table, doing the heavy lifting of compromise, standoff closings, and initiating nonconflict activities following standoffs.

One obvious site for difficult conversations is a high school restorative justice program, where teens talk in a group to try to come to terms with their wrongdoings and community violence. As alternatives to "zero-tolerance" policies such as suspension and expulsion, these programs forge close relationships among students, teachers, and administrators. They encourage young people to develop empathy for one another and to devise reparations for the harm they have caused. U.S. Department of Education civil rights investigations have revealed that African American boys have disproportionately high suspension and expulsion rates and that many disciplinary actions are for "defiance." Research indicates that lost class time due to suspension and expulsion results in alienation and often early involvement with the juvenile justice system; furthermore, zero-tolerance policies do not make schools safer. At Ralph J. Bunch High School in Oakland, where 90 percent of the students had run-ins with the juvenile system or lived in foster homes, restorative justice conversations were emotionally demanding and required an experienced facilitator, Eric Butler. One day, a senior was distraught because her father had been arrested that morning on a charge of shooting at a car. She was prone to anger, and when she got angry she "blanked out." She listed some reasons for her anger on a white board—the names of friends and classmates who had been murdered. One was Kiante Campbell, who had recently been killed during a downtown arts festival. His image was posted around the classroom, along with flowers from a restorative grief circle. "Restorative justice adopts some techniques of the circle practice that is a way of life for indigenous cultures, fostering collaboration. Students speak without interruption, for example, to show mutual respect." An after-school coordinator, whose twenty-one-year-old brother had been shot dead in a nightclub two years earlier, said, "A lot of these young people don't have adults to cry to. So whatever emotion they feel, they go do." One student who had been suspended more than fifteen times had thought it was cool, until he realized that it was almost impossible to catch up on class work. He said that the restorative justice sessions helped him see things in a new way. "I didn't know how to express emotions with my mouth. I knew how to hit people," he said. "I feel I can go to someone now." In their circles, students discussed racism, and one girl told about being molested as a child. "Those boys who looked scary wrapped their arms around this girl," Butler said. "That's what's missing for our kids. It's harder to fight people you feel a closeness to." When two girls got into a fight, one admitted she had an anger problem and burst into tears, saying that her brother had been shot in the head the year before. No one at the school had known.

> A recent circle at Bunche for Jeffrey, who was on the verge of expulsion for habitual vandalism, included an Oakland police officer, and the conversation turned to the probability that Jeffrey would wind up incarcerated or on the streets. The student had told Mr. Butler that he was being pressured to join a gang. "Cat, you got five people right now invested in your well-being," Mr. Butler told him. "This is a matter of life or death." Jeffrey agreed to go to Mr. Butler's classroom every day at third period to do his schoolwork.
>
> Mr. Butler, who grew up in a vast segregated housing project in New Orleans, knows the urge for retribution: Two years ago, his sister was murdered by her boyfriend. "I wanted my quart of blood," he told students disturbed by Kiante Campbell's death. Then the boyfriend's mother showed up, seeking forgiveness. "This brave little woman knocked on the door in her robe and flip-flops," he told his classroom. "The want for revenge in my stomach lifted." Keeping students in school, focused on the future, is at the core of his work. So every Friday afternoon he tells them: "Y'all gotta come back Monday. Come back. I gotta see you." "We're all we've got," he said. "And we need to start thinking that way."[4]

Keeping in mind the three components of difficult conversations (facts, emotions, and identity), restorative justice conversations are challenging, even gut-wrenching, emotionally, and gay rights conversations are especially taxing about identity. It is hard to keep your cool in a conversation when something as basic as your sexual identity is being disparaged. Nevertheless, many gay and lesbian political organizers decided that having difficult conversations with "reachable" voters was an effective strategy for legalizing gay marriage. After the November 2004 elections, when voters in eleven states resoundingly approved amendments to their constitutions banning same-sex marriage, gay rights activists met to discuss how to respond. Evan Wolfson, the executive director of Freedom to Marry, said: "There's a sense out there that there's a group of people that hates us. At the same time, not everyone out there is a hater." He thought of the nation as divided in thirds: one against gays, one supporting gays, and another "reachable but not yet reached" third. He thought that activists needed to spend more time providing information for the reachable group. Activists noted that five years earlier, civil unions were unheard of, and now they have become more accepted. "We're still at the beginning of a conversation that really only started a year ago," said Liz Seaton, senior counsel at the Human Rights Campaign. "People are voting on a topic that they're not yet engaged in. And we know that voters will vote with the status quo unless they've had a chance to have a conversation about what change means." State organizers celebrated victories resulting from those kinds of conversations. In Cincinnati, a city ordinance prohibiting any law that protected gay rights was repealed. Even though they were outspent two to one, activists won by going door to door. Support for gay marriage had increased in Oregon by thirteen points over two months, and in Kentucky by eight points over four months. "We just need to have more conversations," said Rachel Hurst, the statewide field director for the Kentucky Fairness Alliance. "That's what we're excited about because when we did have those conversations, Kentucky voters overwhelmingly wanted to vote with us. Regular folks are on our side. They just need to see the full story."[5]

One topic that many people avoid talking about is death. In terms of difficult conversations, no one denies the fact of death, but that does not make it any easier to come to terms with it emotionally or philosophically. In recent years, Death Cafes have cropped up across the United States. They are not grief groups or support groups—just discussion groups with no agenda. The first Death Cafe in Los Angeles consisted of a group of friends who gathered at Betsy Trapasso's home and concluded their meeting in the kitchen. Her goal was to get people to discuss death so that they would not be afraid when the time came. Talking about it in a comfortable, safe setting over tea, cake, and cookies could "make the prospect less frightening." British-born Leszek Burzynski said he thought that Americans needed to change their approach to death. Instead of seeing it as a postscript, it should be viewed as a chapter in a continuation, as it is in many other cultures. He predicted that the way we die is bound to change since aging baby boomers will demand better options. His mother grew up in a village where, "as a girl, she helped wash and lay out the bodies of the dead. Most deaths used to be at home." Burzynski added, "We all want to make a good death. If you ask anybody, 'How do you want to die?' they'll say, 'In the bosom of my family, with my friends around.' They don't say, 'In a hospital bed with tubes coming out of my nose and my ears, in a semi-coma—that's my perfect death.'" The conversation slid back and forth between life and death. Trapasso had this advice for the group based on her encounters with regretful dying people: she told the group to live fully, without regrets. She "[knew] many a dying person who felt smothered by" regrets, and she advised the group, "If you don't like your job, quit. If you don't like the person you're with, leave that person. Travel now. Don't wait for later. And don't let anyone stop you from living the life you want." After a two-hour discussion, people congregated near the kitchen counter—smiling, laughing, and eating cake.[6]

At most Death Cafe meetings, the point is to have a philosophical discussion about the meaning of life and death, modeled after European salons. Talking about a taboo subject reduces fear and anxiety and enhances a sense of control, agency, and resilience. According to journalist Paula Span, Death Cafes are "casual forums for people who want to bat around philosophical thoughts. What is death like? Why do we fear it? How do our views of death inform the way we live?" She interviewed people who attended monthly meetings at a Manhattan coffee shop. For Lorraine Tosiello, it was the process of dying that puzzled her. "I'm more interested, philosophically, in what is death? What is that transition?" Grief counselor Audrey Pellicano said, "Death and grief are topics avoided at all costs in our society. If we talk about them, maybe we won't fear them as much." Span described the meetings as "part dorm room chat session, part group therapy." They are "styled as intellectual salons, but in practice they tend to wind up being something slightly different—call it café society in the age of the meetup. Each is led by a volunteer facilitator, often someone who has a professional tie to the topic. . . . The participants include people of all ages, working and retired, who are drawn by Facebook announcements, storefront fliers, local calendar listings or word of mouth. Women usually outnumber men."[7]

"In Europe, there's a tradition of meeting in informal ways to discuss ideas—the *café philosophique*, the *café scientifique*," said Jon Underwood, 40, a Web designer in London who said he held the first Death Cafe in his basement in 2011 and has propagated the concept through a Web site he maintains. Mr. Underwood adapted the idea from a Swiss sociologist, Bernard Crettaz, who had organized "*café mortels*" to try to foster more open discussions of death. "There's a growing recognition that the way we've outsourced death to the medical profession and to funeral directors hasn't done us any favors," Mr. Underwood said. He envisioned Death Cafe as "a space where people can discuss death and find meaning and reflect on what's important and ask profound questions."

In practice, people's motives for attending vary, as does the depth of the conversation. Dr. Tosiello, who said she had never lost a close family member, was there for intellectual enjoyment. Others went to ponder the questions and feel-ings that the death of a loved one had raised. . . . Doctors and scholars who study attitudes toward death say that for most people, such conversations are healthy; talking about death can ease people's fears and the notion that death is taboo. . . . The Death Cafe movement has a few ground rules. Meetings are confidential and not for profit. People must respect one another's disparate beliefs and avoid proselytizing. And tea and cake play an important role. "There's a superstition that if you talk about death, you invite it closer," said Mr. Underwood. . . ." But the consumption of food is a life-sustaining process. Cake normalizes things."[8]

Cultural Differences at the Table

Cultural differences can give rise to table conflicts. Elinor Ochs and Meray Shohet describe how Chinese, Samoans, Matsingenka (of the Peruvian Ama-zon), Swedes, Americans, and Italians have different rules about who eats together at which tables, who prepares and serves meals, how much children are expected to eat, who is supposed to speak, and how much narration, interrogation, and criticism are permitted. In China, older-generation fam-ily members eat first, and at formal dinners with guests, children may be excluded until the adults are finished, or they may be seated at a separate table. In Samoa, older children help young untitled adults prepare and serve meals. "During important meals, older, titled adults generally eat the main meal before untitled adults and children, although they may bring a very young child next to them to share their food. During more intimate family mealtimes, adults and children may eat at the same time. A similar pattern holds for the egalitarian Matsingenka . . . where men eat before women and children when several family units assemble, but in smaller nuclear family meals, the entire family eats at the same time."[9]

Ochs and Shohet cite a study comparing American and Italian dinnertime socialization. American parents encouraged children to finish their meal because it was "nutritious and part of a social contract, which [yielded] a reward, namely, dessert." This "emphasis on food as nutrition and eating as a social and moral obligation led to protracted food negotiations and tensions at the dinner table. . . . Children's compliance with eating their meal domi-nated mealtime interaction. Such here-and-now topical focus may preclude children from participating in mealtime discussions that would expose them to family and community frameworks for interpreting past and future events." By contrast, Italian parents emphasized food as pleasure and did not expect children to eat everything on their plates. Both adults and children "used a richer grammar of positive affect to praise both the food and the person who prepared or purchased it. . . . Parents at the Italian family dinners would also recount their own positive childhood memories of particular dishes on the dinner table. In this manner, food items were not only imbued with positive sentiments but also served to link family members across generations, and in some cases to bring family members no longer alive into family members' consciousness."[10]

In all social groups, food was a symbol of care but also a weapon or threat: children refused others' attempts to get them to eat, others rejected children's demands for specific foods, and family members formed alliances around food preferences. Eating disorders reflected conflicts about care and control. Sometimes all participants were silent during the meal, as among the Matsingenka. In some communities, children were expected to remain silent while adults conversed. During New England family mealtimes, parents dominated the conversation; children spoke only one-third of the time. During urban Swedish family dinners, "parents dominated conversation, with mothers providing more than half of all comments." In societies that expected children to serve, be silent, or eat separately, "minimal or no communication may be directed to them, but they may nonetheless acquire critical sociocultural knowledge and skills through observing and overhearing the communication of others."[11]

In most cultures, talk at family meals reinforces what is "right and wrong about both the family and outsiders." "Morality is socialized through grammatical markings of deference and authority, directives, assessments, justifications, excuses, apologies, prayers, storytelling, and other forms of communicative exchange in which children participate . . . For many social groups, family mealtimes are cultural sites for recounting narratives that convey moral messages. That is, exchanging accounts of personal or collective significance is often a central facet of the meal, as important as the food consumed. While in some cases, one family member dominates as narrator, in other cases, the narratives and moral points they highlight are collaboratively produced by family members, including children." In the United States, talking about one's day at dinner was motivated not only by a desire to update others, but also to solicit sympathies for one's moral stance. "Family members frequently positioned themselves as morally superior to others (the 'looking good' principle)" but often found that it was difficult to look good when family members knew about skeletons in their closet. "Indeed, U.S. children often have difficulty garnering and maintaining their moral credibility when parents and siblings begin to probe their role in a narrated episode. Mealtimes in many U.S. and other households turn out to be cultural sites for surveillance not only of children's here-and-now comportment at the table, but also of their past and projected activities narrated during mealtimes. As such, some children come to regard dinnertime as a provocative, even unpleasant moment when they are subjected to interrogation and criticism. In Italian family dinnertimes, in contrast, parents almost always side with their children or position them as justified in their actions."[12]

In the United States, cultural conflicts emerged from the different food traditions of immigrant groups, as illustrated in this comparison of the Irish, Eastern European Jews, and Italians.

> Emigration from Ireland to the United States began during the famine of the 1840s and continued through the 1920s. Given the economic and religious divides in Ireland between Protestant landowners and the Catholic majority, emigrants from the famine years did not bring a food culture to the United States. They lacked a positive memory of people who ate well whom they wanted to emulate, and whose foods would represent the markers of mobility as they fashioned families and communities. They had no reason to remember Ireland by way of food. . . . The preparation of food was a chore that [Irish American women] had to get through, for employers or their own families. Cooking had little connection to self-esteem or to the esteem given them by husbands and children. Few of the Irish American memoirs, autobiographies, or other texts that described first-hand accounts of growing up in Irish-American families included the details of meals as shaping family life. Nor in those remembered fragments did grown daughters and sons of immigrant Irish parents compliment their mothers on the foods they prepared or the commensality of the family table. America-born women of Irish families rarely recalled being taught to cook by their mother, nor did they describe groups of women bonding with each other to prepare community meals.
>
> Eastern European Jews began their immigration to the United States in the 1870s. Food, however scarce, was central to their identity. The preparation and consumption of food informed Judaism and Jewish ritual practice, shaping what foods could be eaten and how. . . . Home and community functioned as overlapping spaces. . . . The vast bulk of east European Jewish narratives, regardless of the writer's sex, class, geography, and ideology, described food in exquisite detail, their words catching tastes, smells, and sights. . . . Better-off Jews bore the responsibility of sharing something fine from their Sabbath and holiday tables with the hungry. . . . Once in America, some Jews challenged and expanded dietary strictures, but they continued food rituals and the tradition of making sure that children got the best and most food.
>
> Most of Italian migration occurred between 1880 and 1920. Migrants brought with them distinctive local cooking traditions, and once they had the means to do

so, they mimicked the foodways of the rich in their home towns. Italian American memoirs, community histories, and fiction all emphasize the family meal as a common social experience. . . . Italian American women resisted attempts by American ameliorative associations to modify their Italian cooking habits and Italian American children expressed little interest in eating non-Italian food, . . . While there was a generational chasm between parents' ideas of obedience and children's desire for freedom and independence, there was generational harmony when it came to food. For many, home cooking represented the most—and often only—element in the cultural repertoire which kept them Italian.[13]

Teacher Barbara Scheifler compared her family's table practices with those of Don, her Filipino American partner of thirty-five years. Her German American father worked from eight to five, and her German French American mother was a full time homemaker. Barbara was the second oldest of four sisters. They always had dinner together, and everyone talked at the same time. Don experienced culture shock the first time he had dinner with her family. One sister chided him for not listening to her, and he replied, "I can't listen to anybody because you are all taking at the same time."

My oldest sister went into the convent when my youngest sister was three. So most of the time it was four kids at the table with Mom and Dad. Dad did not say much. Mom died when she was fifty-three so Dad had to acquire "pleasant dinner conversation" skills. He couldn't just sit there passively or tune out. When there were just two sisters left at home, it was rather a quiet time at the table, and the dinners would not last long. Mom was the conversational model because of how she was raised. Dad was raised in a Germanic household where his father did not say anything either. Dad was actually chattier than grandpa. Family meals were equally important for my dad as for my mom. He was out of the house all day and wanted some quiet time. She was home with the little ones and wanted some adult conversation.

Don is Filipino and the oldest of ten. In our house, food was dished up in the kitchen and you got what you got. Everybody got the same amount and that was all that there was. In Don's family, they cooked huge amounts of everything and put it in the center of the table. But you didn't talk, because if you did, you lost food because you couldn't get more until you ate what was on your plate. Everyone guarded their plates and did not speak.

So when Don and I first had dinner together, he would sit there and read the paper, and I said, "Aren't we going to talk," and he said, "What's there to talk about?" I said (laughing), "There are a million things, pick something." Then he would say, "We weren't raised that way." There was always a little kid they had to focus on and to feed. He eats fast too. It is still a work in progress. He sometimes wants to bring a newspaper to dinner after thirty-five years together. He wants to eat quietly and read and then talk afterwards. The way I was raised, table time is people time; with him table time is quiet time to read.

When he's finished eating, then he can share. I bring an agenda to the table. "I want to talk about these three things." To this day, if I say "agenda," he rolls his eyes, and he will do it, but he never initiates it. When we go to his relatives' houses, he does not bring a newspaper. He was born and raised here. When we went to the Philippines, we saw some of his first cousins that he had never met, but of course we were guests there so it is hard to know how they act without guests. Now that we are both retired, there often is not that much to share at meals, so not every meal has to be a big share.[14]

Hospitality and etiquette differences can get new relationships off to a rocky start. Here is a woman's story about the first meeting between her Czech maternal grandmother and her Argentinian paternal grandmother.

The Czech woman was not aware that in Argentina it is the custom among some to refuse the first three offers of food. The hostess may or may not offer a fourth time; this gives her the chance to be hospitable even if she does not have any food to offer, and it provides the guest an opportunity to decline the first offer as a gesture of modesty. The Argentine woman did not know that many Czechs observe a different etiquette in which food is offered only once; people are not required to accept food, but when they do, they are expected to eat everything given to them. According to the story, the Czech grandmother offered some beautiful pastries to the Argentine grandmother, who, of course, refused. To her surprise, the pastries were whisked away to the kitchen not to be offered a second time, much less a third or fourth. The Czech hostess thought that her Argentine guest was either not hungry or did not find the pastries appealing; otherwise she would have accepted some. At the same time, the Argentine woman was greatly distressed by the Czech's apparent rudeness. Because both parties felt the other lacked proper manners, the relationship between the inlaws was in jeopardy for a short while.[15]

In some cultures, hospitality dictates a full meal, while in others, drinks and snacks suffice. Here is how a Bengali American woman experienced this difference. "An American couple, a friend of my husband, invited us to a party. I thought we would have a full dinner, like our style of hospitality. I found quite a big crowd and they offered us some drinks, crackers, vegetables with dip and some cheese. That's it! My husband after coming home at 1 o'clock in the morning had fish and rice and then went to bed cursing Americans for the lack of hospitality."[16]

Venturing into new cultural table traditions can be both frightening and enlightening. When Jade Snow Wong cooked a Chinese dinner for an interracial group of schoolmates, "she found that the girls were perpetually curious about her Chinese background and Chinese ideologies, and for the first time she began to formulate in her mind the constructive and delightful aspects of the Chinese culture to present to non-Chinese." When she prepared a dinner for a group of world-famous musicians staying with her employer, "she soon lost her shyness in the presence of celebrities and acted naturally. There was no talk about music, only about Chinese food. And Jade Snow ceased thinking of famous people as 'those' in a world apart. She had a glimpse of the truth, that the great people of any race are unpretentious, genuinely honest, and nonpatronizing in their interest in other human beings."[17]

Dispute Mediation Tables

At some tables, people get together for the expressed purpose of mediating conflict. In the legal process of dispute mediation, parties in a conflict are "brought to the table" and a professional mediator works with them to facilitate a resolution. In my interview with mediator Malcolm Sher, he described how he used food in his practice to break the ice, provide something familiar, and show respect to the cultural backgrounds of the disputing parties. Here is how he put his ideas into practice.[18]

Getting People Together and Breaking the Ice

After litigating for forty-one years, I transitioned to full-time mediation about five years ago. It occurred to me from what I had read and from my own upbringing that if you can get people to talk to one another in a familiar setting—with food, refreshment, or drink—it is a way of getting them focused. The mediation process starts when the lawyers call you up, or you talk with the clients on the phone. I ask folks whether they would be willing to spend five or ten minutes together in an informal meet-and-greet before we begin our sessions. For lawsuits that are already in the court system, the parties never see one another again because they're represented by lawyers. They may meet at a deposition, but their lawyers try to keep them apart. In this country the idea is that lawyers should take control of the entire process, and God forbid the clients should actually have any interaction. I personally believe that is not the right way of approaching it. So when we come into a meditative session, I like the disputants to meet one another. I started by bringing something very simple like a sandwich or a salad or cookies or a cake. One has to be flexible and improvisational. When people arrive, I watch body language and try to gauge whether or not I should say, "Go and get cake in that room, all together," or "I'll cut the cake in half and put half in each room." Sometimes it is spur of the moment thinking about what you need to do to make it work. You go in there with bated breath.

Showing Cultural Respect at the Table

As my practice progressed, I found that I was being contacted by lawyers whose clients were from diverse ethnic, cultural, religious backgrounds. Perhaps because I was born in Zimbabwe and schooled in England and practiced law there, I was being contacted by lawyers with clients who were from many of the British Commonwealth countries. I formed this niche of a mediation practice where easily 70-plus percent of the cases that I handled involved folks from different cultural and ethnic backgrounds. It made sense to provide food that was ethnically and culturally appropriate. And so I started studying up and reading.

When lawyers called me up, I'd ask about their clients' background and whether their clients had met in the last few months during the course of this litigation. Most of the time they said no. Then I asked whether their clients were first- or second-generation Americans, and often they wouldn't know, so I gave them some homework to do. "I want you to find out as much about who your client is, not just what this case is about. We can all lawyer the case. We can get the facts. We can look up the law. We can hopefully put the two together and it fits." But so many lawyers didn't know who their clients were; what made them tick; what about the fact that they were culturally, ethnically different was going to impact the way they negotiate.

My first case mediating Sikhs was an interfamily inheritance dispute that was very, very volatile. I asked the lawyers to find out whether our clients had a traditional Sikh background because I wanted to provide food. He called me back and said, "My clients are very traditional and they're vegan." I went on the internet and discovered what food you can and cannot serve, and I got the right food. When they showed up, we chatted for a while, and then I said, "You know, I have some light fare, some food here." One of the people said, "Oh, that's very interesting; we didn't think you did that." And I said, "Well, I think it's a good way of helping break the ice. And I'm hoping that if I bring the food in, we can spend some time continuing our discussions around the table, or if you prefer, I can put the food over there or in a different room, but I'm going to ask you all to go in there and help yourselves and then bring it back here." And that's what they did.

In another case, one of the people was from India and the other was from Pakistan, so we had Hindus and Muslims. I knew from the beginning nothing with ham and pork, and if you are going to serve meat, it's got to be halal. I also knew that the folks from India are not going to eat beef. So I got vegetarian and fruit and dolmas with rice and hummus with pita bread, and that went over very well. The lawyer came up to me afterwards and said, "You know, having food here was a very good idea. It showed my clients that you had taken the time, the energy, and spent the money to go and get the right food to bring here, and above all, it showed them that you had respect for their religious, ethnic, and cultural background." That was the incident and the discussion that really sold me on the idea that I've got to keep doing this and I've done it now for years. I never charge the clients for food. I just bring it.

Making the Disputants Comfortable at the Table

The whole idea is to make the process as easy and comfortable for those whose interests you're serving. My interests are in serving the disputants. They hire me to try and help them resolve their differences. Although I am the mediator, it's not about me because I don't own the problem. They own the problem, and they'll either resolve it if they want to or they won't if they don't. My job is to provide as much value to the process as I can such that the disputants feel comfort; they feel that they are in a safe place; they feel that their needs are being taken care of. And from the standpoint of serving the lawyers, it gives the lawyers a boost in the eyes of their clients if they choose a mediator who is sensitive to these kinds of needs.

In order to negotiate, think clearly, and make decisions that make sense, people need to be properly nourished and hydrated. It's that simple from a physiological standpoint. If you've got folks who have traveled many miles for the mediation, they probably got up at six in the morning. They may have had time for a quick cup of coffee, but probably not for a halfway decent breakfast. By the same token, if you are going through lunch and into the afternoon and maybe into the evening—and I've had mediations that go until ten or eleven at night—there comes a time when physiologically people's bodies begin to just shut down and it's hard to concentrate. It's hard to spend time with others in a setting that is after all litigious and divisive and expect everyone to remain cool and calm and willing to keep talking if their stomachs are rumbling and if they've got a headache because they haven't eaten in four or five hours. I think it's very important to stop, take some time out, and have food.

Tables in Individualistic and Collectivist Societies

The Anglo-American system of negotiation is very individualistic. We come from a society which is all about me and what I need and what I want and what's best for me in the outcome of this dispute. Many collectivist societies see it as part of hospitality to carry out negotiation and deal making around food. You are expected to serve food, and you might be frowned upon if you don't. It doesn't have to be elaborate, although high-level people in some countries will expect and get a more elaborate meal setting.

My view is meet their expectations but don't patronize them by overdoing it. They're not there to see how smart or wealthy I am or whether I can beat the next person in providing the best meal. It's about serving their needs and being sensitive to their cultures and paying deference to status without making it too obvious. When they see that you've brought something for them to eat, *your* status goes up in their eyes. They're much more willing to listen to you. As mediators, we attempt to gently encourage and persuade and to ask difficult "what if" and "have you considered" types of questions. That is much more likely to be heard if you ask in a way that is neither demanding nor rude. If you've sat them down and if you've given them something to eat, it just makes all the difference in the world.

I had a mediation where the plaintiff was an elderly woman from Iran and the defendant was an American whose family had been from Iran, but he was very Americanized. When I talked with the woman's lawyer, I found out that she was in her early seventies and a baker. I went to a bakery, and I bought food that was ethnically appropriate and showed that I had taken the time and effort to go get this stuff. She came up to me afterwards and said, "I want to tell you how pleased I am that you fed us, because in my country, it's the way of showing respect." She asked where I came from and I told her, and then she asked what religion I was and I said, "Well, actually I am traditionally Jewish." And bearing in mind the cultures, I didn't know what I was going to get as a response. And she said, "Well, that explains it."

Using Food to Level the Playing Field

I mediated a case involving a dispute between partners in a Thai restaurant. I didn't know how I was going to match these people's food, so I contacted a friend who lives in Bangkok. He said just keep it simple because they like fairly spicy food and unless you can prepare it, keep it simple. I obtained egg rolls and finger food so that there wasn't going to be a lot of complex sauces that I could be criticized for screwing up. We started the mediation at the restaurant. I had gone there in the early morning because I wanted to take a look at the premises, which is what I usually do if real property is involved. Then I said, "When we go back to my office, I will have a very light lunch." And one of them said, "Well, should we bring something from the restaurant?" My initial reaction was, "That would probably be better," and then I thought, "Oh, no. Let's not do that" because these folks are in a dispute and

I don't want either side to have any sort of advantage, so I said, "No, I will come back to your restaurant one of these days, but today, let me do it." I thought that was a way of leveling the playing field a bit more.

Customize the Table and Improvise in the Kitchen

In another case, the folks were from Europe and it was winter time. In California we still get a lot of fruit, but it's hard and expensive to get fruit in England and France during the winter, and I thought well, what can I get them that isn't ethnic but is something that they might not have had in a while, something a little different? So I served a large fruit salad, and it went over very well. It is important to take the time to think about it, as opposed to a knee-jerk reaction or serving the same sort of stuff every time. Try and customize it.

I did one mediation where I showed up carrying my briefcase and a cooler bag of food. I set my stuff out in the kitchen and one of the lawyers stood there looking, and I don't know whether he thought I was nuts or what, but I said, "I told you I would bring food and here it is." When the clients saw this and I said that I had become somewhat of a carpetbagger, they laughed and it was a conversation starter. I mean, how many mediators do you know are going to show up with food? In this case the lawyer had a small space, just two lawyers' offices and a little file room-cum-kitchen. I set out the food on the kitchen table, and it worked wonders. It just worked perfectly. They loved it. It was part of improvising. There was no big splendid conference room with lots of nice artwork and carpets and secretaries running here and there. It was this guy's kitchen in his office with a Formica kitchen table.

Food Memories Might Help

If the dispute arises out of a partnership or transaction that went wrong, I step back and say to myself, at one time these folks made a deal with one another. They started a business or negotiated a contract for the sale of goods together. They were willing to be in the same room, make a deal, and sign it, even if it was on the back of a napkin, which is often the way deals are made in non-Anglo-American cultures. What we're here to do now is to unravel that deal or dissolve that relationship. It's a bit like a divorce. They got along well enough at one time to get married economically, and now the question is, are they going to be able to undo it in a way that they're both going to have a certain amount of regret that it's over, but they are going to go away feeling comfortable about how that relationship was dissolved, and that *they* were able to do it without too much animosity? And maybe a lawsuit was necessary to start the process going or make everyone sit up and take notice because that's what often happens and that is purely strategic. You can ask, "How are we going to dissolve this relationship that's not working for you anymore?" In some cultures, when they made that deal it was in a restaurant or in an office where they brought food in. In Japan, they would go to a restaurant and maybe be there for hours where deals were made. And you couldn't do it without the benefit of a meal together. And now, we need to have that same get-together with food, but the purpose is different: to unravel and dissolve as opposed to create. And what I tell them is, "You are going to create a new deal today. The deal that you are going to create is going to be different from the one you had before, and it's going to be a deal that allows you to separate in such a way that the deal is sustainable."

Passing Food Creates a Connection

It's almost palpable sometimes in mediation; you can see their anxiety level goes down if they've got something in their hands and they can talk and eat and see the other person is right there doing the same thing. There is still the "we" and "they" in the context of the dispute, but they are doing something that is common, that is mutual. I have seen situations where disputants sitting across the table from each other will say, "Would you mind passing the food?" Or they will get up and try and reach over and the other person who is on the opposite side of this dispute will say, "Here, let me." But for having the food there, that little interaction wouldn't have occurred. There'd have been no reason for it. They'd have both been sitting in their places, and their lawyers would be talking, or they'd be talking or shaking their heads or staring at one another. But the fact that there was food there, and one wanted, and the other got up and helped, that little interaction can be enormous in terms of looking for and finding common ground and common purpose, if just for a second. Sometimes I manipulate it that way. It's part of the tools that you have in your box.

If there isn't something that is common, people fidget. I've been at a mediation where someone will keep tapping, or they'll shift, and the anxiety level is very high. But if there's food—and there is not too much sugar—it lowers the anxiety level. The worst thing one can do is serve junk or sugary food. I never serve sugared sodas at my mediations. I have bottled water or tea. I also have coffee, and it's mostly the lawyers who drink it—the clients know better.

Food Helps Clients Own the Process

Clients accord you a certain status as the mediator. They've asked you to help resolve their case. But you shouldn't be presumptuous. A lot of mediators parachute into the room on the day of the mediation and think they are there to settle the case. "I am the mediator, I own the process, we are going to do it this way because this is the right way and the traditional way to do it, and I am going to tell you how we are going to conduct this mediation." Sometimes it works wonders. But in the kinds of cases I mediate, they do not want retired judges in black robes who come in with a very directive approach. One of the worst things that a mediator can do is to believe that you're better than everybody else. I never say I am here to settle your case for you because it shuts people down, and you get a really lousy reputation. As a mediator, I can be as evaluative as folks want me to be—give my impression or prediction on how a case is going to come out. But I try not to be presumptuous, and a lot of people are very glad that I bring food to level the field.

Sharing Food Is Not a Waste of Time

I have never had a client say that using food was a waste of time. But lawyers have. Some of them are afraid of being criticized by their clients for wasting too much time at a mediation that went longer than it should have because the mediator insisted on serving food. One lawyer said to me, "You shouldn't have done that because it slowed everything down." I asked, "Is that your feeling, or is it something that came from your client?" He said, "Well, it's my view." I thought okay, that's legitimate. I said, "Do you know whether your client felt the same way?" He said, "I don't care. It's my view. We could have gone much quicker." If I recall right, that case did not resolve, but it didn't have anything to do with the fact that there was food. Those folks were not going to resolve their differences anyway. And that happens. So the lawyer was frustrated. The mediator is often the scapegoat. I don't have a problem with that.

Deep Divides at the Table

Tables are places where deep divisions between people can be discussed, rather than swept under the rug. Students at Mount Holyoke College created just such a space after the September 11 attacks, as described in a phone call to the Kitchen Sisters. "Hello, my name is David LaChance at Mount Holyoke College. Here at the college we have a kosher halal dining hall, which means that all of the food served there can be eaten by observant Jews and observant Muslims. It brings together these two groups on our campus to literally break bread together. The dining hall was opened here on September 13, 2001, at the request of students. It was their idea to have such a place. It is a powerful reminder of the connections between these two very ancient faiths."[19]

A table is a constructive place to deal with destructive situations, not only internationally but also within oneself, as Kim Severson recognized about her alcoholism. In hindsight, she said she should have recognized that there was a problem when alcohol became more important than food, something that she loved and that gave her confidence and solace. She believed that "where there was good food, there were usually good people. Making food for other people was something [she] was good at, [and] it gave [her] a sense of peace and belonging." She felt that when she made food, she "made a tribe." Alcohol was destroying all of that.[20]

Even such seemingly intractable problems as the Israeli-Palestinian conflict can be put on the table by citizens who want to promote dialogue. Slim Peace is a nonprofit organization that brings Israeli and Palestinian women together for weight-loss support. Yael Luttwak founded this organization during the second Palestinian uprising and made a documentary about the group. When she visited American Jewish communities to talk about her work, they told her they had problems in their own communities with anti-Muslim and anti-Israeli sentiment, and she brought the Slim Peace model to the United States. Ten women—five Muslims and five Jews—met weekly at a Boston-area high school for lessons and activities around healthy eating and self-esteem. They took turns bringing dinner and said they wanted to promote dialogue. Mrs. Salim wore a long skirt and covered her hair in public. "When people see me they think I'm superreligious, but I have my struggles," she said. "I feel I'm put on this pedestal, and it's hard to live up to that." Mrs. Bailit shared that she had never spent any time with Muslims before this group and that she felt like her "whole life" was Jewish. She was invested in her synagogue and sent her children to a Jewish school. But she wanted to experience diversity. Ms. Wekstein said that a Christian friend of hers thought that she should be afraid to attend these get-togethers, especially if the husbands came. Anne Myers, a Harvard divinity student who had converted to Islam, lamented, "Yet another stereotype of Muslim men being violent. I hear it so many times, but it does not hurt any less." The group "discussed the popular assumption that Muslims and Jews are incapable of getting along." Ms. Myers thought it was insulting and incorrect. The women agreed to meet for monthly dinners at their homes. "A recent meeting closed with each woman choosing one word to express how they were feeling. Words like 'moved,' 'joy' and 'grateful' filled the quiet room. 'Sameach,' announced Ms. Yakubu-Owolewa, her face lit by a wide smile. 'It means "happy" in Hebrew.'"[21]

In another effort to deal with difficult divides at the table, the Potluck Diplomacy website highlighted culinary diplomacy initiatives to connect people "around the world and around the corner." It solicited stories of how food has helped people reach across boundaries of culture, ethnicity, class, and politics. Its philosophy was that everyone brought something to the table, and that torn communities could be repaired through common meals. One story from Afghanistan focused on "salt diplomacy." For Afghans, the expression "I have had water and salt in your home" means "we've eaten together—we are intimates, bonded to one another." Mansoor, who lived in Kabul, employed some salt diplomacy when two of his relatives had a dispute about marriage. One wanted to engage a son to the daughter of another, but the girl's mother preferred another boy and refused the match. The two sides of the family broke off relations. Mansoor and his wife "hatched a plan" for food diplomacy. *Ashak* and *mantu* are dumplings filled with leeks and meat respectively, and they are highly labor intensive. "They are an all-hands on deck operation—so why not get the hands of the two families to make them together? Mansoor fell back on another pillar of Afghan culture—the taboo against saying no to an elder. Both families felt obliged to accept his invitation. And so, the women sat in a room, saying 'please pass the salt' and 'can you hand me the leeks,' while the men sat in the other discussing cordially. It worked. The two branches of the family have been on good terms since." For more serious disputes, local elders are called in to mediate. Sometimes the mediator cooks a meal and invites both sides. If they work out their differences, the next day both families, along with invited community members, return for a communal feast. Particular men cook for free and share in the eating. "When the fabric of [a community] is torn, rifts [can be] repaired through a combination of negotiations and nourishment. Dialogue, and sometimes dumplings, can offer critical and delicious ingredients to ensure harmonious relations."[22]

Another deep divide occurred when a gay rights advocate and an opponent broke bread together. Dan Savage, a columnist and originator of the "It Gets Better" antibullying campaign, invited to his home Brian S. Brown,

In 2012, a difficult conversation about gay rights took place over dinner at the Seattle home of columnist Dan Savage (*right*), whose debate with Brian Brown (*left*), president of the National Organization for Marriage, was moderated by writer Mark Oppenheimer (*center*). Credit: Stuart Isett / *New York Times*.

president of the National Organization for Marriage, an anti–gay marriage advocacy organization. Norms of hospitality played a role, just as they did for the Afghans. But interestingly, Savage concluded these norms may have been counterproductive—preventing him from being more forceful in expressing his views. Journalist Mark Oppenheimer moderated and provided an account of the "dinner table debate."

It was set in motion when Savage gave a speech to a high school journalism convention and "[attacked] the Bible as the root of much anti-gay bullying." Brown challenged Savage to a debate, and Savage offered to hold it at his dining-room table. He told Brown to bring his wife and indicated that his husband would be there. "You have to acknowledge my humanity by accepting my hospitality, and I have to acknowledge yours by extending my hospitality to you," he said. They would have dinner, followed by the debate. Oppenheimer thought that the debate was dispiriting but instructive. They agreed on nothing and failed to change each other's views. They disagreed about such things as whether Savage "had the right to insult the Bible in front of high school students" and "whether the New Testament endorsed slavery." Savage thought that religion was pointless, if not malevolent. Brown believed that the truths of Catholicism were self-evident. Oppenheimer concluded that these were incompatible views and that "the homey setting did little to raise the level of discourse." Several days later, he asked the two men and Terry Miller, Dan Savage's spouse, what they thought about the debate. Miller thought it was a waste of time. "Brian's heartless readings of the Bible, then his turns to 'natural law' when the Bible fails, don't hide his bigotry and cruelty. In the end, that's what he is. Cruel." Brown did not think the dinner-table setting had made a difference. "There's this myth that folks like me, we don't know any gay people, and if we just met them, we would change our views," he stated. "But the notion that if you have us into your house, that all the faith and reason that we have on our side, we will chuck it out and change our views—that's not the real world." Savage maintained that his notion of hospitality had actually worked against him: "Playing host put me in this position of treating Brian Brown like a guest. It was better in theory than in practice—it put me at a disadvantage during the debate, as the undertow of playing host resulted in my being more solicitous and considerate than I should've been. If I had it to do over again, I think I'd go with a hall." Oppenheimer had hoped that Brown might consider a happy family in a bourgeois home as evidence that would affect his reasoning. After all, one of Brown's former allies had "recently changed his views on same-sex marriage, in part . . . because he listened to the stories of gay parents."[23]

This story reminds us that it is unrealistic to think that one dinner conversation can change people's fundamental beliefs, in this case about religion. Both sides resorted to evidence, but they clashed over the nature and validity of biblical evidence. If the dinner's goal was to win a debate, the evening was a draw. If the goal was to have a conversation that did not demonize and went some way toward humanizing the "other," then it was a step in the right direction for civil society.

Cooking for Racial Equality

Slaves were no strangers to conflict and violence, and the social dislocations of slavery often played out at dinner tables. VertaMae Smart-Grosvenor recounted a family story about dinners at stops on the Underground Railroad, the safe houses for escaping slaves. "Sometimes they would be in the middle of their dinner when the stops got word that a slave or slaves were coming through that night. They might even have some neighbors or even members of the family there who were not cool . . . so they had to have signals to let each other know that tonight it would happen. Uncle Costen said they had a special dish they would serve called 'Harriet Tubman Ragout.'"[24]

Segregated restaurants and public facilities, along with hostility from whites, meant that blacks had to be self-sufficient when they drove through the South. The family car was their table. Karen Fields remembered her family's annual trips across the Mason-Dixon Line: "The drive to South Carolina allowed us a transition from our own country to that one. My father always saw to it that we carried huge provisions—fried chicken, potato salad, roast ham, buttered bread, unbuttered bread, big Thermos jugs filled with lemonade, and anything else we could possibly want to eat or drink. We even carried bottles filled with plain water and a special container just for ice. As far as possible, the family car was to be self-sufficient. We carried detailed maps for the same reason that we carried so much food and drink: a determination to avoid insult, or worse."[25]

When civil rights activists began organizing in the segregated South in the 1950s, they often gathered in kitchens for secret meetings, since it was illegal for whites and blacks to eat together in restaurants. The Kitchen Sisters interviewed people who knew Georgia Gilmore, who cooked in her home for civil rights supporters in Montgomery, Alabama. Activists, including Dr. Martin Luther King Jr., got to know and trust each other at her dining-room table, and she coordinated the sale of homemade pies to fund alternative transportation during the bus boycott. Gilmore had worked as a tie changer for the railroad, a midwife in the black community, and a cook in a segregated, white-owned restaurant. She raised six children on her own and fed "half the church" with her fried chicken. Friends said that she could talk at everyone's level and was a confidante of both young and old. She began to do some catering, and one of her clients was Dr. Martin Luther King Jr. She turned part of her home into a dining area. King brought guests for lunch and held meetings at Gilmore's home, some of them in secret. King needed a place where he could not only trust the people around him but also trust the food. She got up at 4:00 in the morning to cook, handwrite the day's menu for the tables, and be ready for lunch. There was often an hour-long wait to be fed. Clients sat around a dining-room table and held conversations on a daily basis. People—black and white—became friends, including Morris Dees with the Southern Poverty Law Center and lawyers from his office, doctors, professors, clerical workers, and policemen. When the place was full, people ate standing up, sometimes in the kitchen, where Gilmore took chops right out of the grease and put them on people's plates. Gilmore cooked throughout the Montgomery bus boycott, which lasted 381 days. In order to raise money for station wagons and gasoline to help boycotters get to and from work, she organized a grassroots bake-and-carry organization called the Club from Nowhere. Women baked at home and took their goods to be sold at beauty shops, groceries, cabstands, and liquor stores. Since many people were afraid to openly support the boycott, the club remained anonymous, but Gilmore knew who actually baked or bought the food. Gilmore's son described how King continued to rely on his mother's house as a meeting room and social hall: "He brought Robert Kennedy, President Johnson, Governor Wallace. All of them—black, white, presidents, plumbers, Ray Charles, Aretha Franklin—all had a chance to eat at my mother's table."[26]

Mixed-race groups of civil rights activists also met illegally at Dooky Chase, a New Orleans restaurant run by Leah Chase, where there was always a table for traveling musicians and artists. "Activists could gather at her place because the police did not want to cross Mrs. Chase." Among the artists and musicians who were regulars were Jacob Lawrence, Elizabeth Catlett, Nat "King" Cole, Count Basie, Duke Ellington, Cab Calloway, Lena Horne, Sarah Vaughan, and Ray Charles.[27]

Conflict Kitchen in Pittsburgh

Two restaurants in Pittsburgh, Pennsylvania, were designed to promote conversations about conflict. The Waffle Shop was opened in 2008 by Jon Rubin, an art professor at Carnegie Mellon University who specialized in using public places as art projects to explore human behavior. In 2010, he and artists Dawn Weleski and John Peña opened the Conflict Kitchen next door.

At the Waffle Shop, employees conducted a live-streamed talk show as customers ate waffles. Guests ranged from local politicians to ordinary diners lured onstage to talk about everything from men wearing Speedos to unrequited love. Rubin used food to "seduce people to get up onstage."[28] The content of the show was determined by the customers, for example, facilitating conversations about the ethnic diversity of Pittsburgh, reading poetry, and discussing monopoly etiquette. As Rubin saw it: "The talk show functions as a platform for people of all walks of life to come together and engage in public conversation about pretty much anything. We often provide a host, who anyone can come up and talk to, but at this point we have people from throughout the city working with us to produce their own spin-off talk shows. It's like amateur dinner theatre meets amateur TV."[29] "Rubin says the idea is that people can be seduced via their stomachs to engage with things that they are otherwise unfamiliar with, be it going up onstage at a talk show or asking questions about a completely alien—and often vilified—foreign culture. Recently at the Waffle Shop, a young black man and an 80-year-old Jewish woman engaged each other in a frank conversation about race. Another man came out to his father."[30]

Conflict Kitchen is a take-out lunch restaurant that serves cuisines from countries in conflict with the United States. Their boxes have wrappers containing interviews with people from the conflict country. The thoughts and opinions expressed in these interviews are often contradictory, reflecting a nuanced range of thought and instigating questions, conversation, and debate among customers. Conflict Kitchen seeks to engage the general public in discussions about countries, cultures, and people that they might know little about outside the "polarizing rhetoric of U.S. politics and the narrow lens of media headlines." The restaurant is also the only one in Pittsburgh that offers Iranian, Afghan, Venezuelan, and Cuban cuisines.[31]

Employees are hired in part for their ability to discuss world affairs. "Our desire is not to simplify, but to complicate the way . . . people think about another country," said Rubin. Employees are prepared to deal with customers' responses to comments on the food wrappers, such as, "Generally speaking, Iranian people have no issues with the Jewish people," or "Most Americans who I have encountered think that Iranians are ugly, aggressive, violent, terrorists, Islamists and uncivilized." Typical comments from customers include: "If you want to understand something more about a country, what better way to do it than through food?" "There's common ground in food.

No matter what kind of conflict it is, no matter which side of it you're on, everyone needs to eat." And "The stomach really clears a path."[32]

Cofounders Dawn Weleski and Jon Rubin said that they wanted to create a space for civilized discourse. As Weleski put it: "In contrast to the polarizing effect of broadcast media, we've sought to create a platform which can support a more subtle exchange of culture and politics. With food as a mediator, it becomes easier for customers to consider the everyday life of people—they become responsive in a different way and consider more nuanced perspectives. They start to consider the people and culture behind conflicts [that are conducted] at a government or military level." Rubin provided this example: "I've watched a Japanese Buddhist and a Muslim start to chat from the takeout window. They ended up in a rich exchange of experiences and perspectives on food, spirituality, rituals and symbolism. Difference doesn't require us to be damning. We're keen to encourage dialogue which doesn't blame or accuse and may be driven by curiosity rather than media-prescribed positions." Weleski has trained the staff in "conversation hosting," handling contentious topics and tricky questions through role playing. "It's not just about inviting people to talk to us but also encouraging interaction between customers," she said. "I remember one woman who had a Pennsylvanian Dutch mother and a Persian father and spoke of the cultural tension this could create. . . . Once these kinds of discussions start happening, people begin to expand their personal insights into social ones and appreciate similarity and difference in a new way."[33]

Weleski and Rubin put a lot of thought into how the sandwich wrappers could be used as conversation starters. They interviewed people who had emigrated to the United States from the focus country. They wanted statements from first-person conversations, not secondhand research, in order to obtain a variety of thoughts and opinions about what daily life in the focus country was like. No single story or identity was presented. Rubin said: "For our Iranian wrapper there are comments about tea, women's rights, Israel, perceptions of the US, and more. The section on Israel includes several quotes from Iranians who are critical of the state of Israel but not of the Jewish people. The section on women's rights presents one Iranian speaking of how women are leaders in government and industry, and another pointing out that they are still considered second-class citizens subject to unfair restrictions, and another pointing out how they have difficult dual roles in society as workers and homekeepers." Weleski noted that they provided multiple levels of engagement for the public to choose from. Just passing by and seeing the sign in Farsi added diversity to the neighborhood. People could choose "to eat the food and read the wrapper, talk with [the] staff or with other customers assembled at the take-out window." According to Weleski, "Some of the best conversations actually happen between customers without our participation. Many of our customers seek out their own information about daily life and politics in Iran and come back and tell us about it. And then, other customers come to our programming and events, which hopefully allows them a different entry point into life and culture in Iran."[34]

The project, Rubin said, is

> a real-time research centre in which we're presenting what we discover in our conversations with Iranians, or Afghans, or Venezuelans, . . . and people are coming to us at the take-out window each day presenting what they know and we're sharing that too. The take-out window often becomes an impromptu platform for discussions on culture and politics. We like to feel that the project creates a space for people to ask questions that they might feel uncomfortable or afraid of asking. We wanted to create a much more nuanced, less polarized discussion about politics, and culture, and daily life and humanize the people who live in these countries.[35]

The employees who work the window play a vital role in stimulating and responding to dialogue. "One of the things about American culture is that people talk sports publicly with strangers but they don't talk politics. So we thought about how we could create a natural environment where people would get into a political discussion in a public space with people that they might not know and share their own viewpoints and cultural background," Rubin noted. Weleski said that they ask focus country people "questions that a typical American might be afraid or embarrassed to ask because they worry they might not have the knowledge about the conflict that most people expect them to have. What [they] are trying to do is create a safe, engaging and comfortable space for a conversation to happen around these topics, and certainly through food [they] are able to do that."[36]

The choice of food is crucial to their enterprise. The Conflict Kitchen's founders wanted everyday fare that tasted good. Weleski said, "We wanted to choose a food that was sort of an everyman's food, a food that you would find on the streets of Tehran. And everyone understands a sandwich. It's something you can take with you—there's a little girl running by right now, skipping and eating her kubideh sandwich at the same time, and a lot of people have said they feel like it's a Persian hamburger." Using simple and delicious food as an entrée to understanding another culture makes sense to customers. "People have a negative image of a lot of countries based on the leadership in that country," said a grad student who stopped by with some friends. "And I think what they are doing here is promoting the idea that what's more important is the people, customs and culture and that sort of thing." "You know what, it's delicious," said a regular customer who worked nearby. "Every bite full, delightful. And it's just smashing that stereotypical myth that just because there is conflict in those countries . . . I don't let it stop me from buying good food." One man said that between his two visits to Conflict Kitchen he read up on Iranian culture and learned about its religion and literature. "We have a lot more in common with Iran than I would have guessed," he said. Ultimately, though, he says he came back because he likes the food.[37]

Food is considered a catalyst for conversation through empathy. Weleski noticed that when customers come to the window, they immediately introduce themselves by identifying their place of birth. "Often, this has sparked conversations between Iranians and non-Iranians from all over the world who happen to be living in or passing through Pittsburgh—about, initially, Persian cuisine, and then, the various cultural and political issues surrounding food."

The Conflict Kitchen in Pittsburgh serves food from countries with which the United States is in conflict. It encourages customers to learn more about these countries through their cuisines and to talk with one another and the staff about why the United States is in conflict with these countries.
Source: Conflict Kitchen.

When Conflict Kitchen searched for what Persian food to serve, its founders contacted a local professor and decided on the *kubideh* sandwich, to keep it simple and get people talking. "Food is a pathway to positive feelings and a humanization of other cultures. I believe eating and sharing new cuisine is a catalyst for the sort of conversations that can lead to deeper understanding and cross-cultural empathy," the professor said.[38]

In 2010, the Conflict Kitchen held its first international dinner conversation. A meal was held simultaneously in Pittsburgh and in Tehran, with diners sitting around long tables joined via live webcam. They shared the same menu and conversations. Weleski said that youth in both countries had a lot in common: "commiserating about their experiences of finishing university, not being able to find a job in the field that they had studied, dating, rock concerts."[39] She said that the conversation started safely, with talk of food—how Americans purchased bread from supermarkets versus how Iranians bought it fresh from the bakery every morning. It then veered into the related topic of growing your own herbs, which was common in Iran, and eventually morphed into edgier discussions about dating, politics, and the difficulty of finding a job after graduating from college. "Eating the same food provided everyone with a level ground. They began to find commonality in their experiences through the way the food smells and tastes," Weleski observed.[40]

Sohrab Kashani, who arranged the event in Tehran, reported, "The dinner lasted almost four hours. People changed seats all the time, and new people joined in to have a conversation. We had such great responses from people on both sides. Everyone here was surprised to see tables from the two countries joining one another. I could see people staring at the projected image on the wall and wondering if that was in fact live footage of a table setting in Pittsburgh!" In order to maximize spontaneity, Kashani did not tell anyone in Tehran about the project until the very last moment. "That is why conversation topics developed very organically and without any help whatsoever. . . . The intention was to open up a dialogue between the two sides of the table, and it did happen very organically in my opinion."[41]

In 2012, the Conflict Kitchen hosted its second Pittsburgh-to-Tehran dinner party, which was filmed by Al Jazeera for distribution on Arabic language channels.[42] "As the doors opened [in Pittsburgh] at noon, guests streamed in and began dishing food onto plates and sitting at one of the long tables set up to accommodate about 60 people. In Tehran, diners gathered in a similarly appointed room, before the exact same meal, and before long, bilingual diners were helping the distant groups talk to each other through microphones passed around the tables. Conversation ranged from America's obsession with Batman to Iranian views of Occupy Wall Street, and it pointed up some similarities between the Iranians and the Americans: distrust of media and government, for instance."[43]

To summarize our discussion of conflict tables, professional mediators remind us that difficult conversations are always three conversations: about facts, emotions, and identity. If we want to make progress in promoting civil conversations, we need to be prepared to operate at all three levels and to realize that problems are bound to arise in all three: Where do you get your facts about the Arab-Israeli conflict? How do you process emotions toward a rival gang member who has murdered a loved one? How can you not take it personally when a conversant thinks your sexual identity is against God's will? At conflict tables such as those in the segregated South or at Pittsburgh's Conflict Kitchen, people have come up with ingenious ways to foster difficult conversations to replace bias and prejudice with understanding and empathy. Food and tables have a leveling potential, and when we sit and eat and talk together, we can be reminded, however briefly, that it might be worth listening and connecting to someone else, even to a hostile "other."

Chapter Six

Civic Engagement and Diplomacy

Community Building

When political conflict occurs, it is easier to deal with in a civil way when people feel connected to, as opposed to alienated from, one another. Common connections are like glue, holding us together even when strong forces operate to pull us apart. Shared food experiences form powerful bonds. In the 1930s, Nelson Algren joined other American writers employed by the Illinois Writers Project, a branch of the federal Works Progress Administration. He was assigned to collect information for the national America Eats program, a set of regional guides to immigrant customs related to the universal language of food. Algren's *America Eats* covered the foodways of the Midwest and was an inspiration for the Kitchen Sisters. They wondered "what happens to a culture when it loses some essential part of itself," such as home cooking, the family table, and small farmers, all "cornerstones of our civilization" that need to be preserved. They hoped that "fifty years from now some other nationwide collaboration will come along and stare into the fire pits and soup kettles of the nation and ask some of these same questions: 'Who glues your community together through food? Who is cooking on your corner? What traditions are vanishing from your neighborhood, your family, the planet?' . . . It's the food, but more than that, it's the fellowship. This improvisational, ingenious, imaginative cooking—alive across America. Food is our universal language; it's what we have in common. When in doubt, cook."[1]

They interviewed "Lou the Glue" Marcelli, so named for hanging out in one spot, cooking for old-timers at the Dolphin Club, a San Francisco swimming and rowing organization established in 1897. Members were mostly retired males of Italian, Spanish, or Portuguese backgrounds. Some had worked as firemen, policemen, painters, chefs, or waiters. The club provided a place where they could get together to exercise, drink wine and cook, and talk about old times. Lou had been the club's "commodore" for thirty-five years. He operated out of a galley kitchen in the boathouse, the club's lodge complete with large dark-paneled rooms. A couple of times a week, he cooked for the older members. He shopped at a wholesale fish market, where everyone knew him. He said that he was not a gourmet cook, that his skills were limited to putting some pasta together. As a long-time bachelor, he cooked for survival. He distinguished between the younger families that just came to swim and row and the people who lived alone and preferred the club to an empty home. "They just want company, the camaraderie. When I cook, I always cook enough for a few more people, and there is always somebody around. They kind of smell it."[2]

A respondent to the Kitchen Sisters from Milwaukee said that potluck dinners were community glue for many lesbians. In her experience, "almost every lesbian community in the country" held regular potlucks. When she typed "lesbian potluck history" into a search engine, there were over seven thousand hits. "It's sort of like when three lesbians get together, it's a potluck."[3]

Another caller shared the story of her father, a doctor in rural Mississippi whose patients were poor and paid him with homegrown produce, which graced their noontime dinner table. They left "paper bags full of ripe corn, beans, tomatoes, turnip greens, cucumbers, green peppers, peas, and everything else imaginable piled up on the porch." Her father taught her "respect for the hard working farmer." They knew that the farmers had left the vegetables out of pride. "We never saw their faces, but Daddy knew who they were and what they did for us."[4]

The Kitchen Sisters heard a story about how campers from across the country and a wide variety of backgrounds bonded over Aunt Ethel's knishes. She fed these delicious potato-stuffed delicacies to camping neighbors who had never met a Jew. Her aunt's gregariousness and a won't-take-no-for-an-answer style encouraged strangers to become friends who met regularly at campsites for decades. Ethel kept kosher, stopping at every kosher butcher and synagogue along the way and always carrying dual sets of cookware, one for meat and one for dairy. Many of these strangers-turned-friends turned up at her funeral—northerners and southerners, blacks and whites, Jews and gentiles—"with their love for Ethel and their wonderful stories about how much fun they had together and about how much they were going to miss those knishes by the campfire."[5]

In Shenandoah, Iowa, two women cooked for all comers—Democrats and Republicans—at the Elks Club. These seventy-year-old women were known not only for their cooking and their humor but also "as the glue for many family and community functions." They prepared food for weddings and funerals, athletic banquets, and political events, sometimes for five hundred people. Anyone who walked into their kitchen could "catch up on everything. Every Thursday they just cook for [whoever] shows up."[6]

In another story the Kitchen Sisters heard, an act of kindness toward an immigrant family was reciprocated every year with cookies and poetry and became a tradition of generosity that spread to an entire community. In a small American town, the Ladies Altar Guild at an Episcopal church had helped an immigrant family from Prague buy a house and furniture. Every year, Mrs. Pouska expressed her gratitude to guild members on St. Nicholas Eve, December 5. Just after dark, she would stealthily approach their houses, bang on the door, and leave a wrapped carton with a return address of "Saint Nicholas." Inside it was a poem and a tin of Czechoslovakian moon cookies. When Mrs. Pouska died, she left each guild member the cookie recipe in her will. One guild member's son said that for twenty-five years he had told this story to his students and given each of them a cookie on St. Nicholas Day, which for him had become a day of generosity. When he attended his former students' weddings, he honored Mrs. Pouska's tradition by giving them a serving tray and her recipe for Czechoslovakian moon cookies.[7]

Holding a community together through food begins with a concerted effort to stay in touch with friends, as described here by a student I interviewed.

> We have friends that we make a point of taking time to go eat food with because it's a beautiful place to share experiences and stories, especially when we haven't seen those people in a long time. My mom is working for a different company now, and a lot of her friends are from that first company. We still get to share a lot of experiences with them even though she does not see them on a regular basis anymore. It is good for all of us to be able to connect with those people over a medium like food. I enjoy going to most of my friends' houses too. A lot of the time I see a very similar situation to my house, which I like. It's nice to experience other people's cooking sometimes. Some people have really nice houses too. I enjoy going to these massive houses because it's fun to act like a king for one day. I think it is good to experience other people's households.[8]

A librarian I interviewed pointed out that a big pot of soup works wonders in forging connections among friends, neighbors, and coworkers.

> I've had teachers come to my house for Shabbat dinner and the holidays—Hanukkah, Sukkoth, the harvest holiday. We have always invited non-Jews, and they love it. In Judaism, eating food is holy. When people are sick here at school or they have babies, I'm known for making matzo ball soup. I brought a huge pot

of it to one of my non-Jewish colleagues the other day because someone in her neighborhood had died. She wanted the recipe because she said it was so good. I said it was really easy to make, and she said, "You make it every time, so can you just give me the recipe?" So I did. Food is a comfort. I have a friend whose husband died a couple weeks ago, and when I brought her the soup last Tuesday, she said, "I've heard you talk about this soup," because I had given it to other people. We have a neighbor in between us who is elderly, and I used to make soup for him. It's just something that I do. My kids know that I do.⁹

Chef Renee O'Harran built a cooking community in a cramped space with her coworkers, and more broadly among students, faculty, alumni, parents, migrant farmworkers, and the sustainability movement.

> Before being at this school, I was in restaurants, and I just feel I am meant to be in the food-service industry. There's my craft part of it, that I cook, and I like to manage people. I like when you are really busy and just on the edge of falling off the cliff. And the relationships that you have with your coworkers—you work very closely together in a small space. And the larger community from the rest of the faculty to the students, the alumni, the parents, I mean it's just a big great relationship. I feel very lucky. We do a locavore lunch in September for the eleventh graders. They take care of migrant farm camps as a service project in the spring. We do a locavore lunch in the fall, and they just think it is fantastic. We have speakers come in, or maybe I give a little talk. I think they love making the connection of how food is connected with just everything.¹⁰

Chef Gillian Clark saw her restaurant as an inclusive community gathering place, where her daughters learned about life by watching the regulars come and go. Colorado Kitchen was a "crossover gathering place" where no one felt excluded—"black, white, Asian, young, old, tattooed cyclist, church lady, heterosexual, homosexual, Republican, Democrat." Her daughters spent so much time at the restaurant that they became part of a community, which included neighbors on the avenue, customers, and staff. It was a large extended family. The girls had "surrogate fathers in employees who [remembered] their birthdays and [drove] them to school band concerts." Regular customers gave them birthday gifts and cards. Her daughters saw customers' lives unfold. One woman grew thin and started wearing a scarf as she battled cancer, and then she finally no longer joined her husband for lunch. Another couple "that took up table five every Sunday night for hours is suddenly MIA. Then she arrives alone, swollen-eyed and awkward by herself at the counter with a book. He appears weeks later with a much younger girl sitting so close to him their knees touch. The gray is mysteriously gone from his hair. [Her daughters have] seen the pair of twenty-somethings come in every Saturday brunch exposing their tattoos with tank tops and midriff shirts. They uncharacteristically arrive on a Wednesday wearing long-sleeve oxford shirts. Her parents are in town. And he's washed his hair for the occasion."[11]

Leah Chase, who ran Dooky Chase in New Orleans, said that many of her clients lived in a nearby large-scale housing project. Friends encouraged her to move to a more upscale area, but she remained committed to staying in order to hold the neighborhood together. Drugs, unemployment, and poverty had taken their toll, but Chase recognized the dignity of the people who struggled to make ends meet. Through her restaurant, she helped keep the neighborhood going. She said, "If we would have moved off this corner, this whole community would have been gone a long time ago." After Hurricane Katrina destroyed her restaurant, Chase vowed to rebuild: "I have to come back. Who else is going to cook for them? If I don't get back in the kitchen, what message am I sending?" She reopened for business two years after the hurricane, thanks to the generous donations of friends and supporters.[12]

Communities are held together by norms of reciprocity, such as keeping track of meals with friends and neighbors and feeling an obligation to reciprocate in kind. For example, Bengali American women "express and maintain their social position in the community through food work. They are the ones who are primarily responsible for managing systems of reciprocity among households. They keep account of friends and neighbors who have invited them for dinner and the number of times they have been invited. They decide when it is time to reciprocate and to what extent—a formal dinner or tea and snacks?"[13]

How we reciprocate depends on our definition of hospitality. Josephine Beoku-Betts notes that many West African cultures prepare an excess amount of food for a meal in case someone should unexpectedly pay a visit. Even with limited economic resources, people uphold this tradition as a mark of prestige for the head of the household and the cook. Although the Gullah in the United States do not necessarily view this tradition as a symbol of prestige, some of its elements were common in many of the homes she visited. As one woman explained: "I'm always able to feed another person in my home. People [here] will automatically cook something more just in case a stranger drops in." Beoku-Betts knew that local residents were beginning to open up to her when, after several visits, she was offered food, whether or not it was mealtime.[14]

For many people, a potluck is the quintessential community meal. What you bring says a lot about you—your age, income, religion, ethnicity, race, gender, education level, and regional origin. At Pisgah, a housing compound for low-income seniors, monthly potluck dinners and a produce market were designed to build community. Alex Dorsey was the general manager of Equitableroots, a Los Angeles–based program that ran a market. Mariana Negara was the market manager who built relations with the seniors by going door to door, getting to know them. She made juice from vegetables that they had difficulty chewing and made three hundred kale quesadillas for a community festival. "Word spreads," she said. "They would say, 'Did you try those quesadillas? Those are so good.'" The market became popular. Shoppers filled their baskets with produce, chatted, tried new food samples and checked out recipes in Spanish and English. Although residents still might be tempted to buy a ninety-nine-cent sack of conventionally grown potatoes, they learned about the value of locally grown food raised without artificial pesticides, herbicides, and fertilizers. "We are building a trust, so that people will transfer their dollars [to the community-based market]," Dorsey said.[15]

Open spaces at Pisgah were planted with fruit trees, tomatoes, corn, green beans, garlic, onions, and herbs. Residents cultivated the garden boxes and left surplus produce on benches for their neighbors. Cooking classes were held the first Friday of each month in Pisgah's community room, and what they made was served at the potluck dinner. Menus were designed "to appeal to Pisgah's cultures, using the ingredients from its produce market and gardens. A recent dinner included a Korean cucumber salad, zucchini-potato soup and rice pilaf with diced vegetables and almonds. Pieces of tilapia were marinated in Asian spices, then wrapped in corn husks, tied and grilled outside." One woman who lived at Pisgah with her ninety-five-year-old father said that she enjoyed trying new foods and came to believe it was healthier to eat organic produce. Her father was grateful because the food reminded him of the dishes he enjoyed in his youth in Mexico. Usually about thirty people attended the potluck dinners, including Spanish and Korean translators. One resident commented, "The food is good, and I know the people who are there, even though there's a little language barrier." The food served as a catalyst for people to communicate despite language differences. For example, residents realized that both Mexicans and Koreans had a rice beverage, *horchata* and *sikhye*. A staff member noted that such discoveries changed the conversation and led to greater understanding. "It's such a natural fit for the racial healing work we are doing. People got talking about misunderstandings."[16]

Adolescent Civic Engagement

Adolescents are frequently characterized as sullen, self-absorbed, and rebellious—anything but community minded. They want to be accepted by peers, and adults get impatient with their need to "find themselves" (forgetting that they too went through this stage) and worry whether youth will ever be civic-minded enough to care about groups other than their peers. Ironically, political scientists who have studied adolescent civic behavior found that young people wanted to feel connected to community institutions, and when they did, they were less likely to get involved in antisocial activities or substance abuse. Constance Flanagan's analysis of longitudinal data about eighth graders found that extensive connections to others through family, religious institutions, and extracurricular activities were significantly related to political and civic involvement in young adulthood. What mattered was not so much the number of groups a young person belonged to but whether their voices were taken seriously in a group that gave them a sense of collective identity. "Young people become aware that their own goals are realized when the group's goals are achieved. In this way, youth come to see themselves as members of the public who share an interest in the common good." In working to gain the trust of group members, they came to see themselves as trustworthy. "At the same time, if other members of the organization also are accountable and contribute to the group rather than look out only for themselves, participants develop social trust or a positive view of humanity as fair, helpful, and trustworthy."[17]

> Non-formal community-based youth organizations (CBYOs) offer a particularly rich opportunity for youth to be exposed to perspectives unlike their own and to learn how to negotiate and reach a compromise. Unlike families or schools where relationships of power tend to be asymmetrical, the structure of CBYOs is more egalitarian . . . [and] . . . the consequences of disagreeing are, at least in principle, the same for everyone in the groups. To achieve collective goals, individual members have to forego some personal preferences . . . Much of relevance to politics—experiences of inclusion and exclusion; stereotypes and prejudice; membership in and identification with a group; rights and accountability; self-determination and respect for differences; status and power; trust and loyalty; and of fairness in process and justice in outcome—are themes that resonate with adolescents. It is incumbent upon those of us who focus on this period of life to be more clever in listening to what young people have to say and in hearing the political insights in their conversations.[18]

Trust is a foundational concept of civil society. It is important to appreciate how it develops among adolescents, since they are citizens in training. Flanagan argues: "In friendships and peer relationships we learn about loyalty, accountability, and the reciprocity between trust and trustworthiness. However, trust among friends is an insufficient basis for social trust. To nurture a faith in humanity, children need to interact and cooperate with people who are different from them and values of equality, tolerance, and empathy have to be high priorities in their families." People will not learn to trust others unless they are given reasons to do so—from caregivers, friends, and organizations. "The essence of trust is the belief that others are fair, that they will not take advantage of us, although they could." There is no guarantee that family, friends, or organizations will treat us fairly and not take advantage of us. But to the extent that they do, it strengthens civil society. Flanagan cautions that friendships are not necessarily a sound basis for developing social trust. If the bonds of trust between friends are reinforced by stereotyping out-groups as less trustworthy, then social trust is eroded. When friendships are not based on out-group exclusion, they promote the virtues of loyalty, reliability, empathy, a cooperative spirit, honesty, and authenticity. "If virtues learned in friendships become integral to identity, then, compared to loners or social isolates, youth who have had close relationships with friends should be better prepared to extend the boundaries of those they trust to a larger segment of their community."[19]

Like friendships, associations are of limited civic value if their strong internal bonds of trust are maintained by excluding newcomers or outsiders. Flanagan says that it is typically not until late adolescence that teens learn to integrate and resolve different points of view. Before then, exposure to such differences has been limited by age-grading, residential segregation, and tracking practices, resulting in homogeneous everyday encounters. In organizations where teens have face-to-face interactions with members of stereotyped groups, it may increase social trust because they learn, as one teen in her study put it, that "they aren't so bad." Another young person reflected, "You should help people because someday you may need the help." These youth are developing an understanding of the "social contract," that citizenship involves sharing the burdens and responsibilities as well as the benefits and rights of living in a political community. They are also learning to empathize. Studies indicate that activists in the civil rights and antiwar movements of the 1950s and 1960s and those who sheltered Holocaust survivors during World War II were raised in families that valued compassion, empathy, and social responsibility. "Not surprisingly, intergroup contact and friendships with members of different social classes was also part of the socialization experience of citizens who chose to harbor holocaust survivors."[20]

Schools also play an important role in the civic development of youth, who benefit when teachers practice a democratic ethic in the classroom—encouraging students to discuss controversial issues and to tolerate dissenting opinions, enforcing fair standards, and challenging all students, not just the high achievers. A study of students from various ethnic backgrounds (African American, Arab American, European American, and Latino American) found that regardless of age, gender, or ethnic background, "youth were more likely to believe that America was a just society and to commit to democratic goals if they felt a sense of community connectedness, especially if they felt that their teachers practiced a democratic ethic at school." The key element was the perception that people who wielded authority over their lives were fair and responsive to them, and that fellow citizens in their community were committed to a common good. When these conditions were present, young people believed that America was fundamentally a fair society worthy of their allegiance to the principles that make democracy work. Young people's confidence in the system occurred through the accumulated classroom experiences of fair (due) process and responsive interaction with adult authorities.

> An open classroom climate in which discussion of controversial issues can take place . . . [is] associated with the development of democratic skills such as perspective taking, tolerance, and trust . . . [and with] knowledge about international affairs, ability to think critically about civic issues, tolerance of dissenting opinions, and commitment to voting in the future when they are of age. . . . [When teachers create a] civil climate for learning, . . . they convey messages about social inclusion (i.e., who belongs, whose opinions count) and about tolerance and respect for differences of opinions, core principles of democracy in the United States. . . . When teachers set standards of civility, respect, and fair and equal treatment, they create a democratic climate for learning. Teachers' behaviors and relationships with their students are key in creating a welcoming climate for learning. Perceptions of teachers as caring, fair, and respectful are positively correlated with motivation, engagement, and achievement, and negatively correlated with dropping out of school. Not surprisingly, students' sense of belonging at school is positively associated with their engagement and motivation to learn. . . .
>
> Students' perceptions that teachers apply fair standards, challenging all students, rather than privileging only the high achievers, actually boosts students' beliefs that they are capable of learning. In short, students' sense of efficacy or agency as learners is highly related to their perceptions of how their teachers treat them and fellow students. [An] open classroom is not a free for all. The rules of social interaction include mutual respect, offering one's own perspective and listening with an open mind to others' perspectives. Such ground rules also reflect an egalitarian and open-minded view about learning and authority—i.e., the authority (teacher) is not "all knowing" but, rather, continues to learn with his or her students. . . . The best way to learn is to be public and open, trusting fellow learners enough to leave oneself vulnerable to their judgments.[21]

Flanagan shares the view of scholars discussed earlier that authoritative teaching and parenting are preferable to both a no-rules free-for-all and an authoritarian refusal to discuss the rules. Children need practice and guidance from knowledgeable and listening adults in developing their political voices.

A wide range of political competencies are nourished in family environments where adolescents are encouraged to think for themselves. Authoritative parenting practices that encourage a give-and-take of opinions between generations are associated with the following outcomes in adolescents: more political knowledge, a greater personal commitment to civic responsibility, social tolerance and support of First Amendment rights, autonomy in the choice of party affiliation, and the ability to see multiple sides of a political issue and to integrate rather than compartmentalize competing points of view. Taken together, these studies suggest that the democratic dimensions of authoritative parenting, that is, respecting children's ideas and accommodating family practices in response to their suggestions, may make children feel both more efficacious personally and more attentive to the rights and perspectives of others.[22]

There are cultural differences in parental views about children's autonomy. Collectivist families put more weight on tradition and obligation than do individualist families, which promote autonomy and independence. One study of these differences concludes that either model can provide adolescents with a path to civic identity.

Asian and Latin American adolescents possessed stronger values and greater expectations regarding their duty to assist, respect, and support their families than their peers with European backgrounds. These differences tended to be large and were consistent across youths' generation, gender, family composition, and socioeconomic background. Whereas an emphasis on family obligations tended to be associated with more positive family and peer relationships and academic motivation, adolescents who indicated the strongest endorsement of their obligations tended to receive school grades just as low or even lower than those with the weakest endorsement. There was no evidence, however, that the ethnic variations in attitudes produced meaningful group differences in the adolescents' development. These findings suggest that even within a society that emphasizes adolescent autonomy and independence, youths from families with collectivist traditions retain their parents' familistic values and that these values do not have a negative impact upon their development.[23]

Martín Sánchez-Jankowski argues that there are cultural differences in types of civic engagement, depending on whether the history of one's ethnic or racial group was one of exclusion, inclusion, or privilege. Civic subcultures have resulted from group experiences with prejudice and with institutions that socialized them into American citizenship.

> For those groups that are in the *exclusion* category . . . civic engagement is centered on the group's interests. The vast majority of this group will believe that their own interest must be surrendered to that of the group because their own personal interest can only be realized if the group's interests are gained. Therefore, helping members of one's ethnic group is considered the civic thing to do. . . .
>
> Civic knowledge for the individuals in the *inclusion* group is provided by the official institutions and reinforced by all of the formal ones. The history of being "excluded" and then gaining inclusion has influenced the individuals of these groups to want to give something back to the society that has been so generous. . . . Civic engagement is understood as not only a debt of gratitude, but also as an opportunity to forget their group's ugly history with discrimination.
>
> Finally, for the groups that have been *privileged* in the system, knowledge about civic engagement comes directly from the formal institutions of the school, family, media, and government. . . . More than the other two groups, knowledge about what is civic engagement assumes an individual orientation, whereas for the "exclusion" group it is focused on the group and for the "inclusion" group it is nation oriented. Thus, for the privileged group it is the obligation of the individual to participate, and as that participation benefits the individual, the larger political system will prosper. . . .
>
> There is a general feeling among the "exclusion" group that their social predicament is not understood or, even worse, is irrelevant to members of the "inclusion" and "privileged" groups. For example, the experience that a significant number of youth in the "exclusion" group have with the government is negative. The police are viewed as being hostile. The court system is viewed as being unfair and punitive toward members of their group while lenient to members of the "inclusion" and "privileged" groups. . . . Civic mindedness, or what it means to be civically engaged, is relative. A person's socioeconomic position and their ethnic group's history in America influence the type and intensity of their civic involvement.[24]

It is important to recognize that there are different civic subcultures and multiple patterns of civic engagement. Just because people think and act differently does not mean that they are not trying to cooperate or contribute to the general good and civil society.

Political Discussions

Most investigations of adolescents' political discussions at home presume that parents initiate the process. However, one study found not only that adolescents who participated in a school-based civics curriculum initiated discussions of politics at home but also that those conversations influenced family communication patterns six months later. The researchers made a distinction between *socio-oriented communication*, which is designed to produce deference, and *concept-oriented communication*, which focuses on topics from outside the family and includes more than one side of an issue—features crucial to developing a political voice. As adolescents' cognitive abilities developed through attention to the news, discussion of politics, and campaign activism, parents decreased their socio-oriented demands for agreement and encouraged concept-oriented discussion. Adolescents whose parents were high in concept-orientation scored highest on tests of political knowledge. "Some parents responded to adolescent-initiated discussion of politics by putting their adolescents in a double bind, [saying] concept-oriented things such as, 'Say what you think about politics, even if the two of us disagree,' and also socio-oriented things such as, 'Don't argue with adults about politics.'" Parent-adolescent interaction led to changes in parents, whose political knowledge, attitudes, and attention to news were stimulated by their children's political development.[25]

Political scientists maintain that, among adults, there is a strong link between political participation and income, education, and religiosity. However, researchers who looked at young people found that these factors were less significant than the impact of political discussions at home and at school. On the home front, "38% of those from homes with frequent political discussions say they always vote, compared to 20% of those without such dialogue. Similarly, more than one third (35%) of those who often heard political talk while growing up are regular volunteers, compared to just 13% of those raised in homes where political talk never occurred. By talking about politics, families teach their children that it is important to pay attention to the world around them—and to take the next step of doing something." School discussions were also critical. About three-quarters of high school students had taken a civics course during the two previous school years, with most indicating that these courses positively influenced them.

> However, simply requiring attention to politics and government is not enough to foster greater involvement among high school students. Instead, it is when students report that teachers encouraged open discussion about these matters that their scores on scales of civic behavior climb. This finding holds up even when other important influences are taken into account. Open discussions are a regular part of the classroom experience for about half of today's high school students. Fully 49% report that teachers often encourage the class to discuss political and

social issues in which people have different opinions; another 27% say that teachers sometimes do. Slightly over half (54%) say that teachers encourage them to make up their own mind about issues; 31% say they sometimes do. Very few students say that open discussions and independent thinking are never encouraged (4% and 1% respectively). Among college students, about half (47%) say that teachers often promote open exchanges and fully 70% say they are encouraged to make up their own mind about issues.

Teachers can have a greater impact on engagement when they require students to develop specific civic skills, but not all students are being taught such skills. Eight-in-ten high school students have given a speech or oral report, but only half (51%) have taken part in a debate or discussion in which they had to persuade someone about something and just 38% have written a letter to someone they do not know. Students who have been taught these skills, especially letter writing and debating, are much more likely than those lacking such education to be involved in a range of participator acts inside and outside the school environment, even when other factors are taken into account. Again, the link between these skills and participation is much stronger than is the more generic course requirement to follow politics and national affairs.[26]

Many other studies have found that political discussions with parents, teachers, and peers influence youth's civic development. Here are the findings of a national study of high school students and their parents.

Adolescents who discuss politics and current events with their parents, peers, or teachers tend to score higher than other youth on measures of civic behavior, attitudes and skills. They develop higher levels of political knowledge, show greater attention to vote in the future, and do better on a range of civic outcomes from petitioning and boycotting to raising money for charities and participating in community meetings. . . . Individuals who grow up in homes where they discussed current events with their parents and saw their parents participating in civic activities become, on average, more involved in political activities in adulthood than do other persons. . . .

Youth who discuss politics more, versus less, frequently with their parents report higher levels of national news monitoring, political knowledge, public communication skill, and community service. . . . The finding that family political discussion is broadly linked to youth civic development conforms to cognitive developmental theory, which argues that young persons construct meaning and knowledge about the political world through social interaction. . . .

[Certain] parent characteristics . . . are linked to youth civic development, including the parents' education, political knowledge, news monitoring, internal political efficacy, giving money to a political cause, and membership in community or professional organizations. . . . In this study, we generally assume that parents develop their civic-related qualities before their children do, owing to the age differences between them, and that the direction of causality runs from parent to child. Causality can, however, flow in the opposite direction, as demonstrated by evaluations of the Kids Voting USA curriculum, which is taught during election years in several states. These studies in four states found that students who participated in the intervention at school often initiated political discussions with their parents that led to enhanced civic outcomes for both youth and parents. In addition, other youth-level factors, such as youth news monitoring or participating in civics courses at school, might lead youth to family political discussions . . . rather than the reverse. . . .

Who parents are in terms of their background characteristics is less important for youth civic development than *what parents do with their adolescent children* and *what parents know* about politics and government. . . . Parents play an especially important role in the development of youth political knowledge when they function both as a source of political information (i.e., they have a high degree of political knowledge) and as a frequent participant in discussions that help youth fashion that information into their own political understanding. Parents' background characteristics do play a role when the outcome is youth civic knowledge. Parent education—a measure of socioeconomic status—was positively associated with this outcome. . . . These parents may . . . provide their children with access to additional sources of civic information such as books, magazines, newspapers, electronic media, and enhanced education from which to draw in constructing their understanding of the political world. The finding that being Black is negatively associated with youth civic knowledge may be linked to a historical lack of access to [these] civic resources.[27]

Other political scientists have underscored the importance of parental education level, which in turn affects virtually every other participatory factor. "Parents who are educated are more likely to expose their children to politics—by taking part in politics themselves and by discussing politics at the dinner table—which has an impact on future political activity by enhancing political interest later in life."[28]

Political scientists are interested in who talks and who listens in family political discussions. A national study found that men were more likely than women to discuss politics nearly every day and to enjoy political discussion. However, there were no gender differences in frequency of political discussions at home when they were young. Political discussions were somewhat more frequent among Anglo-whites and blacks than Latinos. Even though husbands were more likely than wives to say that they could always express their point of view in family discussions, there were no differences in how much attention they felt their spouses paid to their point of view, nor in how satisfied they were with how family decisions were made. For the most part, husbands and wives reported discussing politics with their spouses as often as they discussed politics with others. "For wives, there is a relationship between political activity and being able to express themselves in family discussions. For husbands, financial power is politically enabling: husbands who bring in a larger share of the family income or who exercise greater control over financial decisions are, all else equal, more politically active."[29]

Another question about political voice is who frames political discussions: the elite media or the mass public? In one experimental study, interpersonal conversations reduced the effect of elite framing if they were cross-cutting, that is, introduced alternative frames. Conversations within one frame resulted in polarization—a strengthening of the initial elite frames and more extreme opinions. Alternatively, cross-cutting conversations resulted in depolarization.[30]

Evidence from one national survey indicated that political discussions stimulated interest and involvement in national elections and the local community. Respondents described their networks, people with whom they regularly discussed politics. "The more frequently people discuss[ed] political matters with their intimates, the greater their interest and participation in national campaigns and voting. . . . For members of voluntary associations, having at least one other with whom they frequently discuss[ed] politics strongly boost[ed] mobilization in internal organizational affairs and in the local community."[31]

It is difficult, and expensive, to study the effect of political conversations on people's political activity. Two researchers lamented the demise of the "conversion through conversation" research on neighborhood discussions that had been popular in the 1960s and 1970s, "largely because of the absence of data at the relevant spatial scales and the difficulty (and cost) of mounting surveys designed to provide direct tests of its operation. . . . To ignore social networks and conversations within them, as possible influence on the voting decision, seems premature." In their survey of British voters, people were much more likely to change their votes in a particular direction if those with whom they discussed political issues supported that direction, especially if they were family members or individuals with whom they discussed politics most. Almost half the respondents talked to their spouses or partners about politics, and most named their spouse or partner as their primary discussant. Most others named another relative. Outside the family, people turned to friends and workmates for political discussions. By comparison, neighbors and members of voluntary organizations were chosen very infrequently. The authors concluded that "political conversations formed a distinct context within which people evaluated the parties and decided who to support. Conversations with a party's supporters encouraged respondents to vote for it too, and discouraged them from voting for other parties, especially if those conversations took place within their families. . . . Families who talked together (more or less) voted together."[32]

Political discussions also occur among elected officials: at legislative tables among committee chairs, committee members, and witnesses providing testimony. When political scientist Lyn Kathlene studied committee hearings in the Colorado legislature, she found significant gender differences in the conversational dynamics. For example, compared to their male counterparts, female committee chairs spoke less, took fewer turns, and made fewer interruptions.

> Male chairs, beyond taking the floor away from speakers through interruptions, influenced and controlled committee hearings by offering substantive comments more than female chairs. In one out of six turns, men interjected personal opinions or guided the committee members and witnesses to a topic of their interest. Men used their position to control hearings in ways we commonly associate with positional power and leadership. Conversely, rather than interjecting their own opinions, women used their position of power to facilitate discussion among committee members, the sponsor and witnesses. . . .
>
> In hearings chaired by a woman, witnesses began speaking earlier because chairs tended to move directly to witness testimony. Men chairing committees tended to delay witness testimony through substantive questioning of sponsors, especially female sponsors, during the introduction of their bills. Male witnesses appearing before female chairs or during hearings on family bills (a traditional women's issue area) demonstrated heightened verbal aggressiveness through their use of interruptions—most notably, male witnesses interrupting female chairs. . . . Regardless of who chaired the committee, female witnesses opposed to a bill had significantly less opportunity to participate in hearings than male witnesses opposed to a bill. Female citizens (i.e., nonexperts) spoke less than male citizens, who were asked more questions by committee members. Although we might expect that citizens and witnesses opposed to bills would receive fewer opportunities to participate, this was the case only for females. . . .
>
> Male bureaucrats were engaged by committee members through questioning significantly more than female bureaucrats. . . . Women committee members, on average, waited until more than two-thirds of hearings were over before they

uttered their first words. Men engaged halfway through the hearings. Men spoke longer and took more turns, and men made and encountered more interruptions than did women committee members. . . . As women made up greater proportions of the committee, men became significantly more vocal. . . . Similarly, male committee members engaged earlier than female committee members when the sponsor of the bill was a woman. . . .

Other research in gender and nonverbal actions in group conversations indicate simple methods for neutralizing gender power. Seating arrangements, such as whether males and females are grouped together or interspersed, may be a powerful factor in verbal behavior. Given the importance of political friendships and women legislators' reports that they tend to find other women more friendly toward them, perhaps women on committees would speak earlier and more often if they sat next to each other. In addition, other research has found that women are more aware of and responsive to nonverbal social and emotional cues, suggesting that if the hearing table were shaped so that women could make visual contact with each other, their verbal activity might increase. [In this study,] when women sat next to each other and/or could see each other (as in the case of a V-shaped table), women were more active participants in the committee hearing. Without this arrangement, women's voices were significantly muted.[33]

Conversations and Civility

Conversations are a civil way of expressing points of view. Of course, political conversations can challenge existing power relations, even call for rebellion. Throughout the world, people have met in coffeehouses for lively discussions about overthrowing oppressive regimes. The American colonies were no exception. In the eighteenth century, coffeehouses were associated with news and rebellion in the disturbances that led up to the American Revolution. "In their meetings at coffee-houses, the New York rebels debated their protests against British policy and expressed their support for the foundations of the Continental Congress. To the Sons of Liberty, the egalitarian coffee-house seemed an especially welcoming location for their debates, as a neutral ground in which both wealthy merchants and laboring mechanics might meet together."[34]

In recent years, political theorists have argued that civil conversations are the essence of politics from four different vantage points: Rawlsian liberal, communitarian or civic republican, deliberative democratic, and postmodern. According to Peter Berkowitz, Rawlsian liberals focus on public reason to set boundaries and establish criteria for public discussion. Communitarian

202 · CHAPTER SIX

or civic republican critics think that public reason is too restrictive because it excludes arguments about moral and religious beliefs, which they add to the agenda. Deliberative democrats set procedural constraints on permissible forms of political argument, limit substantive issues that can be appropriately discussed in the public sphere, and promote an engaged political discourse. Postmoderns expand ideas about democratic participation, contest the boundaries of the political, and refocus the public agenda.

> So there is a consensus in America that conversation, properly conceived, is a cure for much that ails our public life. It is not often remarked, however, that this cure, like any other, may have unpleasant side effects or substantial costs. For a start, making talk the essence of politics can be highly destabilizing; you may well come to despise what others have to say, and they may grow disgusted or infuriated when they listen to what you have been thinking. Candor often makes life harder and uglier, not easier and lovelier. And who really benefits from the politics of conversation? The conversants, obviously. The well-educated, the plugged-in and the velvet-tongued have a considerable edge in the burnishing of reputation and the acquisition of power when conversation is made the mark of civic involvement.
>
> Yet the strangest difficulty with the scholarly defense of discourse as our defining political action is not that it takes conversation too seriously, but that it does not take conversation seriously enough. For conversation, an egalitarian activity open to all, and one of life's delights, is an elusive art. Mastering the art of conversation requires a rare combination of gifts: a discerning eye, an alert ear, a generous heart, a disciplined mind, a respect for the weakness of words, an attentiveness to silence's subtle textures.
>
> In the best of circumstances, when friends meet face to face, conversation provides not only a respite from the idle chatter that gets one through the day, but also an opportunity to share memories, form dreams, explore old ways and set out on new paths. And yet every conversation somehow contains the promise of a meeting of hearts and minds, of a self-perfecting world of patience and respect. So conversation is a token of the troubled coexistence in our world of the real and the ideal, an everyday act that holds out the prospect of a mutual trust that transcends words, but more often reminds us rudely of the barriers between us.[35]

Not all political conversations—rude or trusting—are face-to-face. They also occur on television, the dominant medium that exposes citizens to political controversy. Diane Mutz and Byron Reeves point out that its images and sounds mimic real conversations, and viewers tend to apply face-to-face standards of civility to televised conflict. They react as if they are watching a real-life interaction. Their emotional reactions are not mediated by the cognitive realization that this is "only television." But the experience of political conflict on television often differs substantially from real life in a way that exaggerates incivility and erodes trust in government.

> Politeness and civility . . . are a means of demonstrating mutual respect. . . . The distance deemed appropriate for face-to-face interactions with public figures in American culture is beyond 12 feet, yet most citizens' exposure to politicians via television has the appearance of being far closer. When people argue, it is typically unpleasant, and the tendency is to back off, especially if one is personally involved in the argument. In contrast, as televised political conflicts intensify, cameras close in with tighter and tighter perspectives on the people involved. This creates a highly unnatural experience for viewers, one in which they view conflict from an extremely intimate perspective, and one that would be highly unlikely to occur in the real world. When social norms for civility are violated on television, the viewer's intimate perspective intensifies an already negative reaction to incivility. . . . Increased market competition has encouraged political shows to "liven themselves up" in order to increase audience size. . . . The central tendency in the media is to highlight emotionally extreme and impolite expressions, whereas the central tendency in face-to-face communication is toward polite and emotionally controlled interactions. . . . Polite manners and other pleasantries may seem extraneous to political trust, but the need for politeness is particularly great when expressing controversial views.[36]

Mutz and Reeves conducted an experiment in which they exposed viewers to different versions of political disagreements in which they manipulated the level of civility and politeness while keeping the political content intact.

> The civil and uncivil versions of these discussions were perceived as equally informative, and rightly so given that they included precisely the same amount of substantive political information. But overwhelmingly, viewers found the uncivil version of this public affairs talk show more entertaining, indicating that it was more interesting [and] more exciting. They also indicated a much weaker desire to view the program again in the future if they viewed the civil version. Unfortunately, the kind of presentation of political conflict that is likely to attract audiences and build television revenues does not appear to be the one that best serves democratic citizens.[37]

Talk-show host Bill O'Reilly told the authors that incivility contributed to the success of political programs. "If a producer can find someone who eggs on conservative listeners to spout off and prods liberals into shouting back, he's got a hit show. The best host is the guy or gal who can get the most listeners extremely annoyed over and over and over again." Mutz and Reeves explain why political conflict simultaneously attracts and repulses people.

At a very basic psychological level, aggressiveness demands attention. And yet, in a culture where political disagreements are ideally *not* resolved by duels, what will pique viewers' interest in political debate enough to get them to pay attention? . . . [We] are left with the quandary of how to create political programming that is both interesting and exciting to watch yet not likely to damage public attitudes in a significant way. . . . [Our] experiments consistently demonstrate that incivility in political discourse has adverse effects on political trust relative to civil discussions of the same political substance. Not only were attitudes towards politicians and Congress affected, but levels of support for the institutions of government themselves also were influenced.[38]

Politics is a hot topic in online discussion groups. In her study of civility in such groups, media scholar Zizi Papacharissi made a distinction between politeness, that is, interpersonal manners, and civility, which is deference to an individual's social and political identity. Uncivil behaviors threaten democracy, deny people personal freedoms, and stereotype social groups. In her view, conversations should be guided by democratic principles, not just proper manners, which could stifle robust and heated discussion. In her research, 70 percent of messages posted on political newsgroups were neither impolite nor uncivil. Impolite behaviors included aspersions, synonyms for liar, hyperbole, noncooperation, pejorative speak, vulgarity, sarcasm, name-calling, and using all-caps (frequently used online to reflect shouting). The most common type of incivility was the use of stereotypes to offend or undermine an opponent's arguments.

[A discussion would escalate into a debate] when an opinionated participant expressed his/her take on an issue in an uncivil and/or impolite manner, or when a person put forth a fairly unusual or provocative point of view. The next five or six messages that followed would contain heated discussion, with occurrences of impoliteness or incivility. Eventually they would be toned down by the discussants themselves, who realized that their exchanges were reaching the point of nonsensical rants. At this point, the discussants would frequently apologize to each other for unnecessary use of sarcasm or other impoliteness. On the other hand, those discussants who were uncivil never apologized or took back any of their words. This indicates that the expression of incivility stems from strongly-held attitudes. . . .

[Discussants] valued freedom of speech, diversity in discussion, and calls to make the world better. Discussants acknowledged and respected the others' right to disagree with them. To this point, the majority of the participants appreciated these online debates, because they provided them with the opportunity to hone their argumentation skills. . . . Discussants often expressed their disappointment with a fellow discussant that did not structure an effective argument, or said they expected more from a certain person, or commented on the argumentative habits of a certain person. . . . Belief in the power of the best argument prevailed in most newsgroups. Moreover, when discussants focused on structuring a valid argument, they were seldom impolite and rarely uncivil.[39]

This study suggests that in everyday political discussion, most people play by, and self-correct for, agreed-upon rules of politeness and valid argument construction. They apologize for unnecessary use of sarcasm or other impoliteness, and they respect the power of the best argument. Things get more complicated when it comes to breaches of civility, where people neither apologize nor take back their words. I agree that the expression of incivility stems from strongly held attitudes that are resistant to change and difficult for conversants to deal with because they fail to show deference to the social and political identity of an individual. And an attack on one's identity is one of the three components of a difficult conversation.

In recent years, many politicians and pundits have advocated "national conversations" on a host of topics. Some commentators were skeptical about whether such conversations were genuine. *Washington Post* editor Carlos Lozada suspects that they were likely to be political ploys, euphemisms for bitter divisions, and a fail-safe when face-to-face conversations fell short. There were so many national conversations—about gun violence, immigration, income inequality, marriage equality, debt, climate change, obesity, bullying, and race—that "it's hard to know whose turn it is to talk, what everyone is saying or which conversations really matter—especially because they're all 'long overdue.' Politicians love calling for national conversations, but without a doubt, President Obama is our national conversationalist in chief." Former education secretary and drug czar William Bennett first popularized the term in the 1980s, calling for national conversations "on the place of religion in American life, on the proper relationship between the government and the people, on foreign policy and much more. . . . But like many others who have called for national conversations, Bennett always seems to have clear conclusions in mind, whether limited government or the defeat of secularism. And that is precisely what renders such conversations largely non-conversational."[40]

Our so-called national conversations are not about making human connections; they are really discussions, debates, and arguments.

> Fiercely held and mutually exclusive opinions won't magically disappear if we frame them as a feel-good conversation. . . . Just recall the town hall meetings

surrounding President Obama's health-care legislation in 2009. The notion of a town hall (so Athenian!) has become an indispensable element of our conversational stagecraft: citizens gathering in a public square to discuss important issues and engage their political leaders in the timeless tradition of democratic societies. Except that unhappy Americans showed up packing heat, America's first black president was depicted as a Nazi, and the truth got a little muddled in translation. Not very conversational.[41]

In his memoirs, President Obama frequently notes the importance of national dialogue. He believes in the concept of "deliberative democracy," the notion that politics is not just about interest groups and elections but also about discourse, conversation, and deliberation. Individual interests are developed in dialogue with other participants in a democracy.

> In the preface to his memoir "Dreams From My Father," Obama reminisces about working as a state senator in Springfield, Ill.: "Within the capitol building of a big, industrial state, one sees every day the face of a nation in constant conversation: inner-city mothers and corn and bean farmers, immigrant day laborers alongside suburban investment bankers—all jostling to be heard, all ready to tell their stories." And in the book's epilogue, he invokes a similar dialogue as a way to understand his chosen profession: "The law records a long-running conversation, a nation arguing with its conscience." In 2006's "The Audacity of Hope," Obama hails the Constitution "not just as a source of individual rights, but also as a means of organizing a democratic conversation around our collective future."[42]

Lozada thinks that Obama's efforts at national conversation fell short when it came to race and to gridlock in Washington. "Polls show that our partisan gulf is greater than ever, and even the most liberal Republican and the most conservative Democrat in Congress have little in common. . . . And Obama himself seems torn between trying to fix the conversation in the capital or going over his opponents' heads and directly addressing the nation. So, are we just not capable of having real conversations anymore? I'm sure you've heard: Just like we were 'bowling alone' in the 1990s, untethered to the groups that once defined us, now we're 'alone together,' our gadgets linking us only to the like-minded or the ephemeral. So we're too distant, or too distracted, to take seriously political calls for national conversations."[43]

Congresswomen and Civility

During the Obama administration, one place in Washington where civil conversations were alive and well was among female senators. However, this

During President Barack Obama's administration, women in the Senate were described by *Time* magazine as the "only adults left in Washington" because of their ability to work in a bipartisan fashion in a gridlocked Congress. Many of them attributed their willingness to compromise to the trust they built during regular dinners together. In 2013, President Obama invited them to the White House for dinner.
Credit: Official White House photo by Pete Souza.

pocket of civility was not enough to keep moderate Republican Olympia Snowe of Maine from leaving a "dysfunctional and polarized Senate" that obstructed the budget-making process, legislated by "political brinkmanship," and replaced "full debate and an open amendment process in favor of competing, up-or-down, take-it-or-leave-it proposals." She thought that because America's electorate was increasingly divided into Republican and Democratic states, there was no practical incentive for 75 percent of the senators to work across party lines. She urged them "to look past their differences and find common ground if their initial party positions failed to garner sufficient support." She maintained that there was "strength in compromise, courage in conciliation and honor in consensus-building."[44]

Snowe's departure after seventeen years of public service was lamented by both Republican and Democratic women in the Senate, who had developed a tradition of working across party lines, thanks in large part to the monthly dinner parties started by Senator Barbara Mikulski (D-Md.). The dinners were held at their homes or in the Strom Thurmond Room in the Capitol.

The irony was not lost on them that the room's namesake preferred to pinch a woman rather than listen to her. The club was not secret, nor was it a caucus around a particular subject. Rather, it sought "to restore some of the natural camaraderie that existed before so many members left their families behind and spent every free moment of their nights and weekends fundraising." Bipartisan friendships used to be common. "There was a day when Senate Majority Leader Mike Mansfield had breakfast weekly with Republican Sen. George Aiken and when Tip O'Neill had an after-hours whisky with Richard Nixon." Soon after her arrival in Washington, Senator Mikulski launched the dinner group.

> "The other ladies call me Coach Barb. When a new woman is elected to the Senate—Republican or Democrat—I bring her in for my Senate Power Workshop and guide her on how to get started, how to get on the good committees for her state, and how to be an effective senator." And for a meal. Sen. Mary Landrieu lives just a few blocks from the office and serves New Orleans food with pecan pie for dessert. What the off-campus get-togethers do is foster the ability to handle the inevitable conflicts that arise. Sen. Amy Klobuchar, formerly a tough prosecutor for Minnesota's largest county, may not agree with Sen. Lisa Murkowski on everything. "But when we went on family vacation to Alaska," she says, "Lisa had us over to her house."[45]

Capitol observers have noted that female senators never attacked each other on the floor, in committee, or even behind closed doors, simply because they got to know one another and, as a result, said Senator Kay Bailey Hutchison, "resolve conflicts the way friends do." They worked together on a host of issues, from children's health to national security to Supreme Court appointments.

> The complaint you always hear is that there just isn't enough time for lawmakers to get to know their colleagues to create the civility that is in such short supply. Yet, a second X chromosome doesn't give women another couple hours in the day. Women just carve out time for what they know is important. It goes beyond dinner. When Hillary Clinton was a senator, she hosted the group's baby shower for Hutchison. Klobuchar is in charge of games for the upcoming shower for Republican Sen. Susan Collins, who will now be separated from the other Maine twin with Snowe's retirement. When Sen. Claire McCaskill collaborated on Second City's "A Girl's Guide to Washington Politics," at the Woolly Mammoth theater in D.C., a dozen of the group found time to attend the opening. If only the men could pick up on some of this, Congress might get above a 10 percent favorability rating in Americans' eyes. The incivility that is driving Snowe out isn't just atmospherics. It's crippling the body. A dinner or two might help.[46]

New Hampshire senators Jeanne Shaheen, a Democrat, and Kelly Ayotte, a Republican, said that taking part in both the all-female Senate supper club and in other bipartisan dinner parties had helped them build bridges. Senior senators lamented the loss of the kind of one-on-one interactions that previously greased the wheels of law making. "However, Ayotte, who is serving her first term in the Senate, said those informal gatherings are indeed still happening, sometimes in the form of after-hours dinner parties held to strengthen relationships with colleagues." She had already attended about six bipartisan dinner parties, explaining, "I always go, because I always feel like I learn something in every single one of these informal gatherings." Shaheen said female senators from both parties who dined together several times a year operated under "Mikulski's rules": whatever happens at the dinner table stays there. "I actually think that the women of the Senate have done a very good job of working together," she said, "and I think there are a lot of examples we can point to where people work together very well."[47]

Congresswomen in the House also got together for dinners and touted the benefits of sharing meals and conversations. House Speaker Nancy Pelosi's comments about dinners surprised a blogger who attended a Washington conference, "Women 2020."

> I certainly didn't anticipate that she would . . . use this opportunity to speak about dinners she shared with her fellow members of Congress. Eating a meal with other people seems extremely simple. You exchange food, conversation and listen to those you eat with; however, what if others did not listen to you? For Nancy Pelosi, many of her early dinners with Congressmen involved the men talking and the women never being asked for their opinions. This continued during many dinners about topics ranging from politics to childbirth, a topic that the women at the table would have clearly known more about; however, they were still never asked to speak. Instead of being mad about these dinners, Pelosi's humor showed that lessons can be learned from negative experiences. Her best advice to "know your power" taught those in the audience the importance of listening to others, but also speaking up for what you believe in. If you don't speak up, who will?[48]

The "civility pact" among female senators was based on regular social interactions, face-to-face conversations, and adherence to certain ground rules. In 2011, there were seventeen women in the one hundred–member Senate, twelve Democrats, and five Republicans. They had what amounted to

> an informal nonaggression pact. In the male-dominated, tradition-bound Senate chamber, their desire to recapture a long lost sense of civility trumps the constant pressure to score partisan points. It's a bond forged by their common experience as women in the highest level of American politics, reinforced during a regular

dinner meeting. . . . Mikulski set the rules for the dinner group when she launched it years ago: no staff, no memos, no leaks and no men. "We committed to maintaining a zone of civility here within the institution long before it became the chic thing to do," said Mikulski, who, along with Sen. Claire McCaskill (D-Mo.), helped organize the group.[49]

Female senators civilly disagreed about oil drilling. Senator Mikulski said of Senator Lisa Murkowski (R-Alaska), "She wants to drill for oil in Alaska, and I never want to drill off the coast of Ocean City. We disagree, but we both know we need new energy policy in the United States." Sometimes women defended each other's positions, as when "Sen. Maria Cantwell (D-Wash.) leapt to then-Sen. Blanche Lincoln's defense during a closed-door meeting on banking regulation, warning male colleagues that ignoring the Arkansas Democrat's amendments to the Wall Street reform bill would be a big political mistake." In several cases, women "crossed party lines to team up on key legislation [such as] an amendment to protect small-community banks during debate over the Wall Street reform bill."[50]

Senator Kirsten Gillibrand (D-N.Y.) recalled that when she first came to Washington in 2009, a bipartisan group of women met with her individually. "They were very welcoming. They all took the time to show me the ropes of what they had learned." Women had to work hard to create civility "in a political environment where most members choose to spend weekends and spare time in their district or at partisan political events, rather than staying in Washington and mingling with co-workers from across the aisle. 'The bond between the woman senators has been through more difficult and more partisan battles,' [Mary] Landrieu [D-La.] said. 'Sen. Mikulski is our dean, and she insists on everyone trying to get along. That kind of extra effort pays off in the ability to work together when opportunities come up.'"[51]

Before the 1990s, members of Congress socialized on weekends with one another's families. According to Debbie Walsh, director of the Center for American Women and Politics at Rutgers University, "The social relationships really make it possible for some of that discourse to be civil discourse. Women bring something different to the table. Their ability to relate to each other could really set a tone for the rest of Congress." Jennifer Lawless, director of the Women & Politics Institute at American University, was more skeptical: "Having policy differences is fair game. It's when the argument turns personal that it gets problematic. Hanging out might make discourse less personal, but that's not what's causing the problematic wrangling." When Chris Matthews interviewed Senator McCaskill during an episode of *Hardball*, he asked her, "How come that works for your side of the gender aisle and men don't seem to get along? Is it just the testosterone or what?" "Oh, I think part of it is," McCaskill replied. "I think we have got to start talking to each other more. We have got to start being willing to compromise. And that's what's going to be interesting."[52]

Female senators said that their dinner conversations helped them avert legislative gridlock. "We have a very, very respected rule that what we talk about there never leaves the room," McCaskill said. "So these are pretty free-wheeling discussions, and we have averted some legislative logjams by some of our discussions at those dinners. I think we're all determined to use those opportunities to try to move things along." Senator Kay Hagan (D-N.C.) added, "A lot of women, we work well together, not just with women, but obviously with men. Women have a tendency to work in partnerships, and that's something I think the American public would really appreciate us doing, working across the aisle."[53]

In the wake of the 2013 government shutdown, *Time* called female senators the only adults left in Washington, given their ability to break the deadlock. At one low point, "Maine Republican Susan Collins went to the Senate floor to do two things that none of her colleagues had yet attempted. She refrained from partisan blame and proposed a plan to end the crisis." She asked colleagues from both parties to come together. "We can do it. We can legislate responsibly and in good faith." Democrat Barbara Mikulski made a similar plea. "Let's get to it. Let's get the job done. I am willing to negotiate. I am willing to compromise." Ten minutes later, Republican Lisa Murkowski joined in: "I am pleased to stand with my friend from Maine, Senator Collins, as she has described a plan which I think is pretty reasonable. I think it is pretty sensible." The night before, most of the Senate's twenty women had gathered for pizza, salad, and wine in the offices of New Hampshire Democrat Jeanne Shaheen, where they talked about Collins's plan to reopen the government with some basic compromises. "In policy terms, it was a potluck dinner. In the hours that followed, those discussions attracted more Senators, including some men, and yielded a plan that would lead to genuine talks between Senate leaders Harry Reid and Mitch McConnell to end the shutdown." The elements for compromise had been there all along, but it took women to craft them together. As Senator Amy Klobuchar put it during negotiations, "The women are an incredibly positive force because we like each other. We work together well, and we look for common ground."[54]

The women's club offers some of the same benefits that came in the original men's version, as well as some updates: mentor lunches and regular dinners, . . . but also bridal and baby showers and playdates for children and grandchildren. An unspoken rule among what Collins calls "the sisterhood" holds that the women refrain from publicly criticizing one another. And there is a deep sense that more unites them personally than divides them politically. "One of the things we do a bit better is listen," says North Dakota Democrat Heidi Heitkamp. "It is about getting people in a room with different life experiences who will look at things a little differently because they're moms, because they're daughters who've been taking care of senior moms, because they have a different life experience than a lot of senior guys in the room."[55]

The supper club had spillover effects. Once a year it dined with the female Supreme Court justices. "Dianne Feinstein, who chairs the Select Committee on Intelligence, holds regular dinners for women in the national-security world. Even the female chiefs of staff and communications directors have started regular get-togethers of their own. In April [2013] the Senate women breached their no-outsider rule by agreeing to dine at the White House with President Obama. Going around the table, California Senator Barbara Boxer remarked that 100 years ago they'd have been meeting outside the White House gates to demand the right to vote. ('A hundred years ago, I'd have been serving you,' Obama replied.)" Their rules of civility were enforced both in private and in public. At one dinner, Massachusetts Democrat Elizabeth Warren mentioned antiabortion bills pending in the House and complained about the Republican "war against women." She was admonished by her fellow Democrats for this partisan formulation. Two of the women at the dinner were pro-life: New Hampshire Republican Kelly Ayotte and Nebraska Republican Deb Fischer.[56]

Women in the Senate believe in the power of food. "Almost all of the chairs and ranking members have regular meals with their top counterparts. Barbara Boxer goes so far as to spend her own money catering mark ups and hearings for the staffs on both sides of the aisle. When a big bill passes, she springs for lobster rolls. 'Food was an important part of my upbringing,' Boxer says. 'I try to take particular staff out on both sides of the aisle.'"[57]

State Department Culinary Diplomacy

Nation-states also believe in the power of food. "Public diplomats" engage in people-to-people "gastrodiplomacy," defined as winning hearts and minds through stomachs, establishing an emotional connection through food, demonstrating commonality, and creating "a shared safe space where a conversation can begin." It could be used as tool for conflict resolution by beginning a "peace from below, starting a movement towards a constructive conversation during which some of the other more difficult issues and fundamental disagreements can be negotiated."[58] Proponents contend that you cannot win hearts and minds solely through rational information; you need emotional connections that are sensual, visceral, and intimate.[59] One effort to put this principle into practice is Mealsharing, an online network where people share home-cooked meals with strangers for free in more than three hundred cities. Its purpose is to create "an equal playing field" to pursue the common goal of sharing a meal and conversation: "There's no meal, unless it's the most awkward meal in the history of meals, where there's no conversation."[60] Gastrodiplomacy can also be used to promote a country's image on the world stage. Some countries have used their cuisines to create a national brand and encourage tourism. There is some evidence that this might be working. In one survey, half the respondents reported that they had changed their opinion of a country based on eating its national cuisine, and over three-quarters indicated that they had considered traveling to a country based on its food.[61]

Some people refer to the use of food to create international understanding and cooperation as "culinary diplomacy," which has figured in diplomatic history since the Bible and the Greeks and loomed large during the advent of modern diplomacy in early nineteenth-century France.[62] It is an example of what the United States Institute of Peace defines as Track 3 Diplomacy: "People to people diplomacy undertaken by individuals and private groups to encourage interaction and understanding between hostile communities and involving awareness raising and empowerment within these communities." It "does not specifically aim to resolve the wider conflict, but instead focuses on the concepts of contact and understanding as a way of setting the table for resolution."[63] It is a form of what political scientist Joseph Nye calls "soft power," or the ability to get what you want through attraction rather than through the threat of force or the exchange of money.[64]

When she was secretary of state, Hilary Rodham Clinton used food for what she called "smart diplomacy": viewing meals for foreign dignitaries as opportunities to show respect for their culinary traditions. Clinton explained, "Showcasing favorite cuisines, ceremonies and values is an often overlooked and powerful tool of diplomacy. The meals that I share with my counterparts at home and abroad cultivate a stronger cultural understanding between countries and offer a unique setting to enhance the formal diplomacy we conduct every day." Her deputy chief of protocol said that food was crucial "because tough negotiations take place at the dining table." Menus for visiting officials required careful planning. "We are sharing our culture with our guests," chief of protocol Capricia Marshall said. "At the same time, we don't want to serve them their food, because they can do it better. But we want to give a nod to their culture in a fusion dish." A good example was the soy-marinated black cod and eight-treasure rice packet with dried fruit and pork sausage served to Chinese vice president, Xi Jinping. It was cooked by Chinese American chef Ming Tsai. When Xi met the chef, "his eyes lit up," Marshall said. "They spoke Chinese, and according to the translator, he said, 'Isn't this wonderful.'" At the start of each meal, Clinton insisted that tables have culturally appropriate snacks for guests to nibble while they waited for the speeches to be over.[65]

In 2012, Secretary Clinton launched the Diplomatic Culinary Partnership with the James Beard Foundation to promote a "culinary engagement" of intercultural dialogue, and the American Chefs Corps, composed of chefs who shared their cooking here and abroad. She said that food was not traditionally thought of as a diplomatic tool, "but sharing a meal can help people transcend boundaries and build bridges in a way that nothing else can. Some of the most meaningful conversations I've had with my counterparts around the world have taken place over lunch and dinner." Exploring the idea of culinary engagement led to the identification of new opportunities to further intercultural dialogue and strengthen bilateral relationships, right at the dinner table.[66] Members of the American Chef Corps relished their role as citizen diplomats, outfitted in navy blue jackets with an American flag, the seal of the State Department, and their names embroidered in gold on the front.[67]

Culinary diplomacy struck a delicate balance between showcasing American food and reminding diplomats of their home cuisine. Chief of protocol Marshall said that the French food that once dominated diplomatic functions had been replaced by American food with fresh local ingredients, along with some subtle reminders of home. The chefs used spices that visitors were accustomed to, or they presented dishes in a way that had never been seen before in their country. "It's really important because they're going to talk about some tough issues with one another," Marshall said. "We want the framework of those tough discussions to be relaxing, to be welcoming, to be inviting." When chef José Andrés designed the menu for a meeting of protocol chiefs from all over the world, he served Louisiana Gulf shrimp to remind them of the tragic losses and recovery from Hurricane Katrina. "I believe that dinner, gathering people around a table, you have a true opportunity to send hidden messages," he said. The State Department was "sending a message that we need to be supporting American ingredients, we need to be supporting our fishermen. With better food and a happy table, probably, probably, we will have a better world, a happier world."[68]

Presidential Barbecue Diplomacy

Two presidents, Democrat Lyndon B. Johnson and Republican George W. Bush, were famous for barbecue diplomacy at their Texas ranches. Johnson survived the gaffe of serving pork ribs to a Muslim dignitary and diplomatically insisted on inviting both Democrats and Republicans. An invitation to Bush's ranch was a prized honor for a head of state. What follows are lively descriptions of their use of this diplomatic tool.

In April 1961, newly elected Vice President Lyndon Johnson held a barbecue for West German chancellor Konrad Adenauer. "The American West held a romantic appeal to Europeans, and the attraction was greater to Adenauer because Hill Country had been settled by many German families. . . Ranching, its barbecues, beans, and chuck wagons, had a cross-cultural resonance that allowed even those raised in other parts of the world to participate in an American myth made universal by popular fiction and the movies. Foreigners could see their preconceived vision of the 'real America' in the vistas, settings, entertainment, and libations of the LBJ Ranch." Later that year, Johnson hosted Field Marshall Mohammed Ayub Khan of Pakistan, who "deftly averted a diplomatic incident by ignoring the fact that pork ribs were served. Pork is forbidden to Muslims. But a connection was made between men of rocky soil and poor farmers. Khan later became President of Pakistan."[69]

A month after the assassination of President John Kennedy on November 22, 1963, the Johnson family retreated to their ranch. "West German Chancellor Ludwig Erhard was scheduled to visit the President to discuss the Soviet threat, the Berlin Wall, and other important matters. Rather than return to Washington for a formal State Dinner, Lyndon invited Erhard and his entourage on down to what historians claim was the first official Presidential barbecue in history." Johnson's first state dinner was a barbecue for three hundred on December 29, 1963. Because of the chilly weather, the feast was moved inside a high school gymnasium about two miles away. "Workers did an admirable job of creating an outdoorsy feel with bales of hay, red lanterns, red-checkered table cloths, saddles, lassos, and mariachis."

There were pinto beans, barbecued spareribs, coleslaw, apricot fried pies, coffee, and beer. "The food was served on paper plates, buffet style." Fellow Texan Van Cliburn played classical music. "Erhard presented Johnson with a bottle of 1959 Piesporter Goldtröpchen Feinste Spätlese by Reichsgraf von Kesselstatt, a superb sweet white wine. Johnson presented Erhard and his entire delegation with Stetsons." A Texas humorist who served as master of ceremonies "jokingly apologized to the German delegation because they could not find a recipe for barbecued sauerkraut. Johnson's cookouts strove for authenticity with 'the look and feel of a chuck wagon dinner.' . . . Unfortunately that included cowpies that the Air Force was asked to remove. For future events it was decided that the cattle should be kept on the south side of the river."[70]

The phrase "barbecue diplomacy" was coined by W. D. Taylor of the *New York Herald-Tribune*. Johnson liked the symbolism. It conveyed the sense of an everyday man as President, the same image conveyed by Truman. It was so effective the Johnsons occasionally staged barbecues at the White House, also a first. . . .

A month after the assassination of President John Kennedy in 1963, German chancellor Ludwig Erhard visited President Lyndon B. Johnson at his Texas ranch to discuss global issues. Johnson's first state dinner was a barbecue for three hundred served on paper plates buffet style to encourage conversation.
Credit: White House Photo Office, 30930, LBJ Presidential Library.

One of the largest barbecues was on April 1, 1967, with 35 Latin American ambassadors and their wives. There was a huge re-enactment of the settling of Texas by Native Americans, followed by Spaniards, then Anglo cowboys, complete with buckboards and cattle. Johnson spoke briefly of his War on Hunger and he pledged three million tons of food grain to India and another $25 million in food for distribution by CARE. . . . When told that Congressman Gonzales was unhappy because so many Republicans had been invited to the barbecue, Johnson replied that he was "President of all the people, Republicans and Democrats."[71]

President George W. Bush entertained many heads of state at his 1,600-acre Prairie Chapel Ranch in Crawford. When Australian prime minister John Howard paid a visit in 2003, he and Bush ate "smoked beef tenderloin, traded compliments, and took a rambling walk under the gray central Texas skies with a Scottie frolicking at their heels while the birds chirruped and a storm brewed. . . . It was down-home Texas hospitality at its best, and if the routine by now runs like clockwork, the results never fail to hit the mark." The morning after his arrival at the ranch, the often-dour Howard "was all smiles at a bucolically picture-perfect press briefing. Paying tribute to Bush's leadership style, the Australian 'man of steel' called it resolute and clear under 'great obstructionism.' Distinguished guest and famous host then swapped souvenirs—a pair of monogrammed cowboy boots bearing a map of Australia for Howard and a classic Down Under whip and rancher hat for Bush."[72]

According to George Stephanopoulos, news anchor and former adviser to President Clinton, "For a foreign leader, a visit to Crawford has become the ultimate honor—the place to be seen. For Bush, it's an invaluable part of his diplomatic toolbox." He noted that an invitation to the ranch had served many purposes throughout the Bush presidency. It helped start a new relationship with Russian president Vladimir Putin in November 2001, to smooth a rocky relationship with Crown Prince Abdullah of Saudi Arabia in April 2002, and to reward heads of state such as Howard and Spanish prime minister José María Aznar who had supported Bush's war in Iraq despite widespread domestic opposition.[73]

> Deep in the heart of Texas, inevitably buoyed up by a hearty (if haute) barbecue, a select few world leaders over the past several years have engaged in a brand of personal diplomacy—call it barbecue diplomacy—that has the capacity to shape the forces of history. In a world divided by often conflicting interests, ideologies and geopolitical goals, personal chemistries between statesmen—or the lack thereof—can sometimes make the difference between peace, war and dangerous impasses. And sometimes, a physical and mental distance from the crush of na-

tional capitals, ringing telephones, prying journalists and demanding staffs have pressed arch enemies to acts of supreme statesmanship. It was in the idyllic Catoctin Mountains of Maryland that President Jimmy Carter got Egyptian President Anwar Sadat to sign the landmark Camp David accord with Israeli Prime Minister Menachem Begin in 1978. More than a decade later, the tranquility of the Nordic countryside—coupled with the quiet diplomacy of Norwegian officials—paved the way for the Oslo accords and the subsequent historic handshake between Israeli Prime Minister Yitzhak Rabin and Palestinian leader Yasser Arafat on the White House lawn on Sept. 13, 1993.[74]

Conclusion

We have come full circle from kitchen tables to congressional, presidential, and diplomatic tables. Along the way, we have raised some important ethical questions about table talk and democracy. When do we have an ethical obligation to converse with strangers or to frame what we want to say in a polite way? What obligation do we have to engage in meaningful conversations, where we listen and learn, show respect and create trust between people with whom we may not have much in common? What rules should we set about who gets to talk, and how, at the table? At what age should children have a say about table processes? Who gets included and who gets excluded in our commensality? How should conflict and difficult conversations be handled? When should matters be confronted head on and when should they be avoided or tabled until later?

The democratic potential of tables cannot be realized without some order and rules regarding listening, turn taking, respectful language, and adherence to cultural conventions. Democracy requires a habit of thinking beyond one's own wants and needs and valuing a group of people we can trust. Respectful conversation builds good will. But it comes at a price of restraints on individual expression. When does the need to be polite and to attend to the needs of the group become counterproductive to democracy by stifling a robust exchange of ideas, perpetuating group think, and preventing the speaking of truth to power?

Conversants have different levels of verbal ability. Democratic speech requires listeners to be sensitive to these differences and to try to minimize them. Highly educated professionals and wealthy people tend to be verbal and to raise children with verbal privileges: a large vocabulary, conversational skills, and participatory classrooms. These privileges need to be broadly shared for democracy to work. What obligation do adults and teachers have to make sure that verbal privileges are shared among all children?

There may be times when it is too emotionally difficult for people to sit at a table and converse. When family members retreat to different rooms for dinner, it is often to avoid tense interactions because the family lacks someone with the requisite conflict-resolution skills to defuse potentially inflammatory situations. Without skilled conversationalists and conflict mediators at the table, things can get uncomfortable, volatile, and abusive, perhaps doing more harm than good. Under what conditions is it unrealistic, even ill-advised, to expect people to sit at tables and converse? Which of these conditions are temporary and amenable to change if enough people at the table have conversational skills?

It can be quite daunting to develop the conversational and conflict-resolution skills needed for democratic tables. Just consider this practical "how-to" list from linguists: listen, show interest, take turns, sequence interactions, manage miscommunication, express and interpret expressions of affect, make tacit rules explicit, call attention to breaches of etiquette, correct or expand children's utterances to be socially appropriate and grammatical, repeat and rephrase your speech and that of others, model linguistic behavior, promote moral theorizing and stance taking, engage in both narrative and explanatory talk, avoid others' loss of face, build group cohesion without denigrating others, be authoritative and not authoritarian or rule-less, mitigate requests, ask "wh questions" (who, what, when, why) rather than yes-or-no questions, scaffold speech to help others join in, and be prepared for cross-cultural differences. Once we appreciate the features of respectful conversations needed for democratic tables, how can we avoid feeling overwhelmed when we speak and resentful of all the work it takes, especially when others are not pitching in to help?

Conflict resolution between unequals has distinctive political dynamics. The point of a democracy is for all people to find their political voice, and in so doing they need to be given an increasing say in things when they are cognitively, socially, and emotionally capable of doing so. The dinner table abounds in daily opportunities to let people have a say. How much should children be forced to eat certain foods, what should the punishment be if they don't, and at what point is the decision theirs to make? How should parents deal with the double bind of interrogating children: they need to know what their children are up to, but an overbearing inquisition can seem unjust, especially if parents are not forthcoming about their own lives. How should the relatively powerful at the table use power differences to enhance democracy rather than stymie it?

Conflict resolution between equals is also political. At all tables, people need to clarify rights and obligations, for example, the right to have a turn speaking and the obligation to use respectful language; to mark interpersonal boundaries, for instance, where to sit and how to share; and to recognize specializations or hierarchies in decision making, for example, who cooks and who sets the table. Conversants have to decide which conflict-resolution strategy to adopt. Submission means someone loses face. Compromise takes a lot of work to find a position that allows each person to give a little. Withdrawal disrupts the social occasion. It is not surprising that most dinner-table conflict ends in a standoff, without resolution, winners, or losers. It is cognitively and emotionally the simplest way to end a table conflict, but it also keeps open the possibility of eventual resolution. How do we decide which conflict-resolution strategy to use at a table: submission, compromise, withdrawal, or standoff?

I have suggested answers to these ethical and practical questions that would promote democracy and civility along the lines advocated by "civic constitutional" legal scholars. When we think of the U.S. Constitution, what comes to mind is a formal document that is occasionally amended and whose meaning is interpreted by courts. But the meaning of constitutional principles such as liberty, equality, and justice has changed thanks to the efforts of engaged citizens: colonial revolutionaries, antifederalists, abolitionists, and suffragists.[1] Our constitutional order presupposes that citizens possess the capacities for democratic and personal self-government, that families are the seedbeds of civic virtue, and that both government and civil society have a responsibility to foster capacities for self-government.[2] The Constitution is both created by and creates "we the people": "a *deliberative* community knowledgeable of its constitutional commitments, and an *engaged* community, alive with civic concern and actively occupied in the work of self-government." Constitutional practice occurs on a regular, recurrent basis when citizens seek liberty, justice, and equality in everyday practices. Citizenship requires civility and tending to constitutional responsibilities.[3]

I have also provided evidence about what makes us resilient. In the introduction, I asked: why do people keep having democratic hopes, given the inevitability of setbacks and adversity in politics? My answer is that there is a cumulative positive effect of being respected, listened to, taken seriously, and trusted, and that these experiences create a reservoir of value and strength for the common good, for a collectivity beyond those in our immediate contact, that can be drawn on in hard times. We become resilient when we feel connected, and stories, conversations, and table activities are important and everyday ways of connecting and empathizing with others. A vibrant civil society depends on feelings of respect, trust, and empathy, which in turn make possible the idea of a common good that is worth working toward.

In the social sciences, the concept of resilience was first employed in the 1970s by psychiatrists, psychologists, and other mental-health professionals. In the 1980s, the term began to be used in educational studies, and in the 1990s, research increasingly focused on the ethnic and socioeconomic status of at-risk populations. Most definitions of resilience have three fundamental components: (1) in the face of risk or adversity (2) protective factors and processes (3) help people adapt. Studies of risk and adversity range from the individual to the social and political: mental illness, death of a loved one, drug addiction, family violence, poverty, and community and wartime traumas. Protective factors and processes are individual and social resources, competencies, talents, and skills. And adaptation is measured by using interviews, questionnaires, and tests to determine the extent to which someone is "doing okay" on developmental tasks appropriate for that person's age, social context, and historical time.[4]

These studies are relevant for our consideration of civil and political resilience. What enables people to stay engaged in difficult conversations in the face of the setbacks? A consideration of protective factors and processes sheds light on this question. The list researchers have come up with bears a striking resemblance to the factors and processes we have described as fostering civility and democracy in table conversations.

Resilient individuals have certain personal characteristics: flexibility, tolerance for negative affect, self-efficacy, self-esteem, internal locus of control, sense of humor, hopefulness, enduring values, fortitude, conviction, tenacity, resolve, the ability to plan, and language and reading skills. At the interpersonal level, what matters is attachment and responsiveness to others, empathy, ability to elicit positive responses from others, and ability to move between different cultures. From families, protective factors include parental warmth, encouragement, assistance, cohesion and care, a close relationship with at least one caring adult, belief in the child, nonblaming, and talents valued by others. Material resources are protective factors. From schools, it is important to have positive teacher role models, supportive peers, and success (academic or otherwise). And communities create protective factors to the extent that they take an individual's stress seriously, provide resources for assistance, and are nonpunitive.

Consider how table conversations foster these protective factors. Active listeners have to be flexible. Skilled conversants expect negative affect as part of any difficult conversation. Self-efficacy and self-esteem are enhanced when everyone's story matters at the table. Internal locus of control develops when children construct their own narratives to add to family stories. Adolescents frequently describe family dinner conversations as fun, with lots of jokes, laughter, and games, and fun conversations are hopeful. Even when there is conflict at the table, it is usually dealt with in a way in which people neither lose face nor exit the table. Conflict is aired even if it is not resolved, with the expectation that it will be revisited later. Every table has rules about what is valued in terms of listening, showing respect, and sharing. The virtues of fortitude, conviction, tenacity, and resolve are fostered when people "stick it out" at tables, even when the conversation is boring or unsettling; when strong views are aired, attacked, and defended; and when skilled conversants model conflict resolution. The ability to plan characterizes every shared meal. Language skills are developed at tables. People are attached to family food practices, rituals, and recipes, and they pay attention to the different kinds of needs of those at the table. When adults tell children that they, too, have been down a difficult road, it models empathy. Skilled conversants are able to redirect nonconstructive interchanges in more productive directions. Cultural differences crop up at most tables. Adult warmth, encouragement, and assistance characterize most tables, except when people are too tired or lack the skills to tend to everyone's needs, moods, and developmental stages. Authoritative parenting and teaching value everyone's voice and talents and downplay blame in enforcing rules. Material resources help when it comes to producing table competencies, talents, and skills. To the extent that teachers listen to students, allow them to express their views, and insist on rules for civil discourse, they are positive role models, not only for taking students seriously, but also for creating a climate where students show each other respect. At the community level, nonpunitive assistance is provided at tables at addiction-recovery meetings, conflict-themed restaurants, and housing for seniors and veterans.

In addition to resilience, another social science idea relevant to our concerns here is intergroup contact theory, which states that, under the right conditions, contact between groups reduces prejudice. According to social psychologist Gordon Allport, these conditions are (1) equal status of the groups in the situation, (2) common goals, (3) intergroup cooperation, and (4) the support of authorities, law, or custom.[5] A review of over five hundred intergroup-contact studies found that these conditions facilitated a reduction in prejudice. There were also other positive outcomes, including greater trust and forgiveness for past transgressions. Positive contact effects occurred for ethnic groups, homosexuals, the disabled, and the mentally ill. Intergroup friendships were especially important in reducing prejudice. The positive effects of contact extended beyond the immediate member to the group as a whole and even to other out-groups not involved in the contact, and they occurred across nations, genders, and age groups. Intergroup contact had a negative effect when it was nonvoluntary and threatening.[6]

As we have seen, just sitting at a table with someone does not guarantee that prejudice will magically disappear. However, much empirical evidence suggests that voluntary, nonthreatening, face-to-face contact can break down barriers between people. Most meals are face-to-face, voluntary, and non-threatening; they have common goals of hunger reduction and conviviality; they involve coordination in their planning and execution; and they are immersed in the informal rules of customs. These conditions bode well for a reduction in prejudice and an increase in trust, forgiveness, and intergroup friendship.

In *The Audacity of Hope*, President Obama endorsed "a shift in metaphors, one that sees our democracy not as a house to be built but as a conversation to be had," adding that "all citizens are required to engage in a process of testing their ideas against an external reality, persuading others of their point of view, and building shifting alliances of consent."[7] I agree that citizens in a democracy have a moral obligation to bring others into conversations about our social contract—an understanding that citizenship involves sharing the burdens and responsibilities, along with the benefits and rights, of living in a political community. Conversations have the potential to build trust and empathy among strangers, especially if conversants are caring, respectful, fair, and open to learning. Conversations take work, but they are well worth the effort because they are the building blocks of democracy, fashioned one meal at a time.

Notes

Chapter One. Setting the Table

1. Wilk, "Power at the Table," 428.
2. Ibid., 430.
3. Ibid., 432.
4. Musick and Meier, "Assessing Causality and Persistence," 476, 488.
5. David, *Family Dinner*, 6.
6. Parker, *Idella Parker*, 107–8.
7. Sharpless, *Cooking in Other Women's Kitchens*, 145.
8. Severson, *Spoon Fed*, 182–84.
9. Batsell et al., "You Will Eat," 211, 215.
10. Colt, "Sibling Rivalry."
11. Counihan, "Food Rules," 60.
12. Ibid.
13. Ibid., 61.
14. Fiese and Schwartz, "Reclaiming the Family Table," 7.
15. Ludvigsen and Scott, "Real Kids Don't Eat Quiche," 428, 430–31.
16. Bossard, "Family Table Talk."
17. Schieffelin and Ochs, "Language Socialization."
18. Blum-Kulka, *Dinner Talk*, 9–10.
19. Ibid., 10–12, 14, 32.
20. Ibid., 37–39.
21. Ibid., 49, 51–52, 102.
22. Ibid., 75, 81.
23. Ibid., 142–43, 168, 181, 184.
24. Ibid., 264–65.
25. Ibid., 51, 265–67.
26. DeVault, *Feeding the Family*, 49.
27. Ibid., 49–50.
28. Ibid., 50.

29. Ibid., 50–51.

30. Ibid., 52–53.

31. Ibid., 52–54.

32. Ibid., 54.

33. Ibid., 188–89.

34. Ibid., 190.

35. Cinotto, "Around the Table," 18–21.

36. Ibid., 22–23.

37. Ibid., 23–24.

38. Ibid., 27, 29–30.

39. United States Department of Agriculture, "Economics of Food."

40. Schor, "Why Americans Should Rest."

41. Castle, "Overworked No More."

42. De Graaf, "Workweek Woes."

43. Greenhouse, "Demands on Workers Grow."

44. Samuelson, "Europe Surpasses America."

45. Harjo, "World Ends Here."

46. Rabbi Morley Feinstein, quoted in David, *Family Dinner*, 200.

47. Silva and Nelson, *Hidden Kitchens*, 255.

48. Gopnik, *Table Comes First*, 52–53.

49. Barbour and Rogers, "You Can't Hack a Steakhouse."

50. Smith, "Cohousing Coming of Age."

51. Herrera, "Let's Eat In!"

52. J. Brown, *World Café*, 40.

53. http://worldwide.feastongood.com/, accessed October 2013.

54. Gopnik, *Table Comes First*, 250–51.

55. Bambara, "Salvation Is the Issue," 41.

56. Silva and Nelson, *Hidden Kitchens*, 248, 251.

57. Hauck-Lawson, "Introduction," 24.

58. Hood, "My Dinner with Dr. King."

59. Fishel, "Power of Table Talk."

60. Stone, Patton, and Heen, *Difficult Conversations*.

61. Fishel, "Power of Table Talk."

Chapter Two. Conversations and Narratives

1. Tannen, *Conversational Style*, 5–6.

2. Tannen, "Gender Differences in Conversational Coherence," 178.

3. Fishman, "Interaction," 402.

4. Ibid.

5. Lareau, "Invisible Inequality," 748–49.

6. Ibid., 756, 758–59.

7. Ibid., 766, 770–71.
8. Ibid., 774.
9. Hart and Risley, "Early Catastrophe."
10. Talbot, "Talking Cure."
11. Eliasoph, *Avoiding Politics*, 20–21.
12. Walsh, *Talking about Politics*.
13. Ackerman, "Why Dialogue?," 10, 12.
14. Ibid., 16.
15. Ibid., 17, 19–20, 22.
16. Engel, "Playing to Learn."
17. Lei-Anne Ellis, quoted in Weinstein, *Surprising Power of Family Meals*, 213–14.
18. David, *Family Dinner*, 157.
19. Michael Curtis, student at the Northwest School, Seattle, Washington, personal interview, November 8, 2012.
20. David, *Family Dinner*, 158; list of games 159–60, 161–64.
21. Ibid., 167–68.
22. Ibid., 168–69.
23. Weinstein, *Surprising Power of Family Meals*, 3–5.
24. Curtis interview.
25. Seamus O'Leary, student at the Northwest School, Seattle, Washington, personal interview, November 8, 2012.
26. Severson, *Spoon Fed*, 26.
27. Duke et al., "Ketchup and Kin," 3.
28. Ibid., 5.
29. Ibid., 6–7.
30. Ibid., 8.
31. Ibid., 9–12.
32. Erickson, "Social Construction of Discourse Coherence," 208–11, 226–27.
33. Fiese, Foley, and Spagnola, "Routine and Ritual Elements," 82–84.
34. Ibid., 84–85.
35. Minami, "Long Conversational Turns."
36. Ochs and Taylor, "Family Narrative as Political Activity," 301.
37. Ibid., 303.
38. Ibid., 308–9.
39. Ibid., 332–33, 335.
40. Paugh, "Learning about Work at Dinnertime," 57.
41. Ibid., 65–66, 68, 70–71.
42. Snow and Beals, "Mealtime Talk," 52–53.
43. Ibid., 53–54.
44. Ibid., 54–55, 59.

Chapter Three. Tables at Home

1. hooks, *Talking Back*, 21.
2. hooks, "Homeplace," 41–42, 47.
3. Hollows, *Domestic Cultures*, 10, 12–13, 55–56.
4. Gorman-Murray, "Gay and Lesbian Couples," 153–54, 156, 158.
5. Carrington, *No Place Like Home*, 30, 62.
6. Ibid., 63.
7. Ibid., 64–65.
8. Holtzman, "Jewish Lesbian Parenting," 333–34.
9. Kent, "Effects of Television Viewing," 124–25.
10. Ibid., 125–26.
11. Kibria, "Migration and Vietnamese American Women," 257.
12. Matchar, "New Domesticity."
13. Newman, *Accordion Family*, 132, 72–74.
14. Olsen and Fuller, *Home-School Relations*, 29–32.
15. Marshall, "From the Poets in the Kitchen."
16. Finn, "Kitchen Voice as Confessional," 87–88.
17. Sharpless, *Cooking in Other Women's Kitchens*, 143.
18. Ibid., 143–44.
19. Kousha, *Best Friends*, 11–12, 129.
20. Moody, *Coming of Age in Mississippi*, 34.
21. Clark, *Out of the Frying Pan*, 8, 45–46.
22. Ibid., 180–81, 200.
23. Abarca, *Voices in the Kitchen*, 36, 39, 44–46.
24. Abarca, "Charlas Culinarias," 184–88, 201, 203–4.
25. Kraut, "Ethnic Foodways," 413, 415.
26. Severson, *Spoon Fed*, 6–7.
27. Weinstein, *Surprising Power of Family Meals*, 17.
28. Silva and Nelson, *Hidden Kitchens*, 248–49.
29. Dr. Harvey Karp, quoted in David, *Family Dinner*, viii–ix.
30. Mary Hartzell, quoted in David, *Family Dinner*, 16.
31. Nora Ephron, quoted in David, *Family Dinner*, 93.
32. Stephanie Bonham, college student in Pleasanton, California, personal interview, September 10, 2012.
33. Barbara Scheifler, elementary school teacher, in Berkeley, California, personal interview, February 28, 2013.
34. Curtis interview.
35. Wizenberg, *Homemade Life*, 1–3.
36. Weinstein, *Surprising Power of Family Meals*, 177.
37. Beoku-Betts, "We Got Our Way," 551.
38. Hoffman, "Guilt-Trip Casserole."

39. Ibid.
40. Lou Szucs, quoted in David, *Family Dinner*, 179.
41. Marshall Duke and Laurie David, quoted in David, *Family Dinner*, 181.
42. Bryant Terry, quoted in David, *Family Dinner*, 180.
43. Davia Nelson and Nikki Silva, quoted in David, *Family Dinner*, 186.
44. Nikki Silva, quoted in David, *Family Dinner*, 186.
45. Davia Nelson and Nikki Silva, quoted in David, *Family Dinner*, 186.
46. Harris, *Iron Pots and Wooden Spoons*, xx–xxii.
47. Bonham interview.
48. Scheifler interview.
49. O'Leary interview.
50. Sharpless, *Cooking in Other Women's Kitchens*, 102–3.
51. Nancy Highiet, librarian, the Northwest School, Seattle, Washington, personal interview, November 6, 2012.
52. Ray, *Migrant's Table*, 52–54.
53. Fingerman, "Nice Little Chat," 102.
54. Carothers, "Catching Sense," 320–24.
55. Maricel Presilla, quoted in David, *Family Dinner*, 71.
56. O'Leary interview.
57. Clark, *Out of the Frying Pan*, 65–66.
58. Severson, *Spoon Fed*, 2–3.
59. Weinstein, *Surprising Power of Family Meals*, 120–22.
60. Ibid., 235–36.
61. Pooni, "*Saag* and *Makhi de Roti*," 104, 106.
62. Bonham interview.
63. Curtis interview.
64. Kaplan, "Using Food as a Metaphor," 485–87.
65. Ibid., 488–89.
66. Ibid., 490–91.
67. Ibid., 492–94.
68. Ibid., 489–500.
69. Magee, "Cooking with Children."
70. Judith Martin (Miss Manners), quoted in David, *Family Dinner*, 15.
71. Feiring and Lewis, "Ecology," 377, 386.
72. Severson, *Spoon Fed*, 1–2.
73. Scheifler interview.
74. Ibid.
75. Clark, *Out of the Frying Pan*, 47–48.
76. Chao, *How to Cook*, 5, 12–13.
77. Grieshaber, "Mealtime Rituals," 657–58.
78. Ibid., 659–62.
79. Fraser, "Perspectives on Politeness."

80. Snow et al., "Developmental Perspectives on Politeness," 289–90.
81. Ibid., 303.
82. Shuman, "Rhetoric of Portions," 75–76, 79.
83. Bonham interview.
84. O'Leary interview.
85. Clark, *Out of the Frying Pan*, 49, 127–28.
86. Ibid., 101–2.
87. Ibid., 193–94.
88. Arianna Huffington, quoted in David, *Family Dinner*, 183.
89. Furger, "Edible Schoolyard."
90. Carol Smith, quoted in David, *Family Dinner*, 15–16.
91. Robert F. Kennedy Jr., quoted in David, *Family Dinner*, 170–71.
92. Soledad O'Brien, quoted in David, *Family Dinner*, 201.
93. In "The Forms of Capital," Pierre Bourdieu defined "cultural capital" and "social capital" as assets that promoted social mobility, with the former consisting of knowledge and skills and the latter based on group membership and relationships.
94. Emma Le Du, sixth-grade parent, the Northwest School, Seattle, Washington, personal interview, November 8, 2012.
95. Curtis interview.
96. Beals, "Sources of Support," 690–91.
97. Patrick et al., "Benefits of Authoritative Feeding Style," 243–44.
98. Fisher, Wallace, and Fenton, "Discrimination Distress during Adolescence," 681, 691.
99. Julier, *Eating Together*, 23–24, 94.
100. Ephron, "How I Learned."
101. Norwich, "Who Killed Entertaining?," 62.
102. Ibid.
103. Quoted in Norwich, "Who Killed Entertaining?" 62–63.
104. Trebay, "Guess Who Isn't Coming."
105. Ibid.
106. Ibid.
107. Ibid.
108. West, "Pacific Heights."
109. Ibid.
110. Maguy Le Coze, quoted in Rubenstein, "Maguy by the Sea," 133–36.
111. Saffo, "How to Save Democracy."
112. Nancy Wilson, quoted in David, *Family Dinner*, 35.
113. Mary Ann Hoberman and Paul Cummins, quoted in David, *Family Dinner*, 172.
114. Young, *Hungry Ear*, v., 3.
115. Gold, "These Little Toe Shoes."

116. Lindsay, "Engineering Serendipity."
117. Schweitzer, "Where Musicians Bask."
118. Le Du interview.
119. Clark, *Out of the Frying Pan*, 62–64.
120. Severson, *Spoon Fed*, 131–32.
121. O'Leary interview.
122. Bonham interview.
123. Curtis interview.
124. Highiet interview.
125. Clark, *Out of the Frying Pan*, 25.
126. David, *Family Dinner*, 189–90.
127. Ibid., 190.
128. Weinstein, *Surprising Power of Family Meals*, 172–73.
129. Ibid., 235.
130. Clark, *Out of the Frying Pan*, 142, 238–41.
131. Wizenberg, *Homemade Life*, 141, 155.
132. Pham, "Family Comforts."
133. Ebaugh and Curry, "Fictive Kin as Social Capital," 199, 204.
134. Sidenvall, Nydahl, and Fjellström, "Meal as Gift," 415.
135. Ibid., 415–16.

Chapter Four. Tables Away from Home

1. Renee O'Harran, chef at the Northwest School, Seattle, Washington, personal interview, November 6, 2012.
2. Ibid.
3. Ibid.
4. Ibid.
5. Ibid.
6. O'Leary interview.
7. Highiet interview.
8. Le Du interview.
9. Clark, *Out of the Frying Pan*, 69.
10. William Doherty, quoted in Gibbs, "Magic of the Family Meal."
11. Scheifler interview.
12. Ibid.
13. Ibid.
14. Ibid.
15. Ibid.
16. Ibid.
17. Ibid.
18. Hesser, "Dude, Where's My Spice Grinder?"

19. Ibid.
20. Graham, "Let's Eat!," 58–59.
21. Ibid., 59–60.
22. Ibid., 62–63.
23. Korandanis, "Sit at the Same Table."
24. Locher et al., "Comfort Foods," 281–83, 286.
25. Ibid., 282–83.
26. Sharon M. K. Kugler, quoted in Saum, "God & Woman," 19.
27. Dodson and Gilkes, "Church Food," 521–22, 532–33.
28. Wu, "Amazing Grace."
29. Ibid.
30. Ibid.
31. Ibid.
32. Ibid.
33. Brawley, "Table Fellowship," 29–30.
34. Bill Huebsch, quoted in Weinstein, *Surprising Power of Family Meals*, 145–48.
35. Wendy Mogel, quoted in Weinstein, *Surprising Power of Family Meals*, 165–67.
36. Severson, *Spoon Fed*, 150–51.
37. David, *Family Dinner*, 194–95.
38. Mechling, "Boy Scouts," 83–85.
39. Deutsch, "'Please Pass the Chicken Tits,'" 94–95, 98–99.
40. Ibid., 101.
41. Ibid., 104–8.
42. Ibid., 108–9.
43. Ibid., 110–12.
44. Steffen, "Life Stories and Shared Experiences," 101–2, 105, 107.
45. Valverde and White-Mair, "One Day," 402–4.
46. Mäkelä, "International Comparisons of Alcoholics Anonymous," 230.
47. Kohn and Bryan, "Ritual Practice," 720–24.
48. Johnson, "Unorthodox Advocate."
49. "Jefferson Award Winner."
50. Penn's Station, "Homies Empowerment Dinner."
51. Fagan, "Homeless Veterans."
52. Zinder, "Hard Tack."
53. Rick Lynch, quoted in David, *Family Dinner*, 15.
54. Silva and Nelson, *Hidden Kitchens*, 252–53.
55. Kiang and Loo, "Food in Racial Experiences," 10, 7, 11–12.
56. Ibid., 10–11, 13.
57. Ibid., 13–14.

Chapter Five. Tables and Conflict

1. Vuchinich, "Spontaneous Family Conflicts," 591, 594–95.
2. Ibid., 598–99.
3. Ibid., 599.
4. P. L. Brown, "Students Let Guard Down."
5. Zernike, "Sobered Gay Rights Groups."
6. Lelyveld, "L.A.'s First Death Café."
7. Span, "Death Be Not Decaffeinated."
8. Ibid.
9. Ochs and Shohet, "Cultural Structuring of Mealtime Socialization," 38.
10. Ibid., 39–41.
11. Ibid., 42.
12. Ibid., 42–46.
13. Diner, *Hungering for America*, 112, 114, 120, 151–53, 178, 52, 78, 80, 82.
14. Scheifler interview.
15. Shuman, "Rhetoric of Portions," 76–77.
16. Ray, *Migrant's Table*, 80.
17. Jade Snow Wong, quoted in Goldman, *Take My Word*, 10–11.
18. Malcolm Sher, mediator in San Ramon, California, personal interview, July 23, 2013. The text in the following ten subsections is taken from the interview.
19. Silva and Nelson, *Hidden Kitchens*, 251.
20. Severson, *Spoon Fed*, 14–15.
21. Kraft, "Jewish and Muslim."
22. "Dumpling Diplomacy."
23. Oppenheimer, "After Dinner, the Fireworks."
24. Smart-Grosvenor, *Vibration Cooking*, 29.
25. Fields, *Lemon Swamp*, xiii–xiv.
26. Silva and Nelson, *Hidden Kitchens*, 195–206.
27. Severson, *Spoon Fed*, 144.
28. Susman, "Pittsburgh Café."
29. Landgraff, "Talking Politics with Strangers."
30. Shah, "Culinary Diplomacy."
31. Conflict Kitchen website, http://www.conflictkitchen.org/, accessed July 15, 2013.
32. Susman, "Pittsburgh Café."
33. Kadri, "Conflict Kitchen."
34. Landgraff, "Talking Politics with Strangers."
35. Ibid.
36. Ibid.
37. Beras, "Taste of Iran."

38. Gandhi, "Conflict Cuisine."
39. Landgraff, "Talking Politics with Strangers."
40. Shah, "Culinary Diplomacy."
41. Gandhi, "Conflict Cuisine."
42. Conflict Kitchen website.
43. Susman, "Pittsburgh Café."

Chapter Six. Civic Engagement and Diplomacy

1. Silva and Nelson, *Hidden Kitchens*, 256–57.
2. Ibid., xvi–xvii.
3. Ibid., 249–50.
4. Ibid., 250–51.
5. Ibid., 254.
6. Ibid., 258.
7. Ibid., 260.
8. Curtis interview.
9. Highiet interview.
10. O'Harran interview.
11. Clark, *Out of the Frying Pan*, 224, 242.
12. Severson, *Spoon Fed*, 145–46.
13. Ray, *Migrant's Table*, 122.
14. Beoku-Betts, "We Got Our Way," 549.
15. MacVean, "Eden's Garden."
16. Ibid.
17. Flanagan, "Developmental Roots of Political Engagement," 257–58.
18. Ibid., 258, 261.
19. Flanagan, "Trust, Identity," 165–67.
20. Ibid., 168–70.
21. Flanagan et al., "School and Community Climates," 421–23.
22. Flanagan and Gallay, "Reframing the Meaning," 38.
23. Fuligini, Tseng, and Lam, "Attitudes toward Family Obligations," 1030.
24. Sánchez-Jankowski, "Minority Youth and Civic Engagement," 237–38, 240–41, 243, emphasis mine.
25. Saphir and Chaffee, "Adolescents' Contributions," 87–90, 102–3, 105.
26. Andolina et al., "Habits from Home," 277–78.
27. McIntosh, Hart, and Youniss, "Family Political Discussion," 495–98.
28. Verba, Scholzman, and Brady, *Voice and Equality*, 20, 459.
29. Burns, Scholzman, and Verba, *Private Roots of Public Action*, 102, 141, 287, 192, 313, 329.
30. Druckman and Nelson, "Framing and Deliberation."
31. Knoke, "Networks of Political Action," 1041.
32. Pattie and Johnston, "People Who Talk," 41, 58, 62.

33. Kathlene, "In a Different Voice," 224–27.
34. Ellis, *Coffee-House,* 202–3.
35. Berkowitz, "Politic Moralist," 37–38.
36. Mutz and Reeves, "New Videomalaise," 2–3.
37. Ibid., 4–5, 11.
38. Ibid., 11–13.
39. Papacharissi, "Democracy Online," 276–78.
40. Lozada, "President Obama."
41. Ibid.
42. Ibid.
43. Ibid.
44. Snowe, "Why I'm Leaving."
45. Carlson, "Senate's Women."
46. Ibid.
47. Haddadin, "Forging Friendships."
48. Minielly and Finnie, "Nancy Pelosi."
49. Lovley, "Senate Women's Civility' Pact."
50. Ibid.
51. Ibid.
52. Ibid.
53. Foley, "Women Senators."
54. Newton-Small, "Women Are the Only Adults."
55. Ibid.
56. Ibid.
57. Newton-Small, "Things You Don't Know."
58. Osipova, "From Gastronationalism to Gastrodiplomacy."
59. Rockower, "State of Gastrodiplomacy."
60. Wenzel, "Potlucks for Peace?"
61. Ruddy, "Hearts, Minds, and Stomachs."
62. Chapple-Sokol, "Culinary Diplomacy."
63. Chapple-Sokol, "War and Peas."
64. Nye, *Soft Power*, 7.
65. Burros, "Diplomacy Travels."
66. Clinton, video remarks.
67. Sietsema, "Chefs Are the New Diplomats."
68. Reid, "Hillary Clinton."
69. Meathead, "Barbecue Diplomacy."
70. Ibid.
71. Ibid.
72. Jacinto, "Barbecue Diplomacy."
73. Ibid.
74. Ibid.

Conclusion

1. Beaumont, *Civic Constitution.*
2. McClain, "Domain of Civic Virtue."
3. Finn, *Peopling the Constitution,* 6.
4. This discussion of resilience is based on Benard, "Fostering Resilience in Children"; Masten, "Ordinary Magic"; Olsson et al., "Adolescent Resilience"; and Wang, Haertel, and Walberg, "Educational Resilience in Inner Cities."
5. Allport, *Nature of Prejudice.*
6. Pettigrew et al., "Recent Advances."
7. Obama, *Audacity of Hope,* 92.

Bibliography

Abarca, Meredith E. "*Charlas Culinarias*: Mexican Women Speak from Their Public Kitchens." *Food and Foodways* 15:3/4 (2007): 183–212.

———. *Voices in the Kitchen: Views on Food and the World by Working-Class Mexican and Mexican-American Women.* College Station, Tex.: Texas A&M University Press, 2006.

Ackerman, Bruce. "Why Dialogue?" *Journal of Philosophy* 86:1 (January 1989): 5–22.

Algren, Nelson. *America Eats.* Iowa City: University of Iowa Press, 1992.

Allport, Gordon W. *The Nature of Prejudice.* Reading, Mass.: Addison Wesley, 1954.

Andolina, Molly W., Krista Jenkins, Cliff Zukin, and Scott Keeter. "Habits from Home, Lessons from School: Influences on Youth Civic Development." *PS: Political Science and Politics* 36:2 (2003): 275–80.

Bambara, Toni Cade. "Salvation Is the Issue." In *Black Women Writers (1950–1980): A Critical Evaluation*, edited by Mari Evans, 41–47. New York: Anchor Books, 1984.

Barbour, Haley, and Ed Rogers. "You Can't Hack a Steakhouse: What China Doesn't Get about How Washington Works." *Foreign Policy*, February 25, 2013, http://foreignpolicy.com/2013/02/25/you-cant-hack-a-steakhouse/, accessed January 3, 2016.

Batsell, W. Robert, Jr., Alan S. Brown, Matthew E. Ansfield, and Gayla Y. Paschall. "'You Will Eat All of That!': A Retrospective Analysis of Forced Consumption Episodes." *Appetite* 38:3 (June 2002): 211–19.

Beals, Diane E. "Sources of Support for Learning Words in Conversation: Evidence from Mealtimes." *Journal of Child Language* 24:3 (October 1997): 673–94.

Beaumont, Elizabeth. *The Civic Constitution: Civic Visions and Struggles in the Path toward Constitutional Democracy.* New York: Oxford University Press, 2014.

Benard, Bonnie. "Fostering Resilience in Children." ERIC Digest, Educational Resources Information Center. ERIC Clearinghouse on Elementary and Early Childhood Education, Urbana, Illinois, 1995.

Beoku-Betts, Josephine. "We Got Our Way of Cooking Things: Women, Food, and the Preservation of Cultural Identity among the Gullah." *Gender & Society* 9:5 (October 1995): 535–55.

Beras, Erika. "A Taste of Iran, Whipped Up in the 'Conflict Kitchen'." *All Things Considered*, July 2, 2010.

Berkowitz, Peter. "The Politic Moralist." *New Republic*, September 1, 1997, 36–40.

Blum-Kulka, Shoshana. *Dinner Talk: Cultural Patterns of Sociability and Socialization in Family Discourse*. Mahwah, N.J.: Lawrence Erlbaum, 1997.

Bossard, James H. S. "Family Table Talk—An Area for Sociological Study." *American Sociological Review* 8:3 (June 1943): 295–301.

Bourdieu, Pierre. "The Forms of Capital." In *Handbook of Theory and Research for the Sociology of Education*, edited by John Richardson, 241–58. New York: Greenwood Press, 1986.

Brawley, Robert L. "Table Fellowship: Bane and Blessing for the Historical Jesus." *Perspectives in Religious Studies* 22:1 (Spring 1995): 13–31.

Brown, Juanita, with Davie Isaacs. *The World Café: Shaping Our Futures through Conversations That Matter*. San Francisco: Berrett-Koehler, 2005.

Brown, Patricia Leigh. "Students Let Guard Down to Transform Vicious Circle." *New York Times*, April 4, 2013.

Burns, Nancy, Kay Lehman Schlozman, and Sidney Verba. *The Private Roots of Public Action: Gender, Equality, and Political Participation*. Cambridge, Mass.: Harvard University Press, 2001.

Burros, Marian. "Diplomacy Travels on Its Stomach, Too." *New York Times*, July 2, 2012.

Carlson, Margaret. "How the Senate's Women Maintain Bipartisanship and Civility." *Daily Beast*, March 4, 2012, http://tinyurl.com/75zlm4l, accessed January 2, 2016.

Carothers, Suzanne C. "Catching Sense: Learning from Our Mothers to Be Black and Female." In *Families in the U.S.: Kinship and Domestic Politics*, edited by Karen Hansen and Anita Ilta Garey, 315–28. Philadelphia: Temple University Press, 1998.

Carrington, Christopher. *No Place like Home: Relationships and Family Life among Lesbians and Gay Men*. Chicago: University of Chicago Press, 1999.

Castle, Teresa. "Overworked No More—National Group Working Hard to Give Americans a Break." *San Francisco Chronicle*, October 22, 2005.

Chao, Buwei Yang. *How to Cook and Eat in Chinese*. New York: John Day, 1945.

Chapple-Sokol, Sam. "Culinary Diplomacy: Breaking Bread to Win Hearts and Minds." *Hague Journal of Diplomacy* 8:2 (2013): 161–83.

———. "War and Peas: Culinary Conflict Resolution as Citizen Diplomacy." *Public Diplomacy Magazine* 11 (Winter 2014), http://publicdiplomacymagazine.com/warandpeas/.

Cinotto, Simone. "'Everyone Would Be around the Table': American Family Mealtimes in Historical Perspective, 1850–1960." *New Directions for Child and Adolescent Development* 111 (Spring 2006): 17–34.

Clark, Gillian. *Out of the Frying Pan: A Chef's Memoir of Hot Kitchens, Single Motherhood, and the Family Meal*. New York: St. Martin's Press, 2007.

Clinton, Hillary Rodham. Video remarks for the Diplomatic Culinary Partnership Initiative Launch. U.S. State Department, Washington, D.C., September 10, 2012.

Colt, George Howe. "Sibling Rivalry: One Long Food Fight." *New York Times*, November 25, 2012.

Counihan, Carole M. "Food Rules in the United States: Individualism, Control and Hierarchy." *Anthropological Quarterly* 65:2 (April 1992): 55–66.

David, Laurie. *The Family Dinner: Great Ways to Connect with Your Kids One Meal at a Time.* New York: Grand Central Life and Style, 2010.

Dodson, Jualynne E., and Cheryl Townsend Gilkes. "There's Nothing like Church Food: Food and the U.S. Afro-Christian Tradition; Re-Membering Community and Feeding the Embodied S/pirit(s)." *Journal of the American Academy of Religion* 63:3 (Fall 1995): 519–38.

De Graaf, John. "Workweek Woes." *New York Times*, April 12, 2003.

Deutsch, Jonathan. "'Please Pass the Chicken Tits': Rethinking Men and Cooking at an Urban Firehouse." *Food and Foodways* 13:1/2 (2005): 91–114.

DeVault, Marjorie L. *Feeding the Family: The Social Organization of Caring as Gendered Work.* Chicago: University of Chicago Press, 1991.

Diner, Hasia R. *Hungering for America: Italian, Irish and Jewish Foodways in the Age of Migration.* Cambridge, Mass.: Harvard University Press, 2001.

Druckman, James N., and Kjersten R. Nelson. "Framing and Deliberation: How Citizens' Conversations Limit Elite Influence." *American Journal of Political Science* 47:4 (October 2003): 729–45.

Duke, Marshall P., Robin Fivush, Amber Lazarus, and Jennifer Bohanek. "Of Ketchup and Kin: Dinnertime Conversations as a Major Source of Family Knowledge, Family Adjustment, and Family Resilience." Working Paper 26. Atlanta: Emory Center for Myth and Ritual in American Life, May 2003.

"Dumpling Diplomacy," April 17, 2013, http://potluckdiplomacy.tumblr.com/search/dumpling+diplomacy, accessed February 10, 2016.

Ebaugh, Helen Rose, and Mary Curry. "Fictive Kin as Social Capital in New Immigrant Communities." *Sociological Perspectives* 43:2 (2000): 189–209.

Eliasoph, Nina. *Avoiding Politics: How Americans Produce Apathy in Everyday Life.* Cambridge: Cambridge University Press, 1998.

Ellis, Markman. *The Coffee-House: A Cultural History.* London: Phoenix, 2004.

Engel, Susan. "Playing to Learn." *New York Times*, February 2, 2010.

Ephron, Nora. "How I Learned to Stop Worrying . . . and Entertain with Aplomb." *New York Times Magazine: Style & Entertaining*, November 5, 2000, 48–52.

Erickson, Frederick. "The Social Construction of Discourse Coherence in a Family Dinner Table Conversation." In *Conversation Organization and Its Development*, edited by Bruce Dorval, 207–39. Norwood: N.J.: Ablex, 1990.

Fagan, Kevin. "Homeless Veterans Have Each Other's Backs in New S.F. Digs." *San Francisco Chronicle*, November 10, 2012.

Feiring, Candice, and Michael Lewis. "The Ecology of Some Middle-Class Families at Dinner." *International Journal of Behavioral Development* 10:3 (September 1987): 377–90.

Fields, Mamie Garvin, with Karen Fields. *Lemon Swamp and Other Places: A Carolina Memoir.* New York: Free Press, 1983.

Fiese, Barbara H., Kimberly P. Foley, and Mary Spagnola. "Routine and Ritual Elements in Family Mealtimes: Contexts for Child Well-Being and Family Identity." *New Directions for Child and Adolescent Development* 111 (Spring 2006): 67–89.

Fiese, Barbara H., and Marlene Schwartz. "Reclaiming the Family Table: Mealtimes and Child Wellbeing." *Social Policy Report* 22:4 (2008): 1–19.

Fingerman, Karen L. "'We Had a Nice Little Chat': Age and Generational Differences in Mothers' and Daughters' Descriptions of Enjoyable Visits." *Journal of Gerontology: Psychological Sciences* 55B:2 (2000): 95–106.

Finn, John E. "The Kitchen Voice as Confessional." *Food, Culture and Society* 7:1 (Spring 2004): 85–100.

———. *Peopling the Constitution.* Lawrence: University Press of Kansas, 2014.

Fishel, Anne. "The Power of Table Talk." Family Dinner Project website, http://the familydinnerproject.org, accessed May 26, 2011.

Fisher, Celia B., Scyatta A. Wallace, and Rose E. Fenton. "Discrimination Distress during Adolescence." *Journal of Youth and Adolescence* 29:6 (2000): 679–95.

Fishman, Pamela M. "Interaction: The Work Women Do." *Social Problems* 25:4 (April 1978): 397–406.

Flanagan, Constance. "Developmental Roots of Political Engagement." *PS: Political Science and Politics* 36:2 (April 2003): 257–61.

———. "Trust, Identity, and Civic Hope." *Applied Developmental Science* 7:3 (2003): 165–71.

Flanagan, Constance, Patricio Cumsille, Sukhdeep Gill, and Leslie S. Gallay. "School and Community Climates and Civic Commitments: Patterns for Ethnic Minority and Majority Students." *Journal of Educational Psychology* 99:2 (May 2007): 421–31.

Flanagan, Constance, and Leslie S. Gallay. "Reframing the Meaning of 'Political' in Research with Adolescents." *Perspectives on Political Science* 24:1 (Winter 1995): 34–41.

Foley, Elise. "Women Senators Make History in 113th Congress." *Huffington Post*, January 3, 2013, http://tinyurl.com/byf64a4, accessed January 3, 2016.

Fraser, Bruce. "Perspectives on Politeness." *Journal of Pragmatics* 14 (1990): 219–36.

Fuligini, Andrew, Vivian Tseng, and Mary Lam. "Attitudes toward Family Obligations among American Adolescents with Asian, Latin American, and European Backgrounds." *Child Development* 70:4 (August 1999): 1030–44.

Furger, Roberta. "The Edible Schoolyard: Connecting Students to the Earth—and to Their Community." *Edutopia* (Spring 2004): 10–11, 18.

Gandhi, Jatin. "Conflict Cuisine." *Open Magazine*, July 3, 2010, http://www.open themagazine.com/article/international/conflict-cuisine, accessed January 3, 2016.

Gibbs, Nancy. "The Magic of the Family Meal." *Time*, June 4, 2006.

Gold, Sylviane. "These Little Toe Shoes Are Longing to Stray." *New York Times*, August 7, 2005.

Goldman, Anne. *Take My Word: Autobiographical Innovations of Ethnic American Working Women.* Berkeley: University of California Press, 1996.

Gopnik, Adam. *The Table Comes First: Family, France, and the Meaning of Food*. New York: Alfred A. Knopf, 2011.

Gorman-Murray, Andrew. "Gay and Lesbian Couples at Home: Identity Work in Domestic Space." *Home Cultures* 3:2 (2006): 145–68.

Graham, Andrea. "'Let's Eat!' Commitment and Communion in Co-Operative Households." *Western Folklore* 40:1 (1981): 55–63.

Greenhouse, Steven. "As Demands on Workers Grow, Groups Push for Paid Family and Sick Leave." *New York Times*, March 6, 2005.

Grieshaber, Susan. "Mealtime Rituals: Power and Resistance in the Construction of Mealtime Rules." *British Journal of Sociology* 48:4 (December 1997): 649–66.

Haddadin, Jim. "Senators Forging Friendships at the Dinner Table: All-Female Club Gets Things Done." *Foster's Daily Democrat*, April 21, 2012, http://tinyurl.com/zxq8qep, accessed January 16, 2016.

Harjo, Joy. "Perhaps the World Ends Here." In *The Hungry Ear: Poems of Food and Drink*, edited by Kevin Young, 7. New York: Bloomsbury, 2012.

Harris, Jessica B. *Iron Pots and Wooden Spoons: Africa's Gifts to New World Cooking*. New York: Atheneum, 1989.

Hart, Betty, and Todd R. Risley. "The Early Catastrophe: The 30 Million Word Gap by Age 3." *American Educator* (Spring 2003): 4–8.

Hauck-Lawson, Annie. "Introduction to a Special Issue on Food Voice." *Food, Culture and Society* 7:1 (Spring 2004): 24–25.

Herrera, Tilde. "Let's Eat In! Feastly Startup Brings Diners into the Homes of Ambitious Cooks." *Bay Area News Group*, March 14, 2013.

Hesser, Amanda. "Dude, Where's My Spice Grinder?" *New York Times*, April 23, 2003.

Hoffman, Jan. "The Guilt-Trip Casserole: The Family Dinner." *New York Times*, October 4, 2009.

Hollows, Joanne. *Domestic Cultures*. New York: Open University Press/McGraw Hill, 2008.

Holtzman, Linda J. "Jewish Lesbian Parenting." In *Families in the U.S.: Kinship and Domestic Politics*, edited by Karen Hansen and Anita Ilta Garey, 329–34. Philadelphia: Temple University Press, 1998.

Hood, William. "My Dinner with Dr. King." *New York Times*, April 9, 2013.

hooks, bell. "Homeplace: A Site of Resistance." In *Yearning: Race, Gender and Cultural Politics*, 41–49. Boston: South End Press, 1990.

———. *Talking Back: Thinking Feminist, Thinking Black*. Boston: South End Press, 1989.

Jacinto, Leela. "Can Barbecue Diplomacy Shape World History?" *ABC News*, May 9, 2003.

"Jefferson Award Winner Paves Path for Oakland Gang Harmony." *CBS News*, San Francisco Bay Area, April 6, 2011.

Johnson, Scott. "An Unorthodox Advocate." *Bay Area News Group*, June 13, 2011.

Julier, Alice P. *Eating Together: Food, Friendship, and Inequality*. Urbana: University of Illinois Press, 2013.

Kadri, Meena. "Conflict Kitchen." *Design Observer*, November 1, 2010, http://designobserver.com/feature/conflict-kitchen/21738, accessed January 3, 2016.

Kaplan, Elaine Bell. "Using Food as a Metaphor of Care: Middle-School Kids Talk about Family, School, and Class Relationships." *Journal of Contemporary Ethnography* 29:4 (August 2000): 474–509.

Kathlene, Lyn. "In a Different Voice: Women and the Policy Process," In *Women in Elective Office: Past, Present and Future* edited by Sue Thomas and Clyde Wilcox, 213–29. New York: Oxford University Press, 2005.

Kent, Susan. "The Effects of Television Viewing: A Cross-Cultural Perspective." *Current Anthropology* 26:1 (February 1985): 121–26.

Kiang, Peter Nien-chu, and Chalsa M. Loo. "Food in Racial Experiences of Asian American Pacific Islander Vietnam Veterans." *Amerasia Journal* 32:2 (2006): 7–20.

Kibria, Nazli. "Migration and Vietnamese American Women: Remaking Ethnicity." In *Women of Color in U.S. Society*, edited by Maxine Baca Zinn and Bonnie Thornton Dill, 247–61. Philadelphia: Temple University Press, 1994.

Knoke, David. "Networks of Political Action: Toward Theory Construction." *Social Forces* 68:4 (June 1990): 1041–63.

Kohn, Abigail, and Kathy Bryan. "Ritual Practice in a Social Model Recovery Home." *Contemporary Drug Problems* 25 (Winter 1998): 711–39.

Korandanis, Art. "Because We All Sit at the Same Table: Slow Food Feeds the Stomach and Minds of Students at Holy Cross." *Connections* 9:8 (April 2009): 7.

Kousha, Mahnaz. *Best Friends: Power Relations among Black Domestics and White Mistresses*. PhD diss., University of Kentucky, 1990.

Kraft, Dina. "Jewish and Muslim, Bonding over Dieting," *New York Times*, March 17, 2013.

Kraut, Alan M. "Ethnic Foodways: The Significance of Food in the Designation of Cultural Boundaries between Immigrant Groups in the U.S., 1840–1921." *Journal of American Culture* 2:3 (Fall 1979): 409–20.

Landgraff, Amber. "Talking Politics with Strangers." *Fuse Magazine*, February 4, 2011, http://fusemagazine.org/2011/02/talking-politics-with-strangers, accessed January 3, 2016.

Lareau, Annette. "Invisible Inequality: Social Class and Childrearing in Black Families and White Families." *American Sociological Review* 67:5 (October 2002): 747–76.

Lelyveld, Nita. "Passing Thoughts at L.A.'s First Death Café." *Los Angeles Times*, April 15, 2013.

Lindsay, Greg. "Engineering Serendipity." *New York Times*, April 5, 2013.

Locher, Julie L., William C. Yoels, Dona Maurer, and Jullian Van Ells. "Comfort Foods: An Exploratory Journey into the Social and Emotional Significance of Food." *Food and Foodways* 13 (2005): 273–97.

Lovley, Erika. "Senate Women's 'Civility' Pact." *Politico*, February 4, 2011, http://tinyurl.com/gsp5cn8, accessed January 3, 2016.

Lozada, Carlos. "Please, President Obama, Not Another 'National Conversation.'" *Washington Post*, February 1, 2013.

Ludvigsen, Anna, and Sara Scott. "Real Kids Don't Eat Quiche: What Food Means to Children." *Food, Culture, and Society* 12:4 (December 2009): 417–36.

MacVean, Mary. "Eden's Garden." *Los Angeles Times*, August 7, 2010.

Magee, Elaine. "Cooking with Your Children: Why It's So Important to Spend Time in the Kitchen with Your Children—And How You Can Get Started." WebMD Feature, 2005, http://www.webmd.com/a-to-z-guides/features/cooking-with-your-children, accessed January 3, 2016.

Mäkelä, Klaus. "International Comparisons of Alcoholics Anonymous." *Alcohol Health and Research World* 17:3 (1993): 228–34.

Marshall, Paule. "From the Poets in the Kitchen." *New York Times Book Review*, January 9, 1983, http://tinyurl.com/jdoqrmz, accessed January 10, 2016.

Masten, Ann S. "Ordinary Magic: Resilience Processes in Development." *American Psychologist* 56:3 (March 2001): 227–38.

Matchar, Emily. "The New Domesticity: Fun, Empowering or a Step Back for American Women?" *Washington Post*, November 25, 2011.

McClain, Linda C. "The Domain of Civic Virtue in a Good Society: Families, Schools, and Sex Equality." *Fordham Law Review* 69:5 (April 2001): 1617–66.

McIntosh, Hugh, Daniel Hart, and James Youniss. "The Influence of Family Political Discussion on Youth Civic Development: Which Parent Qualities Matter?" *PS: Political Science and Politics* 40:3 (July 2007): 495–99.

Meathead. "Barbecue Diplomacy at LBJ's Texas White House." *Amazing Ribs* (blog). http://www.amazingribs.com/BBQ_articles/LBJ_and_BBQ.html, accessed January 3, 2016.

Mechling, Jay. "Boy Scouts and the Manly Art of Cooking." *Food and Foodways* 13:1/2 (2005): 67–89.

Minami, Masahiko. "Long Conversational Turns or Frequent Turn Exchanges: Cross-Cultural Comparisons of Parental Narrative Elicitation." *Journal of Asian Pacific Communication* 6:4 (1995): 213–30.

Minielly, Kristy, and Hannah Finnie. "Nancy Pelosi." A Tale of Two Dinners at http://www.tumblr.com/tagged/hannah-finnie, accessed September 18, 2012.

Moody, Anne. *Coming of Age in Mississippi: An Autobiography.* New York: Dell, 1968.

Musick, Kelly, and Ann Meier. "Assessing Causality and Persistence in Associations between Family Dinners and Adolescent Well-Being." *Journal of Marriage and Family* 74:3 (June 2012): 476–93.

Mutz, Diana C., and Byron Reeves. "The New Videomalaise: Effects of Televised Incivility on Political Trust." *American Political Science Review* 99:1 (February 2005): 1–15.

Newman, Katherine S. *The Accordion Family: Boomerang Kids, Anxious Parents, and the Private Toll of Global Competition.* Boston: Beacon, 2012.

Newton-Small, Jay. "11 Things You Don't Know about the Senate Sisterhood." *Time*, October 16, 2013, http://tinyurl.com/l85xfro, accessed January 20, 2016.

———. "Women Are the Only Adults Left in Washington," *Time*, October 16, 2013, http://tinyurl.com/nscbsl9, accessed January 10, 2016.

Norwich, William. "Who Killed Entertaining?" *New York Times Magazine: Style & Entertaining*, November 5, 2000, 54–63.

Nye, Joseph S. *Soft Power: The Means to Success in World Politics*. New York: Public Affairs, 2004.

Obama, Barack. *The Audacity of Hope: Thoughts on Reclaiming the American Dream*. New York: Three Rivers Press, 2006.

Ochs, Elinor, and Merav Shohet. "The Cultural Structuring of Mealtime Socialization." *New Directions for Child and Adolescent Development* 111 (Spring 2006): 35–49.

Ochs, Elinor, and Carolyn Taylor. "Family Narrative as Political Activity." *Discourse and Society* 3:3 (July 1992): 301–40.

Olsen, Glenn, and Mary Lou Fuller. *Home-School Relations: Working Successfully with Parents and Families*. New York: Pearson/Allyn Bacon, 2008.

Olsson, Craig A., Lyndal Bond, Jane M. Burns, Dianne A. Vella-Broderick, and Susan M. Sawyer. "Adolescent Resilience: A Concept Analysis." *Journal of Adolescence* 26:1 (2003): 1–11.

Oppenheimer, Mark. "After Dinner, the Fireworks." *New York Times*, August 23, 2012.

Osipova, Yelena. "From Gastronationalism to Gastrodiplomacy: Reversing the Securitization of the Dolma in the South Caucuses." *Public Diplomacy Magazine* 11 (Winter 2014), http://tinyurl.com/h5vf8z7, accessed January 3, 2016.

Papacharissi, Zizi. "Democracy Online: Civility, Politeness, and the Democratic Potential of Online Political Discussion Groups." *New Media and Society* 6:2 (April 2004): 259–83.

Parker, Idella, with Bud and Liz Crussell. *Idella Parker: From Reddick to Cross Creek*. Gainesville: University Press of Florida, 1999.

Patrick, Heather, Theresa A. Nicklas, Sheryl O. Hughes, and Miriam Morales. "The Benefits of Authoritative Feeding Style: Caregiver Feeding Styles and Children's Food Consumption Patterns." *Appetite* 44:2 (April 2005): 243–49.

Pattie, Charles, and Ron Johnston. "'People Who Talk Together Vote Together': An Exploration of Contextual Effects in Great Britain." *Annals of the Association of American Geographers* 90:1 (March 2000): 41–66.

Paugh, Amy L. "Learning about Work at Dinnertime: Language Socialization in Dual-Earner American Families." *Discourse & Society* 16:1 (January 2005): 55–78.

Penn's Station: A Train of Thought. "Homies Empowerment Dinner." http://ogpenn.wordpress.com/2011/01/20/homies-empowerment-dinner/, accessed April 2013.

Pettigrew, Thomas F., Linda R. Tropp, Ulrich Wagner, and Oliver Christ. "Recent Advances in Intergroup Contact Theory." *International Journal of Intercultural Relations* 35:3 (May 2011): 271–80.

Pham, Mai. "Family Comforts: Cooking Together Threads Past with Present, Grief with Joy." *San Francisco Chronicle*, February 20, 2002.

Pooni, Shavreen. "Saag and Makhi de Roti." *Amerasia Journal* 32:2 (2006): 103–7.

Ray, Krishendu. *The Migrant's Table: Meals and Memories in Bengali-American Households*. Philadelphia: Temple University Press, 2004.

Reid, Chip. "Secretary of State Hillary Clinton Turns to Food for Diplomacy." *CBS This Morning*, July 6, 2012.

Rockower, Paul. "The State of Gastrodiplomacy." *Public Diplomacy Magazine* 11 (Winter 2014), http://publicdiplomacymagazine.com/the-state-of-gastrodiplomacy/, accessed January 3, 2016.

Rubenstein, Hal. "Maguy by the Sea." *New York Times Magazine: Style & Entertaining*, November 5, 2000, 130–36.

Ruddy, Braden. "Hearts, Minds, and Stomachs: Gastrodiplomacy and the Potential of National Cuisine in Changing Public Perception of National Image." *Public Diplomacy Magazine* 11 (Winter 2014), http://tinyurl.com/jgs9uxv, accessed January 3, 2016.

Saffo, Paul. "How to Save Democracy over Dinner." *San Francisco Chronicle*, August 7, 2011.

Samuelson, Robert J. "Europe Surpasses America in Vacations." *Washington Post*, July 7, 2013.

Sánchez-Jankowski, Martín. "Minority Youth and Civic Engagement: The Impact of Group Relations." *Applied Developmental Science* 6:4 (2002): 237–45.

Saphir, Melissa Nichols, and Steven H. Chaffee, "Adolescents' Contributions to Family Communication Patterns." *Human Communication Research* 28:1 (January 2002): 86–108.

Saum, Steven Boyd. "God & Woman at Yale." *Santa Clara Magazine*, Winter 2008, 16–19.

Schieffelin, Bambi B., and Elinor Ochs. "Language Socialization." *Annual Review of Anthropology* 15 (1986): 163–91.

Schor, Juliet. "Why Americans Should Rest." *New York Times*, September 2, 2002.

Schweitzer, Vivian. "Where Musicians Bask in the Luxury of Time." *New York Times*, August 9, 2011.

Severson, Kim. *Spoon Fed: How Eight Cooks Saved My Life*. New York: Riverhead Books, 2010.

Shah, Riddhi. "Culinary Diplomacy at the Axis of Evil Café." *Salon.com*, June 9, 2010, http://www.salon.com/2010/06/09/conflict_kitchen_restaurant/, accessed January 3, 2016.

Sharpless, Rebecca. *Cooking in Other Women's Kitchens: Domestic Workers in the South, 1865–1960*. Chapel Hill: University of North Carolina Press, 2010.

Shuman, Amy. "The Rhetoric of Portions." *Western Folklore* 40:1 (January 1981): 72–80.

Sidenvall, Birgitta, Margaretha Nydahl and Christina Fjellström. "The Meal as Gift: The Meaning of Cooking among Retired Women." *Journal of Applied Gerontology* 19:4 (December 2000): 405–23.

Sietsema, Tom. "Chefs Are the New Diplomats." *Washington Post*, September 4, 2012.

Silva, Nikki, and Davia Nelson. *Hidden Kitchens: Stories, Recipes and More from NPR's The Kitchen Sisters*. Emmaus, Pa.: Rodale, 2005.

Smart-Grosvenor, VertaMae. *Vibration Cooking: Or the Travel Notes of a Geechee Girl*. New York: Ballantine, 1986.

Smith, Charles. "Cohousing Coming of Age." *San Francisco Chronicle*, February 9, 2002.

Snow, Catherine E., and Diane E. Beals. "Mealtime Talk That Supports Literacy Development." *New Directions for Child and Adolescent Development* 111 (Spring 2006): 51–66.

Snow, Catherine E., Rivka Y. Perlmann, Jean Berko Gleason, and Nahid Hooshyar. "Developmental Perspectives on Politeness: Sources of Children's Knowledge." *Journal of Pragmatics* 14 (1990): 289–305.

Snowe, Olympia J. "Olympia Snowe: Why I'm Leaving the Senate." *Washington Post*, March 1, 2012.

Span, Paula. "Death Be Not Decaffeinated: Over Cup, Groups Face Taboo." *New York Times*, June 16, 2013.

Steffen, Vibeke. "Life Stories and Shared Experience." *Social Science and Medicine* 45:1 (1997): 99–111.

Stone, Douglas, Bruce Patton, and Sheila Heen. *Difficult Conversations: How to Discuss What Matters Most*. New York: Penguin, 2010.

Susman, Tina. "Pittsburgh Café Offers Cuisine from the U.S. Conflict du Jour." *Los Angeles Times*, May 7, 2012.

Talbot, Margaret. "The Talking Cure." *New Yorker*, January 12, 2015, 38–47.

Tannen, Deborah. *Conversational Style: Analyzing Talk among Friends*. Norwood, N.J.: Ablex, 1984.

———. "Gender Differences in Conversational Coherence." In *Conversational Organization and Its Development*, edited by Bruce Dorval, 167–206. Norwood, N.J.: Ablex, 1990.

Trebay, Guy. "Guess Who Isn't Coming to Dinner." *New York Times*, November 20, 2012.

United States Department of Agriculture (USDA), Economic Research Service. The Economics of Food, Farming, Natural Resources, and Rural America. Eating and Health Module (ATUS): 2008 Current Findings: American Eating and Drinking Patterns, http://tinyurl.com/pw792py, accessed January 3, 2016.

Valverde, Mariana, and Kimberley White-Mair. "'One Day at a Time' and Other Slogans for Everyday Life: The Ethical Practices of Alcoholics Anonymous." *Sociology* 33:2 (May 1999): 393–410.

Verba, Sidney, Kay Lehman Schlozman, and Henry Brady. *Voice and Equality: Civic Voluntarism in American Politics*. Cambridge, Mass.: Harvard University Press, 1995.

Vuchinich, Samuel. "Starting and Stopping Spontaneous Family Conflicts." *Journal of Marriage and the Family* 49:3 (August 1987): 591–601.

Walsh, Katherine Cramer. *Talking about Politics: Informal Groups and Social Identity in American Life*. Chicago: University of Chicago Press, 2004.

Wang, Margaret C., Geneva D. Haertel, and Herbert J. Walberg. "Educational Resilience in Inner Cities." In *Syntheses of Research and Practice: Implications for*

Achieving Schooling Success for Children at Risk, edited by K. L. Alves-Zervos and J. R. Shafer, 136–67. National Center on Education in the Inner Cities. Philadelphia, Pa.: Temple University, 1993.

Weinstein, Miriam. *The Surprising Power of Family Meals: How Eating Together Makes Us Smarter, Stronger, Healthier and Happier*. Hanover, N.H.: Steerforth Press, 2005.

Wenzel, Andrea. "Potlucks for Peace?" *Public Diplomacy Magazine* 11 (Winter 2014), http://publicdiplomacymagazine.com/potlucks-for-peace/, accessed January 3, 2016.

West, Kevin. "Pacific Heights." *W Magazine*, January 2007, http://tinyurl.com/htwasrm, accessed January 3, 2016.

Wilk, Richard. "Power at the Table: Food Fights and Happy Meals." *Cultural Studies—Critical Methodologies* 10:6 (2010): 428–36.

Wizenberg, Molly. *A Homemade Life: Stories and Recipes from My Kitchen Table*. New York: Simon and Schuster, 2010.

Wu, Olivia. "Amazing Grace." *San Francisco Chronicle*, June 4, 2003.

Young, Kevin. *The Hungry Ear: Poems of Food and Drink*. New York: Bloomsbury, 2012.

Zernike, Kate. "Sobered Gay Rights Groups Vow to Change Public's Mind." *New York Times*, November 14, 2004.

Zinder, Daniel. "Hard Tack." *Open Democracy*, April 17, 2003, 1–5.

Index

Haddadin, Jim, 235n47
Haertel, Geneva D., 236n4
Hagan, Kay, 211. *See also* congresswomen
Harjo, Joy, 29–30
Harris, Jessica B., 84
Hart, Betty, 227n9
Hart, Daniel, 234n27
Hartzell, Mary, 228n30
Hauck-Lawson, Annie, 35
Heen, Sheila, 226n60
Heitkamp, Heidi, 212. *See also* congresswomen
Herrera, Tilde, 226n51
Hesser, Amanda, 231–32nn18–19
Highiet, Nancy, 229n51, 231n124, 231n7, 234n9
Hindus, 142, 168–69
Hitz, Alex, 112–13
Hoberman, Mary Ann, 230n113
Hoffman, Jan, 79–80
Hollows, Joanne, 228n3
Holtzman, Linda J., 228n8
Holy Cross, College of the, 137–38
home-cooked meals, 9, 74, 78, 111; African American, 84; by children, 83, 93–94; elite, 110–14; ideal, 21, 25, 146, 185; immigrant, 73, 91–92, 165; online, 32, 112, 213; student, 136–37, 139
Homies Empowerment dinners, 149–51
honesty, 154, 167, 192
Hood, William, 35–36
hooks, bell, 61–62
hospitality, 35, 107, 139, 166, 170, 176; Afghan, 175; Bengali, 166; congressional, 208–10; Gullah, 189; presidential, 215–18; travelers, 34
Huebsch, Bill, 232n34
Huffington, Arianna, 104
humor, in conversation, 49, 53, 55, 56, 154, 222–23. *See also* family meals; language socialization
Hutchison, Kay Bailey, 208. *See also* congresswomen

identity: difficult conversations and, 36, 156, 184, 205; ethnic, 35, 82, 87, 149–50, 153–54, 194–95; family, 53–55, 73, 81–83, 91, 122, 163; group, 44–45, 62, 136–37, 148, 191, 206; individual, 53–54, 87–88, 147–48, 159, 205

Indians, 168–69; Indian Americans, 90–91
insults, in conversation, 1, 50
intergroup contact, 192, 223–24
interruptions. *See under* conversation
Iranian Americans, 170, 179–82
Irish Americans, 145–47, 164. *See also* European Americans
Italians, 162–64; Italian Americans, 73, 145–47, 164–65, 185. *See also* European Americans

Jacinto, Leela, 235nn72–74
Japanese, 56, 101. *See also* Asian Americans
Jews, 10, 170; food sharing, 112, 164, 173, 174, 186–88; as immigrants, 164; Passover seders, 87, 137, 140; Shabbat, 64, 86–87, 112, 121, 141, 143, 164, 187; tables, 30, 140
Johnson, Lyndon B., 215–17
Johnson, Scott, 232n48
Johnston, Ron, 234n32
Julier, Alice P., 109
justice, 1, 57, 81, 142, 191, 193, 221; restorative, 158–59

Kadri, Meena, 233n33
Kaplan, Elaine Bell, 92–94
Karp, Harvey, 228n29
Kathlene, Lyn, 200–201
Kennedy, Robert F., Jr., 105–6, 143
Kent, Susan, 228nn9–10
Kiang, Peter Nien-chu, 232nn55–57
Kibria, Nazli, 66
Kids Voting USA, 198
King, Martin Luther, Jr., 35–36, 177–78
kitchen: borderless boundary zone, 71–72; civil rights activists, 177–78; comfort, 84, 89, 123–24; community, 73, 151, 186, 187; as confessional, 68–69; confidence, 104–5; culinary chats, 71–72; dancing, 117; death café, 160–61; dinner party, 114; family meals, 65, 70, 72, 73, 78, 96; immigrant, 72–73, 83; partnerships and, 62–64; race, 9–10, 69–70, 87–88, 177–78; restaurant, 69–73; seniors, 125; stories, 35, 83; students, 137; tables, 29–30, 84, 118, 125, 139; talk, 67, 68–73, 83, 103–4, 122–23, 137; therapy, 139; voice, 68–69; as women's space, 71, 73, 87–88; working-class, 22, 24, 70–72

talk about one's day, 16, 62, 80, 101–5; at camp, 133–35; at family meals, 19–22, 75–76, 92, 116, 122, 141; during food preparation, 139; with friends, 52, 78; interrogation, 57–58, 102, 163–64, 220; seniors, 125. *See also* family narratives
Tannen, Deborah, 38–39
Taylor, Carolyn, 56–58
teachers: conversation, 47–48, 130; on cooking, 83; democratic, 192–94, 222–23; family trees, 85; shared meals, 75–77, 91, 130, 134; table manners, 96–98, 133–35
teasing, in conversation, 16, 18, 56, 144
television: arguments, 202–4; as babysitter, 43, 89; conflict avoidance, 13, 49; conversations, 41, 48, 80; cooking, 90, 95; eating alone, 7, 53, 76, 77, 85, 125; as educational opportunity, 13; as entertainment, 203; family meals, 21–22, 64–65, 68, 89, 119, 132; family routine, 80, 92, 138; incivility, 202–4
Terry, Bryant, 82–83
time: meal-, 25, 79, 89, 95; parenting, 20–22, 40–41, 43, 79–80; pressures, 110–11; Take Back Your Time Movement, 26–29
tolerance, 36, 96, 142–43, 192–94
topics. *See* conversation topics
town hall meetings, 72, 197, 205–6. *See also* civic engagement
Trebay, Guy, 112–13
trust: barriers, 202; civil society, 2–3, 191–93, 219–24; conversation, 16, 202, 224; food, 20, 143, 190; friends, 191–92; government, 184, 203–4; group, 45, 191–93; intergroup contact, 224; interracial, 177–78; rituals, 55; schools, 192–93; social, 108, 191–93; trustworthiness, 191
Tseng, Vivian, 234n23
turn taking, 205, 219–21; children, 15–19, 58, 135; as conversation skill, 34, 43, 47, 48, 100; rules, 56, 74, 100, 148, 219; state legislators, 200–201

understanding, 59, 184; as goal of conversations, 35–36, 51, 59–60, 107–8, 184, 190; and need to be understood, 35; political, 1–2
U.S. Department of Agriculture, 25
U.S. Department of State, culinary diplomacy, 212–15

Valverde, Mariana, 232n45
Verba, Sidney, 234nn28–29
Vietnamese Americans, 66, 123–24. *See also* Asian Americans
viewpoints: adolescents, 192–94, 196–97; adults, 107–8, 115–16, 198–99, 224; children, 51, 75, 105–6, 220; respect for, 19, 33, 36, 43, 162, 181
Visser, Margaret, 111
vocabulary, 14, 36, 48, 59–60, 108; word gap, 42–43, 219
voice. *See* food: voice; kitchen: voice; political voice
voluntary associations, 148, 196, 198–200. *See also* civic engagement
voting, 1, 193, 196, 197, 199–200. *See also* civic engagement
Vuchinich, Samuel, 156–58

Waffle Shop, 178–79
Walberg, Herbert J., 236n4
Wallace, Scyatta A., 230n98
Walsh, Katherine Cramer, 227n12
Wang, Margaret C., 236n4
Warren, Elizabeth, 212. *See also* congresswomen
Weinstein, Miriam, 51, 73–74, 78
Weleski, Dawn, 179–83
Wenzel, Andrea, 235n60
West, Kevin, 230nn108–9
White-Mair, Kimberley, 232n45
Wilk, Richard, 225nn1–3
Wilson, Nancy, 116
Wizenberg, Molly, 77–78, 123
women. *See* gender
Wong, Jade Snow, 166–67
work, 26–29; multiple-job households, 20, 29, 43, 77, 93; overworked Americans, 20–22, 25–29, 93; part-time and piecework, 27, 73; poverty, 42–43, 189, 222; vs. unemployment, 27, 189; women's unpaid, 62, 66; workplace flexibility, 21–22, 28–29
World Café, 32–33
Wu, Olivia, 140–42

Young, Kevin, 117
Youniss, James, 234n27

Zernike, Kate, 233n5
Zinder, Daniel, 232n52

JANET A. FLAMMANG is Professor Emerita in the Department of Political Science at Santa Clara University. Her books include *The Taste for Civilization: Food, Politics, and Civil Society*.